Qualifications and Credit Framework (QCF)

LEVEL 4 DIPLOMA IN ACCOUNTING

TEXT

Financial Statements

2012 Edition

First edition July 2010

Third edition June 2012

ISBN 9781 4453 9463 3
(Previous ISBN 9781 7517 9735 0)

British Library Cataloguing-in-Publication Data
A catalogue record for this book is available from the British
Library

Published by

BPP Learning Media Ltd
BPP House
Aldine Place
London
W12 8AA

www.bpp.com/learningmedia

Printed in the United Kingdom

CONTENTS

A NOTE ABOUT COPYRIGHT

Dear Customer

What does the little © mean and why does it matter?

Your market-leading BPP books, course materials and e-learning materials do not write and update themselves. People write them: on their own behalf or as employees of an organisation that invests in this activity. Copyright law protects their livelihoods. It does so by creating rights over the use of the content.

Breach of copyright is a form of theft – as well being a criminal offence in some jurisdictions, it is potentially a serious breach of professional ethics.

With current technology, things might seem a bit hazy but, basically, without the express permission of BPP Learning Media:

- Photocopying our materials is a breach of copyright

- Scanning, ripcasting or conversion of our digital materials into different file formats, uploading them to facebook or emailing them to your friends is a breach of copyright

You can, of course, sell your books, in the form in which you have bought them – once you have finished with them. (Is this fair to your fellow students? We update for a reason).

And what about outside the UK? BPP Learning Media strives to make our materials available at prices students can afford by local printing arrangements, pricing policies and partnerships which are clearly listed on our website. A tiny minority ignore this and indulge in criminal activity by illegally photocopying our material or supporting organisations that do. If they act illegally and unethically in one area, can you really trust them?

BPP LEARNING MEDIA'S AAT MATERIALS

Since July 2010 the AAT's assessments have fallen within the **Qualifications and Credit Framework** and most papers are now assessed by way of an on demand **computer based assessment**. BPP Learning Media has invested heavily to ensure our ground breaking materials are as relevant as possible for this method of assessment. In particular, our **suite of online resources** ensures that you are prepared for online testing by allowing you to practice numerous online tasks that are similar to the tasks you will encounter in the AAT's assessments.

The BPP range of resources comprises:

- **Texts**, covering all the knowledge and understanding needed by students, with numerous illustrations of 'how it works', practical examples and tasks for you to use to consolidate your learning. The majority of tasks within the texts have been written in an interactive style that reflects the style of the online tasks we anticipate the AAT will set. Texts are available in our traditional paper format and, in addition, as ebooks which can be downloaded to your PC or laptop.

- **Question Banks**, including additional learning questions plus the AAT's practice assessment and a number of other full practice assessments. Full answers to all questions and assessments, prepared by BPP Learning Media Ltd, are included. Our question banks are provided free of charge in an online environment containing tasks similar to those you will encounter in the AAT's testing environment. This means you can become familiar with being tested in an online environment prior to completing the real assessment.

- **Passcards**, which are handy pocket-sized revision tools designed to fit in a handbag or briefcase to enable you to revise anywhere at anytime. All major points are covered in the Passcards which have been designed to assist you in consolidating knowledge.

- **Workbooks**, which have been designed to cover the units that are assessed by way of project/case study. The workbooks contain many practical tasks to assist in the learning process and also a sample assessment or project to work through.

- **Lecturers' resources**, providing a further bank of tasks, answers and full practice assessments for classroom use, available separately only to lecturers whose colleges adopt BPP Learning Media material. The practice assessments within the lecturers' resources are available in both paper format and online in e format.

This Text for Financial Statements has been written specifically to ensure comprehensive yet concise coverage of the AAT's new learning outcomes and assessment criteria. It is fully up to date as at June 2012 and reflects both the AAT's unit guide and the practice assessments provided by the AAT.

Each chapter contains:

- Clear, step by step explanation of the topic

- Logical progression and linking from one chapter to the next

- Numerous illustrations of 'how it works'

- Interactive tasks within the text of the chapter itself, with answers at the back of the book. In general, these tasks have been written in the interactive form that students can expect to see in their real assessments

- Test your learning questions of varying complexity, again with answers supplied at the back of the book. In general these test questions have been written in the interactive form that students can expect to see in their real assessments

The emphasis in all tasks and test questions is on the practical application of the skills acquired.

If you have any comments about this book, please e-mail paulsutcliffe@bpp.com or write to Paul Sutcliffe, Senior Publishing Manager, BPP Learning Media Ltd, BPP House, Aldine Place, London W12 8AA.

A NOTE ON TERMINOLOGY

On 1 January 2012, the AAT moved from UK GAAP to IFRS terminology. Although you may be used to UK terminology, you need to now know the equivalent international terminology for your assessments.

The following information is taken from an article on the AAT's website and describes how the terminology changes impact on students studying for each level of the AAT QCF qualification.

What is the impact of IFRS terms on AAT assessments?

The list shown in the table that follows gives the 'translation' between UK GAAP and IFRS.

UK GAAP	IFRS
Final accounts	Financial statements
Trading and profit and loss account	**Income statement or Statement of comprehensive income**
Turnover or Sales	Revenue or Sales Revenue
Sundry income	Other operating income
Interest payable	Finance costs
Sundry expenses	Other operating costs
Operating profit	Profit from operations
Net profit/loss	Profit/Loss for the year/period
Balance sheet	**Statement of financial position**
Fixed assets	Non-current assets
Net book value	Carrying amount
Tangible assets	Property, plant and equipment
Reducing balance depreciation	Diminishing balance depreciation
Depreciation/Depreciation expense(s)	Depreciation charge(s)
Stocks	Inventories
Trade debtors or Debtors	Trade receivables
Prepayments	Other receivables
Debtors and prepayments	Trade and other receivables
Cash at bank and in hand	Cash and cash equivalents
Trade creditors or Creditors	Trade payables

UK GAAP	IFRS
Accruals	Other payables
Creditors and accruals	Trade and other payables
Long-term liabilities	Non-current liabilities
Capital and reserves	Equity (limited companies)
Profit and loss balance	Retained earnings
Minority interest	Non-controlling interest
Cash flow statement	**Statement of cash flows**

This is certainly not a comprehensive list, which would run to several pages, but it does cover the main terms that you will come across in your studies and assessments. However, you won't need to know all of these in the early stages of your studies – some of the terms will not be used until you reach Level 4. For each level of the AAT qualification, the points to bear in mind are as follows:

Level 2 Certificate in Accounting

The IFRS terms do not impact greatly at this level. Make sure you are familiar with 'receivables' (also referred to as 'trade receivables'), 'payables' (also referred to as 'trade payables'), and 'inventories'. The terms sales ledger and purchases ledger – together with their control accounts – will continue to be used. Sometimes the control accounts might be called 'trade receivables control account' and 'trade payables control account'. The other term to be aware of is 'non-current asset' – this may be used in some assessments.

Level 3 Diploma in Accounting

At this level you need to be familiar with the term 'financial statements'. The financial statements comprise an 'income statement' (profit and loss account), and a 'statement of financial position' (balance sheet). In the income statement the term 'revenue' or 'sales revenue' takes the place of 'sales', and 'profit for the year' replaces 'net profit'. Other terms may be used in the statement of financial position – eg 'non-current assets' and 'carrying amount'. However, specialist limited company terms are not required at this level.

Level 4 Diploma in Accounting

At Level 4 a wider range of IFRS terms is needed, and in the case of Financial statements (FNST), are already in use – particularly those relating to limited companies. Note especially that an income statement becomes a 'statement of comprehensive income'.

Note: The information above was taken from an AAT article from the 'assessment news' area of the AAT website (www.aat.org.uk).

ASSESSMENT STRATEGY

The Financial Statements (FNST) assessment is normally a two and a half hour computer based assessment.

Learners must be able to demonstrate that they possess the requisite knowledge and skills to be able to accurately draft singular and consolidated financial statements of limited companies, and analyse and interpret the financial statements of limited companies using ratio analysis.

The FNST assessment consists of eight tasks. The first section of the assessment focuses on the drafting of financial statements and the second on analysis and interpretation.

Competency

Learners will be required to demonstrate competence in both sections of the assessment. For the purpose of assessment the competency level for AAT assessment is set at 70 per cent. The level descriptor in the table below describes the ability and skills students at this level must successfully demonstrate to achieve competence.

BPP
LEARNING MEDIA

QCF Level descriptor	**Summary**
	Achievement at level 4 reflects the ability to identify and use relevant understanding, methods and skills to address problems that are well defined but complex and non-routine. It includes taking responsibility for overall courses of action as well as exercising autonomy and judgment within fairly broad parameters. It also reflects understanding of different perspectives or approaches within an area of study or work.
	Knowledge and understanding
	■ Use practical, theoretical or technical understanding to address problems that are well defined but complex and non routine
	■ Analyse, interpret and evaluate relevant information and ideas
	■ Be aware of the nature and approximate scope of the area of study or work
	■ Have an informed awareness of different perspectives or approaches within the area of study or work
	Application and action
	■ Address problems that are complex and non-routine while normally fairly well defined
	■ Identify, adapt and use appropriate methods and skills
	■ Initiate and use appropriate investigation to inform actions
	■ Review the effectiveness and appropriateness of methods, actions and results
	Autonomy and accountability
	■ Take responsibility for courses of action, including where relevant, responsibility for the work of others
	■ Exercise autonomy and judgment within broad but generally well-defined parameters

AAT UNIT GUIDE

Financial Statements (FNST)

Introduction

Please read the information below in conjunction with the QCF standards for the unit.

The purpose of the unit

This unit is concerned with competence in drafting and interpreting the financial statements of limited companies. Learners will have attained competence at Levels 2 and 3 in the process of identifying and recording financial transactions in accounts and ledgers following the principles of double entry bookkeeping. They will also be able to draft the financial statements of sole traders and partnerships. This unit develops and applies these competences further by focusing on the drafting and interpretation of financial statements of limited companies from the records and accounts prepared.

It ensures that learners understand what information is required to be provided, how it is to be presented to users of the financial statements and how the rules and principles established in IFRSs apply to the process of drafting financial statements. The unit also ensures that learners appreciate why financial statements are prepared and communicated so that their significance is understood. They need to understand who these users are and why they are interested in this information.

The unit also introduces learners to tools and techniques that can be used to analyse and interpret the financial performance and financial position of a company.

Learning objectives

The unit has two learning objectives:

- To develop learners' knowledge and skills so that they able to understand and apply international financial reporting standards and relevant legislation in the drafting of financial statements of limited companies and consolidated financial statements.

- To develop learners' knowledge and skills so that they are able to analyse and interpret financial statements using ratio analysis.

Learning outcomes

This unit consists of seven learning outcomes in total. To achieve overall competency in the unit, learners must be able to carry out the three skills based tasks to a competent standard and demonstrate that they are competent in respect of the four underpinning knowledge and understanding requirements.

QCF Unit	Learning Outcome	Assessment Criteria	Covered in Chapter
Financial statements (knowledge and understanding)	Understand the regulatory framework that underpins financial reporting	Explain the scope, elements and purpose, for different users, of preparing financial statements for external reporting.	**1**
		Describe legislation and regulation which must be complied with in the preparation of the financial statements.	**1**
		Explain the reasons for governance by legislation and regulation	**1**
		Explain the relevance of accounting standards	**Through out**
		Explain the duties and responsibilities of the directors or other responsible parties, of a corporate organisation	**2**
	Understand the key features of a published set of accounts	Describe the key components and the purpose of a statement of financial position (balance sheet).	**1,2,3**
		Describe the key components and the purpose of a statement of comprehensive income	**1,2,4**
		Describe the key components and the purpose of a statement of cash flows (cash flow statement).	**5**
		Explain the content and purpose of disclosure notes to the accounts.	**4**
		Identify accounting standards and the effect of these on the preparation of the financial statements	**3 – 11**

QCF Unit	Learning Outcome	Assessment Criteria	Covered in Chapter
	Understand basic principles of consolidation	Describe the key components of a set of consolidated financial statements – parent, subsidiary, non-controlling interest (minority interest), goodwill, fair values, pre and post acquisition profits and equity	**10,11**
		Explain the process of basic consolidation for a parent and subsidiary	**10,11**
		Describe the effect of consolidation on each of the key elements - parent, subsidiary, non-controlling interest (minority interest), goodwill, fair values, pre and post acquisition profits and equity	**10,11**
		Explain the key features of a parent / associate relationship	**11**
	Appreciate the analysis and interpretation of financial statements	Demonstrate an understanding of the relationship between the elements of the financial statements – assets, liabilities, equity, income, expenses, contributions from owners and distributions to owners	**2**
		Explain how to calculate accounting ratios – profitability, liquidity, efficiency, financial position	**12**
		Explain the inter-relationships between ratios	**12**
		Explain the purpose of the interpretation of ratios	**12**
		Describe how the interpretation and analysis of accounting ratios is used in a business environment	**12**

QCF Unit	Learning Outcome	Assessment Criteria	Covered in Chapter
Financial statements (skills)	Draft statutory financial statements for a limited company	Apply accounting standards and relevant legislation to correctly identify, and accurately adjust, accounting information	3 – 9
		Use appropriate information to accurately draft a statement of comprehensive income	4
		Use appropriate information to accurately draft a statement of financial position (balance sheet)	3
		Prepare notes to the accounts which satisfy statutory current disclosure requirements, in respect of accounting policies, fixed assets, current and long term liabilities, equity	3 – 9
		Draft an accurate statement of cash flows (cash flow statement)	5
	Draft simple consolidated financial statements	Draft a consolidated income statement for a parent company with one partly owned subsidiary	11
		Draft a consolidated statement of financial position (balance sheet) for a parent company with one partly owned subsidiary	10
		Apply current standards to accurately calculate and appropriately deal with the accounting treatment of goodwill, non-controlling interest (minority interest) and post acquisition profits, in the group financial statements	10,11

QCF Unit	Learning Outcome	Assessment Criteria	Covered in Chapter
	Interpret financial statements using ratio analysis	Calculate and interpret the relationship between the elements of the financial statements with regard to profitability, liquidity, efficient use of resources and financial position	12
		Draw valid conclusions from the information contained within the financial statements	12
		Present clearly and concisely issues, analysis and conclusions to the appropriate people	12

Knowledge and understanding

1   Understand the regulatory framework that underpins financial reporting

Learners must be able to demonstrate a knowledge and understanding of the International Accounting Standards Board's (IASB) *Conceptual Framework for Financial Reporting (Conceptual Framework)* and the legislation and regulation which must be complied with when preparing financial statements. The assessable areas within the *Conceptual Framework* are:

Introduction

■   The purpose and status of the *Conceptual Framework*

■   The scope of the *Conceptual Framework*

Chapter 1: The objective of general purpose financial reporting:

■   Objective, usefulness and limitations of general purpose financial reporting

■   Information about the reporting entity's economic resources, claims, and changes in resources and claims

Chapter 3: Qualitative characteristics of useful financial information:

■   Introduction
■   Qualitative characteristics of useful financial information
■   Fundamental qualitative characteristics
■   Enhancing qualitative characteristics

Chapter 4: The Framework (1989): the remaining text:

- Underlying assumption
- The elements of financial statements
- Recognition of the elements of financial statements
- Measurement of the elements of financial statements

With regard to the legal and regulatory framework learners must be able to demonstrate an appreciation of:

- The reasons for the existence of a regulatory framework

- The sources of regulation, (international financial reporting standards and company law (Companies Act 2006))

- The role and functions of the IASB and the process by which standards are set

- The purpose of accounting standards

2 Understand the key features of a published set of accounts

Learners must be able to describe the key components and purpose of the statement of financial position and the statement of comprehensive income, and explain the content and purpose of disclosure notes to the accounts, all of which are stipulated in IAS 1.

Learners must also be able to describe the key components and purpose of the statement of cash flows as presented in IAS 7.

Further, learners must be able to identify international financial reporting standards relevant to given scenarios and appreciate their impact upon the financial statements.

3 Understand basic principles of consolidation

Learners must be able to describe the key components of a set of consolidated financial statements and explain the process of basic consolidation, including the elimination of inter company balances and profit, the treatment of non-controlling interest, goodwill, fair values, pre and post acquisition profits and equity as specified in IFRS 3 and IAS 27.

4 Appreciate the analysis and interpretation of financial statements

Learners must be able to demonstrate that they understand the relationship between the elements of the financial statements, namely assets, liabilities, equity, income, expenses, contributions from owners and distributions to owners as set out in the IASB *Conceptual Framework* and in IAS 1.

Accounting ratios are a means of presenting information in a form which facilitates comparisons. Learners must be able to explain how to calculate ratios in respect of profitability, liquidity, efficiency and financial position and how these ratios are inter-related; also why and how interpretation of financial statements is used in a business context and the potential limitations of ratio analysis.

Skills

1 Draft statutory financial statements for a limited company

Learners must be able to accurately draft a statement of financial position and a statement of comprehensive income as per IAS 1. Such statements will typically be drafted from a trial balance or an extended trial balance, with learners then being asked to appraise and adjust for other information about balances or transactions related to the period under consideration.

Such adjustments may relate to the application of specified accounting standards and relevant legislation.

Pro-formas for the statement of financial position and statement of comprehensive income, with analysis of expenses based solely upon functionality, will be provided for learners in the assessment if required which will include the items learners will be expected to deal with. Only a single statement of comprehensive income will be asked for in respect of single companies in this unit as opposed to a separate income statement and a statement of comprehensive income.

Learners must also be able to accurately draft a statement of changes in equity in accordance with IAS 1 and a statement of cash flows in accordance with IAS 7. Learners may be required to draft the statement of cash flows using either the direct or the indirect method, with a pro forma of the statement being given in the assessment if required.

2 Draft simple consolidated financial statements

Learners must be able to draft a consolidated income statement and a consolidated statement of financial position (balance sheet) for a parent company with one partly owned subsidiary. Learners may be required to calculate and appropriately deal with goodwill, non-controlling interest and post acquisition profits in accordance with IFRS 3 and IAS 27. The consolidation of sub-subsidiaries or acquisitions where shares in subsidiary undertakings are acquired at different times will not be assessable. Non-controlling interest will only be measured at the non-controlling interest's proportionate share of the acquiree's identifiable net assets for the purposes of this unit. Pro formas for the statements will again be provided for learners in the assessment as and when these are required which will include the items learners will be expected to be able to deal with.

3 Interpret financial statements using ratio analysis

Learners must be able to calculate and analyse and interpret accounting ratios with regard to profitability, liquidity, efficiency and financial position.

Furthermore, in order to assess a company's performance and financial position in respect of an accounting period, learners must be able to compare the calculated ratios to:

(i) Ratios of a previous accounting period for the same company
(ii) Ratios of another company
(iii) Industry average ratios.

Learners must be able to draw valid conclusions from their calculations and analysis, and be able to present these clearly to appropriate parties.

Note: The AAT have provided further delivery guidance covering details of the international financial reporting standards (both IFRSs and IASs) which are assessable and are therefore covered in this Text. The guidance also lists appropriate formulas for the ratios (which are also reflected in this Text). You can view the latest version of the AAT's full delivery guidance on the AAT's website (www.aat.org.uk).

chapter 1:
LIMITED COMPANIES

─── **chapter coverage** 📖 ───

In this first chapter we look at the reasons why a limited company is different from a sole trader or a partnership, before moving on to explain some of the items which appear in limited company accounts. The format of the income statement and statement of financial position for a limited company are introduced in this chapter and are covered in more detail in Chapters 3 and 4. The topics covered are:

✍ The purpose of financial statements

✍ The different types of organisation

✍ The nature of limited companies

✍ How the accounts of limited companies differ from those of sole traders and partnerships

✍ Share capital

✍ Reserves

✍ Loan finance

✍ Preparing accounts for limited companies

THE PURPOSE OF FINANCIAL STATEMENTS

The purpose of financial statements is to provide useful information about an organisation's:

- Financial position (its assets and liabilities)
- Financial performance (its profit or loss)
- Changes in financial position (its cash flows)

to a wide range of users. Users need this information for two reasons:

- To make economic decisions. For example, information in the financial statements may help a user to decide whether or not to invest in a company.

- To assess the STEWARDSHIP of the organisation's management. This is relevant where an organisation is managed by people other than its owners. Management is accountable to the owners of the organisation. It must safeguard the organisation's resources and use them properly in order to generate profits or other benefits.

THE DIFFERENT TYPES OF ORGANISATION

There are several broad types of organisation. These can be classified into **profit-making** organisations and **not-for-profit** organisations. You will already have met some of these in your earlier studies.

Profit-making organisations

These consist of:

- SOLE TRADERS: businesses owned and managed by one person.

- PARTNERSHIPS: businesses owned and managed by two or more people together, sharing profits and losses.

- COMPANIES: businesses that are a **separate legal entity** from their owners.

Later in this chapter, we look more closely at the nature of limited companies and the reasons why they are different from sole traders and partnerships.

Not-for-profit organisations

These consist of:

- **Charities, clubs and societies**: owned by their members or trustees and created for a specific non-commercial purpose (eg, to give grants to the homeless, to enable members to enjoy a particular sport).

- **Public sector organisations**: these are owned by the general public and include central government; local government; the National Health Service; and public corporations.

Financial statements are always prepared for a business or other organisation as a **separate entity** from its owners. This applies regardless of whether the organisation is legally separate from its owners or not. Accounting regulations often use the term ENTITY to refer to an organisation that prepares financial statements as a separate entity from its owners. An entity may be a sole trader, a partnership, a limited company, or a not-for-profit organisation.

It is useful to have a broad awareness of the different types of entity. However, this paper is concerned specifically with one important type of business organisation: the limited company.

THE NATURE OF LIMITED COMPANIES

There are several ways in which a limited company differs from a sole trader or a partnership, the two types of entity that you have already met.

Separate legal personality

- A company has a **separate legal personality** from those of its owners. It can enter into contracts, acquire assets and incur liabilities in its own name.

- This contrasts with the situation of sole traders and partnerships. For accounting purposes the **business** is treated as a separate entity (the separate entity concept), but the legal position is that it is the owners themselves who enter into contracts and who are personally liable for any debts incurred.

Limited liability

- A limited company gives its owners **limited liability**. Limited liability means that the owners' liability is limited to the amount that they have paid for their shares. If the company becomes insolvent, the maximum amount that the owners lose is the amount of capital that they have invested in the company.

- Sole traders and partners have **unlimited liability**. If the business does not have the resources to repay its liabilities as they fall due, the owners must sell their personal property in order to satisfy creditors and to meet claims against the business.

Size

- Most sole traders and partnerships are small businesses. (There are exceptions, such as large law and accountancy firms.)

- Although many limited companies are small businesses, a limited company may be a very large concern. Large public companies may have several hundred individual shareholders, most of whom have invested in them in order to obtain a share of their profits and possibly to realise a gain on the eventual sale of the shares. They are not involved in the day-to-day running of the companies in which they have invested.

Owners and managers

- Sole traders and partners normally own and manage their business themselves

- Limited companies (particularly large ones) are often managed by persons other than their owners (see above):

    - Limited companies are owned by **shareholders**

    - The shareholders appoint **directors** to manage the company on their behalf

One of the objectives of financial statements is to enable the shareholders to assess the way in which management is safeguarding the assets of the company and using them to generate profit (the **stewardship** of management).

In practice, the directors and the shareholders may be the same people, particularly if the company is small. Even in large public companies directors and key management often have at least a small number of shares.

Types of limited company

There are two types of limited company:

- PUBLIC COMPANIES can invite members of the general public to invest in their shares. The shares of a public company may be (and usually are) traded on a Stock Exchange. Public companies have 'plc', which stands for 'public limited company' at the end of their name. They are generally very large businesses.

- PRIVATE COMPANIES cannot invite members of the general public to invest in their shares. They have the word 'limited' at the end of their name. Most UK companies are private companies.

Advantages of trading as a limited company

The main advantage is limited liability (see above), however, there are other potential benefits:

- It is easier to raise finance:

  - There may be any number of shareholders

  - Investing in a listed company is less risky and therefore more attractive than investing in a partnership or a sole trader (limited liability).

  (In practice, shareholders in small companies are often asked to give personal guarantees to lenders, so that the advantage of limited liability no longer applies.)

- A limited company continues to operate regardless of the identity of the owners (unlike a partnership, where the old partnership ceases and a new one is formed whenever a partner is admitted or retires).

- Limited companies are taxed as separate entities (tax is treated as an appropriation of profits). Partners and sole traders are personally liable for tax on their share of the business profits.

- It is reasonably easy to transfer shares from one owner to another.

Disadvantages of trading as a limited company

- Limited companies must publish their annual accounts. This means that in theory they can be seen by anybody, including competitors. Sole traders and partnerships do not have to publish their accounts.

- Limited companies must comply with a great many legal and administrative formalities (although some of the rules do not apply to small companies). In particular, they must prepare accounts in accordance with the Companies Act 2006. The accounts must comply with the requirements of accounting standards. Sole traders and partnerships may comply with accounting standards, but are not obliged to do so.

- The accounts of larger companies must be **audited** (subjected to independent examination to ensure that they present fairly the company's financial position and performance). This can be inconvenient, time consuming and expensive.

- Companies must comply with the requirements of the Companies Act 2006 when they issue shares or reduce their share capital. Sole traders and partnerships can increase or withdraw capital whenever the owners wish.

HOW THE ACCOUNTS OF LIMITED COMPANIES DIFFER FROM THOSE OF SOLE TRADERS AND PARTNERSHIPS

The income statement of a sole trader or a partnership

The income statement provides information about the financial performance of a business. It shows the income generated and the expenditure incurred during an accounting period. The income statement is often known as the profit and loss account, because it is a calculation of the profit or loss for the period.

The exact format of the income statement varies according to the type of business, but the basic structure is always the same:

Sales	X
Less: cost of sales	(X)
Gross profit	X
Less: other expenses	(X)
Net profit	X

There are two parts.

- The first part shows the gross profit generated by the business, in other words, sales less expenses directly incurred in producing or purchasing goods or services for sale.

- The second part shows the other items of income and expenditure earned and incurred by the business. These are deducted from gross profit to arrive at net profit.

Example

Income statement for the year ended 31 December 20X0

	£	£
Sales		774,000
Less: cost of sales		
Opening inventories	156,000	
Purchases	612,000	
	768,000	
Closing inventories	(180,000)	
		(588,000)
Gross profit		186,000
Less: other expenses		
Wages and salaries	109,200	
Office expenses	9,000	
Rates	7,200	
Electricity	8,000	
Depreciation	4,350	
Bad and doubtful debts	3,600	
		(141,350)
Net profit		44,650

The statement of financial position of a sole trader or a partnership

The statement of financial position provides information about the financial position of a business. It shows the assets, liabilities and capital (ownership interest or equity) of a business at the end of an accounting period. The statement of financial position is often known as the balance sheet, because it has two parts which balance and because it is a summary of the main ledger balances at the period end.

The statement of financial position reflects the accounting equation:

ASSETS – LIABILITIES = CAPITAL; or

ASSETS = LIABILITIES + CAPITAL.

The statement of financial position of a sole trader or a partnership is normally structured as follows:

- The first part shows assets and liabilities. Assets and liabilities are always shown in the same order: non-current assets (property, plant and equipment); current assets; current liabilities; long-term liabilities.

- The second part shows the ownership interest in the business. For a sole trader, this is normally capital, plus profits, less drawings.

Example

Statement of financial position as at 31 December 20X0

	£	£
Non-current assets:		
Leasehold premises		67,500
Fixtures and fittings		10,800
		78,300
Current assets:		
Inventories	180,000	
Trade receivables	311,640	
Prepayments	1,800	
Cash at bank	24,300	
Cash in hand	300	
	518,040	
Current liabilities:		
Trade payables	390,000	
Accruals	2,000	
	392,000	
Net current assets		126,040
		204,340
Represented by:		
Capital at 1 January 20X0		174,090
Net profit for the year ended 31 December 20X0		44,650
		218,740
Less: drawings		(14,400)
		204,340

Task 1

The following trial balance has been extracted from the accounts of Amelia, a sole trader.

Trial balance as at 30 June 20X1

	Dr £	Cr £
Sales		350,000
Purchases	221,200	
Wages and salaries	55,000	
Rent and rates	9,600 − 900	
Heat and light	4,500 +700	
Inventories at 1 July 20X0	12,700	
Drawings	15,600	
Equipment at cost	91,000	
Motor vehicles at cost	39,000	
Accumulated depreciation:		
Equipment		20,500
Motor vehicles		8,000
Trade receivables	48,000	
Trade payables		33,000
Bank	4,800	
Sundry expenses	7,300	
Cash	500	
Capital		97,700
	509,200	509,200

The following information as at 30 June 20X1 is also available.

(a) £700 is owing for heat and light.

(b) £900 has been prepaid for rent and rates.

(c) Depreciation is to be charged for the year as follows:

Equipment   – 10% on cost
Motor vehicles – 20% on cost

(d) Inventories were valued at £14,900 on 30 June 20X1.

Using the proforma below, draft Amelia's income statement for the year ended 30 June 20X1 and her statement of financial position at that date.

Amelia: Income statement for the year ended 30 June 20X1

	£'000	£'000
Sales		
Cost of sales		
Gross profit		
Total expenses		
Net profit for the year		

Amelia: Statement of financial position as at 30 June 20X1

	£'000	£'000
Non-current assets		
Current assets		
Current liabilities		
Net current assets		
Capital		
Balance at 1 July 20X0		
Balance at 30 June 20X1		

The income statement of a limited company

This is prepared in exactly the same way as that of a sole trader or partnership, down to net profit.

The tax payable on the profits, which in the UK is known as CORPORATION TAX, is deducted from net profit. This is because a company is taxed as a separate entity from its owners. Tax does not appear in the accounts of sole traders and partnerships, because the owners are taxed, rather than the business itself.

The statement of financial position of a limited company

The sections of the statement of financial position which list the assets and liabilities of the business are prepared in exactly the same way as for a sole trader or a partnership.

The section of the statement of financial position which shows ownership interest consists of:

- Share capital
- Reserves

The ownership interest in a limited company is normally referred to as its **equity**.

SHARE CAPITAL

SHARE CAPITAL is the capital invested in a company by its owners. The capital of a company is divided into a number of identifiable units, called shares. When a company is formed, it issues shares, which are purchased by investors.

Nominal value and market value

Shares have a nominal value and a market value.

- The nominal value of a share (sometimes known as par value) is its 'face value'. The nominal value of shares is decided when the shares are issued and always remains the same from then onwards. Shares are stated in the statement of financial position at their nominal value.

- The market value of a share is the value at which it is traded on the Stock Exchange. This changes over time and bears no relation to the nominal value. The market value of a company's shares is irrelevant to the accounts.

HOW IT WORKS

On 1 January 20X0 X plc issues 200,000 50p ordinary shares. At 31 December 20X0 A, who purchased 200 shares, sells her shares to B for £2.25 each.

- The nominal value of the shares is 50p. (To have the same amount of share capital, X plc could have issued 100,000 £1 ordinary shares or 400,000 25p ordinary shares.) The double entry to record the issue is:

  DEBIT   Bank (200,000 × 50p)   £100,000

  CREDIT Share capital   £100,000

- The shares are shown in the statement of financial position at £100,000.

- At 31 December 20X0, the market value of the shares is £2.25 each.

- When A sells her shares to B, the transaction is between A and B and X plc does not receive any further cash as a result. The shares continue to be shown in the statement of financial position at £100,000.

Task 2

On 1 April 20X3 Pulsar plc issues 500,000 25p ordinary shares at their nominal value. At 31 March 20X4 the market price of one ordinary share in Pulsar plc is £1.50.

At 31 March 20X4, these shares are included in Pulsar plc's statement of financial position at:

£125,000	
£500,000	
£750,000	

Issued share capital

ISSUED SHARE CAPITAL is the nominal amount of share capital that has actually been issued to shareholders.

The term **allotted share capital** is sometimes used. Shares are allotted to shareholders when shares are issued. Allotted share capital is the same as issued share capital.

Ordinary shares

The majority of shares issued are **ordinary shares**.

ORDINARY SHARES are shares which entitle the holders to share in profits after all prior claims have been satisfied. They entitle the holder to **vote** in general meetings.

This means that:

- Ordinary shareholders cannot be certain of the amount of their dividend as it depends on the level of profit.

- If the company ceases trading, the ordinary shareholders are entitled to any capital remaining after creditors and other classes of shareholder (if any) have received the amounts due to them. (A creditor is any person or entity to which the company owes money.) They may lose their original investment or (in theory) they may receive more than their original investment.

- Because ordinary shareholders can vote, in theory they can determine the policies of the company. (Whether they can do this in practice depends on the percentage of shares that they hold and the percentage held by other ordinary shareholders. In a small company, an individual shareholder is likely to have at least some power; in a large public company, individual shareholders have very little power and the company's policies are generally determined by the directors.)

Ordinary shareholders are therefore the effective owners of the company and bear the risk associated with trading.

Ordinary shares are often known as **equity shares**. EQUITY is the same as ownership interest. A company's equity is its ordinary share capital and its reserves.

Preference shares

PREFERENCE SHARES are shares which carry the right to a fixed rate of dividend.

- The preference dividend must be paid out of available profits before any ordinary dividend is paid.

- In the event of a liquidation, preference shareholders normally have the right to return of their capital before any capital is returned to ordinary shareholders.

- Preference shares **do not** carry the right to vote.

Most types of preference share are actually liabilities of the company, rather than part of equity. This is because the company has an obligation to pay the dividend

and may eventually have an obligation to redeem the shares. If this is the case, the preference shares are not included in share capital, but presented as non-current (long-term) liabilities in the statement of financial position.

RESERVES

All limited companies have at least one reserve: RETAINED EARNINGS.

Retained earnings is the cumulative total of the company's retained profits.

Retained profits are profits after deducting corporation tax and after deducting DIVIDENDS.

The retained earnings reserve is sometimes called the **profit and loss account reserve** or **accumulated profits**.

Dividends

A company's profit after tax is available for distribution to the shareholders, in the form of dividends.

- The dividend received by each shareholder depends on the number of shares that they hold. A dividend is normally expressed as an amount per share.

- Dividends can be viewed as the equivalent of drawings in a sole trader or a partnership. They are a return on a shareholder's investment.

- Any profit not distributed as dividends is retained by the company.

Dividends are not shown in the income statement because they are not an expense, but a distribution to the shareholders. Instead, dividends that are paid during the year are deducted from the retained earnings reserve. This is similar to the way in which drawings (also a distribution to owners) are deducted from capital in accounts of a sole trader.

It is extremely unusual to distribute the whole of the profit after tax for the year:

- Some profits are retained in the business to enable it to continue to operate and to finance future growth (for example, by financing the purchase of new non-current assets).

- The Companies Act 2006 places restrictions on the amount of profits that can be distributed.

- The company may not have sufficient cash to pay the whole amount.

Retained earnings and other reserves

A company has:

- DISTRIBUTABLE RESERVES (sometimes called **revenue reserves** or **non-statutory reserves**) which can be used for paying dividends to shareholders; and may have

- NON-DISTRIBUTABLE RESERVES (sometimes called **capital reserves** or **statutory reserves**) which cannot be used for paying dividends to shareholders.

As well as retained earnings, reserves may consist of:

- Share premium account
- Revaluation reserve
- Capital redemption reserve

} Reserves which the company is legally obliged to set up in certain circumstances; these are not distributable

- General reserve (which may be set up by the directors)

- Other reserves set up by the directors and designated for a specific purpose (for example, non-current asset replacement reserve).

General reserves and other designated reserves can be used to pay dividends. However, the fact that the reserves have been set up suggests that the directors do not intend to use them for this purpose.

All reserves, whether they are distributable or not, are part of equity and 'belong' to the equity (ordinary) shareholders.

HOW IT WORKS

A company wants to transfer £20,000 to a general reserve. Retained profit for the year is £35,000.

The double entry is:

DEBIT	Retained earnings reserve	£20,000	
CREDIT	General reserve		£20,000

LOAN FINANCE

As well as issuing shares, a company can raise finance by taking out a bank loan or by issuing LOAN STOCK.

Like share capital, loan stock is divided into a number of identifiable units and may be held by a large number of individuals. Each unit has a nominal value (at which it is shown in the statement of financial performance) and a market value.

Loan stock may also be known as debentures, debenture stock, loan capital or loan notes.

Loan stock and other long-term loans normally carry a fixed rate of interest. Loans may be secured on particular assets of the company or they may be unsecured. If a loan is secured, the lender has the right to make the directors sell the asset(s) in order to repay the debt.

Loan stock and other long-term loans differ from share capital in a number of important ways:

- Lenders are creditors, while shareholders are members (owners) of the company.

- Lenders normally receive a fixed rate of interest regardless of the profits or losses made by the company. Interest is calculated on the nominal value of the loan stock or the outstanding amount of the bank loan and usually paid half-yearly. The amount of dividend received by ordinary shareholders depends on the level of profit made by the company.

- Loan interest is an expense and charged in the income statement, while dividends on ordinary shares are a distribution to owners (sometimes called an appropriation of profit).

- Lenders can take legal action against a company if their interest is not paid when it is due or repayment of the loan is not made on the due date. Ordinary shareholders are not automatically entitled to receive a dividend and therefore cannot take action against the company if no dividend is paid.

- Loans normally have a fixed repayment date, whereas share capital is only repaid when the company is wound-up.

- Lenders are not entitled to vote in general meetings of the company. Ordinary shareholders can vote in general meetings and therefore (at least in theory) have some influence on the company's policies.

HOW IT WORKS

A company issues £100,000 8% loan stock.

The double entry to record the issue is:

DEBIT	Bank	£100,000	
CREDIT	Loan stock		£100,000

Annual interest on the loan stock is £8,000 (8% × £100,000). The double entry to record the interest payment is:

DEBIT	Interest expense	£8,000	
CREDIT	Bank		£8,000

Task 3

A company has £200,000 12% loan stock. The year-end is 31 December. Interest is payable half-yearly on 31 July and 31 January.

Calculate the total interest payable for the year.

£ [   ]

State what accounting adjustment must be made at the year-end.

Journal

Account name	Debit	Credit
	£	£

PREPARING ACCOUNTS FOR LIMITED COMPANIES

Example of accounts for a limited company

An illustration of the format of an income statement and a statement of financial position for a limited company is shown below. These are simplified versions of the statements that you will be required to draft in your assessment. We will look at these in much more detail in Chapters 3 and 4.

Limited companies are required to publish their accounts. This means that their accounts must be presented in such a way that they provide useful information to users.

Limited company accounts for internal use only can, of course, be prepared in any format that the directors or managers wish.

There are two things to notice:

- The statement of financial position is presented differently from the examples shown earlier. The first part shows total assets and the second part shows total equity and total liabilities:

  ASSETS = EQUITY + LIABILITIES

- The statements use some terms that are different from the ones that you will have learned in your earlier studies, when preparing accounts for sole traders and partnerships. We explain some of the other differences below.

Income statement for the year ended...

	£
Revenue	X
Cost of sales	(X)
Gross profit	X
Operating expenses	(X)
Profit from operations	X
Finance costs	(X)
Profit before tax	X
Tax	(X)
Profit for the year	X

Statement of financial position as at...

	£
Assets	
Non-current assets	
Property, plant and equipment	X
	X
Current assets	
Inventories	X
Trade and other receivables	X
Cash and cash equivalents	X
	X
Total assets	X
Equity and liabilities	
Equity	
Share capital	X
Retained earnings	X
	X
Non-current liabilities	
Bank loans	X
Current liabilities	
Trade and other payables	X
Tax payable	X
	X
Total liabilities	X
Total equity and liabilities	X

The income statement

In the income statement, items cannot be listed out, but must be analysed under the various headings.

Revenue is sales.

Finance costs are normally interest payable on bank loans and on other loans.

The statement of financial position

Trade and other receivables are trade receivables (amounts owed by customers), prepayments and other receivables.

Cash equivalents are short-term investments that can be very easily converted into cash.

Trade and other payables normally consist of trade payables (amounts owed to suppliers) and accruals.

HOW IT WORKS

Tycho Ltd is a private limited company. The trial balance for the year ended 31 March 20X1 is shown below:

	£	£
Ordinary shares of £1 each		50,000
Land and buildings	141,000	
Motor vehicles	15,200	
Plant and machinery	28,900	
Inventories at 1 April 20X0	38,600	
Trade receivables	31,900	
Prepayments	4,200	
Bank current account		2,600
Petty cash	200	
Trade payables		28,300
Accruals		5,600
10% Loan stock		50,000
Sales		304,700
Purchases	221,500	
Operating expenses	52,700	
Loan stock interest	2,500	
Dividend paid	1,500	
Share premium		25,000
Retained earnings at 1 April 20X0		72,000
	538,200	538,200

The following information is also available:

(a) Inventories at 31 March 20X1 were £42,100

(b) Corporation tax for the year has been estimated at £12,500

The adjustments

We need to make three adjustments to the figures shown in the trial balance. Remember that each adjustment affects the financial statements in two places: there is a debit entry and a credit entry.

Inventories

DEBIT	Inventories (statement of financial position)	£42,100	
CREDIT	Inventories (income statement)		£42,100

Being the adjustments for closing inventories

Tax expense

Tax charged on the profits made by a limited company is an expense of the company as a separate legal entity. It is a charge against profits and a liability in the statement of financial position.

DEBIT	Tax expense (income statement)	£12,500	
CREDIT	Tax payable (statement of financial position)		£12,500

Being the tax charge for the year ended 31 March 20X1

Loan stock interest

The charge in the income statement is £2,500, in other words only half the year's interest has been charged. Total loan stock interest for the year is £5,000 (10% × 50,000). A further £2,500 must be accrued.

DEBIT	Loan stock interest (income statement)	£2,500	
CREDIT	Accruals (statement of financial position)		£2,500

Being an accrual for loan stock interests

The accounts

We can now draw up the income statement and the statement of financial position.

Income statement for the year ended 31 March 20X1

	£
Revenue	304,700
Cost of sales (£38,600 + £221,500 − £42,100)	(218,000)
Gross profit	86,700
Operating expenses	(52,700)
Profit from operations	34,000
Finance costs (£2,500 + £2,500)	(5,000)
Profit before tax	29,000
Tax	(12,500)
Profit for the year	16,500

Statement of financial position as at 31 March 20X1

	£	£
Property, plant and equipment		185,100
(£141,000 + £28,900 + £15,200)		
Current assets:		
Inventories	42,100	
Trade and other receivables (£31,900 + £4,200)	36,100	
Cash and cash equivalents	200	
		78,400
Total assets		263,500
Equity:		
Share capital		50,000
Share premium		25,000
Retained earnings (£72,000 + £16,500 − £1,500)		87,000
		162,000
Non-current liabilities:		
Loan stock		50,000
Current liabilities:		
Trade and other payables (£28,300 + £5,600 + £2,500)	36,400	
Tax payable	12,500	
Bank overdraft	2,600	
		51,500
Total liabilities		101,500
Total equity and liabilities		263,500

CHAPTER OVERVIEW

- The purpose of financial statements is to provide information about an entity's financial performance and financial position that is useful to a wide range of users for making economic decisions and assessing the stewardship of the entity's management

- There are several broad types of organisation:

  Profit-making

  - Sole traders
  - Partnerships
  - Companies

  'Not-for-profit'

  - Charities, clubs and societies
  - Public sector organisations

- A limited company:

  - Has a separate legal personality from those of its owners
  - Gives its shareholders (owners) limited liability

- Limited liability means that the owners' liability is limited to the amount that they have paid for their shares. This is the maximum amount that they can lose if the company is wound-up

- Limited companies are owned by shareholders and managed by directors

- There are two types of limited company:

  - Public companies
  - Private companies

- Advantages of trading as a limited company:

  - Limited liability
  - It is easier to raise finance
  - The company continues even if the owners change
  - There may be tax advantages
  - It is easy to transfer shares

- Disadvantages of trading as a limited company:

  - Publication of annual accounts

  - Legal and administrative formalities (including compliance with accounting standards)

  - Restrictions on issuing shares and reducing capital

- Limited companies pay corporation tax, which is deducted from net profit in the income statement

CHAPTER OVERVIEW CONTINUED

- The ownership interest of a limited company is called equity and consists of:
  - Share capital
  - Reserves
- Share capital is reported in the statement of financial position at its nominal ('face') value
- A company's retained earnings reserve is its cumulative profits after tax less dividends paid to shareholders
- Reserves are either:
  - Distributable (including retained profits); or
  - Non-distributable (including share premium and revaluation reserve)
- Loan stock is used to raise finance. Loan stock holders are creditors. They receive a fixed rate of interest, which is an expense in the income statement
- The income statement and statement of financial position of a limited company must follow a specific format
- To adjust for the tax expense for the period:

  DEBIT   Tax expense (income statement)   X

  CREDIT   Tax payable (statement of financial position)   X

Keywords

Stewardship – the accountability of management for the resources entrusted to it by the owners of an entity

Sole trader – a business owned and managed by one person

Partnership – a business jointly owned and managed by two or more people

Company – a business that is a separate legal entity from its owners

Entity – any organisation (whether profit-making or not-for-profit) that prepares accounts as a separate entity from its owners

Public companies – companies that can invite members of the general public to invest in their shares

Private companies – companies that cannot invite members of the general public to invest in their shares

Corporation tax – the tax payable on the profits of a limited company

Share capital – the capital invested in a company by its owners, divided into a number of identifiable shares

Issued share capital – the nominal amount of share capital that has been issued to shareholders (allotted share capital)

Ordinary shares – shares which entitle the holders to share in profits after all prior claims have been satisfied

Equity – ownership interest. A company's equity is its ordinary share capital and its reserves

Preference shares – shares which carry the right to a fixed rate of dividend

Retained earnings – the cumulative total of the company's retained profits

Dividends – amounts paid to shareholders from profits or distributable reserves

Distributable reserves (revenue reserves, non-statutory reserves) – reserves which can be used for paying dividends to shareholders

Non-distributable reserves (capital reserves, statutory reserves) – reserves which cannot be used for paying dividends to shareholders

Loan stock (debentures) – long-term loans made to a company, which normally carry a fixed rate of interest

TEST YOUR LEARNING

Test 1

If a limited company becomes insolvent, the maximum amount that the shareholders can lose is the amount that they have invested in the company.

Is this statement true or false?

True	
False	

Test 2

In a company's statement of financial position, the amount shown as 'Share capital' represents the total market value of the company's shares.

Is this statement true or false?

True	
False	

Test 3

Which ONE of the following items is included in the statement of financial position of a limited company but not in the statement of financial position of a partnership or a sole trader?

Accruals	
Drawings	
Loan stock	
Sales	

Test 4

Which one of the following statements is True?

The general reserve is non-distributable	
The retained earnings reserve is non-distributable	
The revaluation reserve is non-distributable	
The share premium account is distributable	

Test 5

Diamond Ltd made a profit from operations of £140,000 for the year ended 31 December 20X5. Throughout the year the company has had 250,000 £1 ordinary shares and £150,000 9% loan stock. Corporation tax has been estimated at £74,000 for the year. During the year, Diamond Ltd paid a dividend of 5p per ordinary share.

What is the profit for the year ended 31 December 20X5?

£40,000	
£52,500	
£66,000	
£126,500	

Test 6

The trial balance of Hearts Ltd at 31 December 20X2 is shown below:

	£'000	£'000
Bank		420
Bank loan		2,100
Loan interest	105	
Retained earnings reserve		3,955
Operating expenses	3,912	
Purchases	10,493	
Revaluation reserve		1,365
Sales		16,100
Share capital (£1 ordinary shares)		840
Inventories (at 1 January 20X2)	4,515	
Property, plant and equipment (net carrying amount)	5,852	
Trade payables		3,675
Trade receivables	3,578	
	28,455	28,455

Inventories were £5,292,000 at 31 December 20X2.

Corporation tax on profits for the year is estimated to be £280,000.

Required

(a) Draft the income statement for Hearts Ltd for the year ended 31 December 20X2.

Hearts Ltd: Income statement for the year ended 31 December 20X2

	£'000
Revenue	
Cost of sales	
Gross profit	
Operating expenses	
Profit from operations	
Finance cost	
Profit before tax	
Tax	
Profit for the year	

(b) Draft the statement of financial position for Hearts Ltd as at 31 December 20X2.

(Complete the left hand column by writing in the correct line items from the list provided.)

Hearts Ltd: Statement of financial position as at 31 December 20X2

	£'000	£'000
Assets		
Non-current assets:		
▼		
Current assets:		
▼		
▼		
Total assets		
Equity and liabilities		
Equity:		
▼		
▼		
▼		
Non-current liabilities:		
▼		
Current liabilities:		
▼		
▼		
▼		
Total liabilities		
Total equity and liabilities		

Picklist for line items:
Bank loan
Bank overdraft
Inventories
Property, plant and equipment
Receivables
Retained earnings
Revaluation reserve
Share capital
Tax payable
Trade payables

chapter 2:
THE FRAMEWORKS

— chapter coverage 📖 —

In this chapter we put the drafting of limited company financial statements in context by considering why we prepare financial statements, who uses them, and what makes them useful. We also look at several important ideas that underpin the preparation of financial statements. These ideas are set out in the IASB's *Conceptual Framework for Financial Reporting*.

Limited companies have to publish their financial statements, and, unlike sole traders and partnerships, are obliged to comply with company law and accounting standards when preparing them. We begin this chapter by briefly explaining these.

The topics covered are:

✍ The regulatory framework

✍ Accounting standards

✍ Duties and responsibilities of the directors

✍ The purpose and scope of the *Conceptual Framework*

✍ The objective of general purpose financial reporting

✍ The qualities that make financial information useful

✍ The underlying assumption

✍ The elements of financial statements

✍ Recognising the elements of financial statements

✍ Measuring the elements of financial statements

THE REGULATORY FRAMEWORK

Limited companies are required to observe various rules and regulations when preparing financial statements. These regulations govern the accounting treatment of items and the way in which information is presented.

The need for accounting regulation

As we have seen, the purpose of financial statements is to provide useful information about the performance and financial position of an entity. Accounting regulations ensure that financial statements actually do provide useful information.

- Users of the financial statements need to be able to compare the financial statements of different entities and financial statements of the same entity over time. If preparers of financial statements were able to adopt whatever accounting practices they chose it would be impossible to do this in any meaningful way.

- Managers normally wish to show the performance of a company in the best possible light. Without regulation, information might be deliberately presented in such a way as to mislead users.

- The owners or providers of finance to a company are often external to the company and separate from its management. They depend on financial statements for information about a company's performance and position. Accounting regulations ensure that the financial statements provide all the information that users need in order to make decisions.

Sources of regulation

In the UK, the most important sources of regulation for limited companies are:

- Companies legislation (the Companies Act 2006)
- Accounting standards

The detailed requirements of accounting standards will be covered in later chapters.

ACCOUNTING STANDARDS

What are accounting standards?

ACCOUNTING STANDARDS are authoritative statements of how particular types of transactions and other events should be reflected in financial statements. An entity normally needs to comply with accounting standards in order to produce financial statements which give a fair presentation of its performance and financial position.

It follows that unless there are exceptional circumstances, limited companies must comply with all relevant accounting standards. Sole traders and partnerships often adopt accounting standards, even though they may not be legally obliged to do so.

Although accounting standards state how particular items should be dealt with, many accounting standards set out principles, rather than detailed rules. Preparers of financial statements should be guided by the spirit and reasoning behind accounting standards and not simply regard them as a set of rules to circumvent.

Two sets of accounting standards operate in the UK:

- UK accounting standards issued by the UK Accounting Standards Board (ASB). These are known as Financial Reporting Standards (FRSs) or Statements of Standard Accounting Practice (SSAPs).

- International accounting standards (IASs) or International Financial Reporting Standards (IFRSs) issued by the International Accounting Standards Board (IASB).

In your assessment, you will be expected to prepare financial statements that comply with **International Accounting Standards and International Financial Reporting Standards**.

International Accounting Standards

Businesses increasingly operate across national boundaries and users need to be able to make comparisons between the financial statements of entities located in different countries. It follows that there is a need for a 'common language' of accounting practice, so that all companies throughout the world follow broadly similar accounting regulations.

Although the IASB has no power to enforce its standards, most major industrialised nations, including the UK, ensure that their domestic standards reflect the requirements of international standards as far as possible.

Since January 2005, all quoted companies operating within the European Union (EU), including the UK, have been required to use international accounting standards. (A quoted company is a company whose shares are listed on a recognised stock exchange.) For the time being, other companies in the UK can choose whether to change to international standards or to continue to apply UK accounting standards. However, this situation will probably change within the next few years.

The standard-setting structure

International accounting standards are of two types:

- International Financial Reporting Standards (IFRSs): issued by the International Accounting Standards Board (IASB) since 2001.

- International Accounting Standards (IASs): issued before 2001 by the IASB's predecessor, the International Accounting Standards Committee (IASC).

When the IASB succeeded the IASC it adopted all the extant IASs so that they remained in force and it has since improved many of them.

The IASB is part of a larger organisation consisting of several operating bodies:

- **International Financial Reporting Standards Foundation (IFRS Foundation)** (previously the International Accounting Standards Committee Foundation (IASCF))

  This is an independent, not-for-profit organisation working in the public interest. It is overseen by 22 **Trustees**, who appoint the members of the IASB and the other bodies. The IFRS Foundation and the Trustees govern and direct the work of the IASB and are responsible for fundraising and raising public awareness of the IASB's work. The IFRS Foundation is in its turn overseen by a Monitoring Board which consists of representatives of public authorities such as the European Commission and the US Securities and Exchange Commission.

- **The International Accounting Standards Board (IASB)**

  The IASB develops, issues and withdraws accounting standards. Its 15 members are chosen for their technical expertise and include preparers and users of financial statements, auditors and academics. Members are also chosen so as to ensure a broad mix of nationalities.

- **The International Financial Reporting Standards Interpretations Committee (IFRS Interpretations Committee)** (previously the International Financial Reporting Interpretations Committee (IFRIC))

The IFRS Interpretations Committee provides timely guidance on issues not covered by IASs and IFRSs and on applying and interpreting existing IASs and IFRSs. It issues Interpretations (sometimes known as IFRICs) setting out the accounting treatment that should be adopted for specific items.

- **The International Financial Reporting Standards Advisory Council (IFRS Advisory Council)** (previously called the Standards Advisory Council (SAC))

  The IFRS Advisory Council advises the IASB during the standard-setting process. It has about 50 members and it consists of groups and individuals from many different countries and backgrounds.

The IASB's objectives

The objectives of the IFRS Foundation and the IASB are:

- To develop, in the public interest, a single set of high quality, understandable, enforceable and globally accepted financial reporting standards based upon clearly articulated principles. These standards should require high quality, transparent and comparable information in financial statements and other financial reporting to help investors, other participants in the world's capital markets and other users of financial information to make economic decisions

- To promote the use and rigorous application of those standards

- To take account of the needs of a range of sizes and types of entities in diverse economic settings.

  (For example, although IFRSs are mainly designed for large public companies, the IASB has also developed a standard for small and medium sized entities.)

- To promote and facilitate adoption of International Financial Reporting Standards (IFRSs).

  (For example, the IASB works closely with national standard-setters to bring about convergence of national accounting standards and IFRSs.)

The standard-setting process

International Financial Reporting Standards normally pass through several stages as they are developed:

- A topic is identified; *then*

- The topic is discussed at a Board meeting and if the Board decides to proceed with the project; *then*

BPP
LEARNING MEDIA

- The IASB may set up a working group of experts and other interested parties to give advice on issues arising in the project. It decides whether to carry out the project alone or jointly with a national standard-setter; *then*

- A Discussion Paper may be issued. This is circulated to interested parties, who comment on the issues discussed and any proposals made; *then*

- An Exposure Draft (ED) is published. An Exposure Draft is a draft version of the proposed standard. This is circulated to accountancy bodies, governments, regulatory bodies and other interested parties. All interested parties have an opportunity to comment. The IASB also consults with the IFRS Advisory Council, working groups and national standard-setters and may carry out trials or field tests to ensure that what it is proposing will work in practice; *then*

- The IASB examines the comments and suggestions received and may revise the proposals; *then*

- The International Financial Reporting Standard (IFRS) is issued.

DUTIES AND RESPONSIBILITIES OF THE DIRECTORS

Publishing the accounts

The Companies Act 2006 states that the directors of a limited company are responsible for preparing and approving its annual accounts, having them audited (where this is required) and circulating them to the shareholders. Every shareholder is entitled to receive a copy of the company's annual accounts. If the company is a public company, the accounts must be presented to the shareholders in a general meeting.

The shareholders approve the accounts and the directors must then **file** (deposit) them with the Registrar of Companies. The Registrar of Companies keeps copies of the annual accounts of all limited companies and any member of the public may inspect them for a small charge.

If the company is a **public company**, the accounts must be filed **within six months** of the end of the accounting period. If the company is a **private company**, the accounts must be filed within **nine months** of the end of the accounting period.

In addition to filing accounts with the Registrar of Companies, most public limited companies publish an Annual Report, including a Chairman's Statement which comments on the activities of the company during the year and its future plans and prospects. This is circulated to shareholders (who may choose to receive

'summary financial statements' instead). Quoted companies (companies whose shares are listed on a recognised stock exchange) are now required to publish their annual report and accounts on their web site, so that members of the public can obtain them easily. For public limited companies, the published accounts are an important method of promoting the company to potential investors.

Smaller companies do not normally 'publish' their accounts in this way. However, because of the potential 'publicity' that can follow from filing accounts with the Registrar, the financial statements of limited companies prepared for external use are often known as PUBLISHED ACCOUNTS or PUBLISHED FINANCIAL STATEMENTS.

Because they are required by statute (law), they may also be referred to as STATUTORY ACCOUNTS.

What must be published

Unless they are quoted companies, UK companies have a choice when preparing accounts for publication:

- They can follow UK standards. This means that they must follow certain rules set out in the Companies Act itself; these set out the format of the profit and loss account and the balance sheet, the accounting principles to be followed, and other disclosures that must be made. The Companies Act describes these accounts as COMPANIES ACT ACCOUNTS.

- They can follow IASs and IFRSs. This means that they comply with IAS 1 *Presentation of Financial Statements*, which contains requirements that are very similar to those in the Companies Act. The Companies Act describes these accounts as IAS ACCOUNTS.

Quoted companies must prepare IAS accounts. The EU Regulation actually states that IAS accounts are required for the **consolidated** accounts of a quoted company. (Consolidated accounts are accounts that present information for a group of companies as if they were a single entity. They are covered in Chapters 10 and 11.)

Companies Act accounts

The Companies Act 2006 states that the following items must be filed with the Registrar of Companies:

- A **profit and loss account** (income statement) showing the profit or loss for the accounting period
- A **balance sheet** (statement of financial position) showing the state of the company's affairs on the last day of the accounting period
- A directors' report
- An auditors' report
- **Group accounts** (if the company has subsidiaries)

The profit and loss account and balance sheet are supported by notes, which analyse the figures in the main statements and may disclose additional information.

IAS accounts

IAS 1 states that a complete set of financial statements comprises:

- A **statement of financial position** at the end of the period (see Chapter 3)
- A **statement of comprehensive income** for the period (see Chapter 4)
- A **statement of changes in equity** for the period (see Chapter 4)
- A **statement of cash flows** for the period (see Chapter 5)
- **Notes**, comprising a summary of significant accounting policies and other information

IAS 1 also states that an entity should present all the financial statements with equal prominence.

The Companies Act also requires:

- A directors' report
- An auditors' report
- **Group accounts** (if the company has subsidiaries)

Adequate accounting records

Whichever set of regulations the directors follow, they also have a legal duty to **keep adequate accounting records**.

A company's accounting records must be sufficient

- to show and explain the company's transactions,
- to disclose with reasonable accuracy, at any time, the financial position of the company at that time, and
- to enable the directors to ensure that any accounts required to be prepared comply with the requirements of the Companies Act (and with the requirements of IFRSs)

Accounting records must contain

- entries of all sums of money received and expended by the company and the matters in respect of which the receipt and expenditure takes place, and
- a record of the assets and liabilities of the company

A true and fair view

The Companies Act states that published accounts must show a **true and fair view** of the company's results for the period and its assets and liabilities at the end of the period. This normally means that they must comply with the requirements of the Companies Acts and applicable accounting standards.

Where IAS accounts are prepared, this requirement is met if the accounts **present fairly** the financial position and financial performance of the entity (as required by IAS 1).

However, (in very exceptional circumstances), the directors may override any of these rules if following them would result in the financial statements not showing a true and fair view (the 'true and fair view override').

THE PURPOSE AND SCOPE OF THE *CONCEPTUAL FRAMEWORK*

A CONCEPTUAL FRAMEWORK is a set of concepts and principles that underpin the preparation of financial statements.

The IASB's *Conceptual Framework for Financial Reporting* sets out the principles and concepts that the IASB believes should underlie the preparation and presentation of financial statements that are prepared to assist their users in making economic decisions, for example:

- to decide when to buy, hold or sell an equity investment.
- to assess the stewardship or accountability of management.
- to assess the ability of the entity to pay and provide other benefits to its employees.
- to assess the security for amounts lent to the entity.
- to determine taxation policies.
- to determine distributable profits and dividends.
- to prepare and use national income statistics.
- to regulate the activities of entities.

The *Conceptual Framework* is not an accounting standard and entities are not required to comply with it. It has been developed by the IASB in order to:

- Assist it in its development of future IFRSs and in its review of existing IFRSs
- Assist it in promoting harmonisation of regulations, accounting standards and other procedures

- Assist national standard-setters (such as the UK ASB) in developing national standards
- Assist preparers of financial statements in applying IFRSs and in dealing with topics that do not yet form the subject of an IFRS
- Assist auditors in forming an opinion as to whether financial statements comply with IFRSs
- Assist users of financial statements in interpreting the information contained in financial statements prepared in compliance with IFRSs
- Provide those who are interested in the work of the IASB with information about its approach to the development of IFRSs

The *Conceptual Framework* covers the following topics:

- The objective of financial reporting
- The qualitative characteristics of useful financial information (the qualities that make financial information useful)
- The definition, recognition and measurement of the elements from which financial statements are constructed.

Many of the IASB's standards have been strongly influenced by the ideas set out in the *Conceptual Framework*.

THE OBJECTIVE OF GENERAL PURPOSE FINANCIAL REPORTING

The IASB's *Conceptual Framework* states that:

'The objective of general purpose financial reporting is to provide financial information about the reporting entity that is useful to existing and potential investors, lenders and other creditors in making decisions about providing resources to the entity. Those decisions involve buying, selling or holding equity and debt instruments, and providing or settling loans and other forms of credit.'

General purpose financial reporting means published financial statements.

A reporting entity is a company or other organisation that prepares financial statements.

Task 1

At the beginning of Chapter 1, we set out two reasons why users need financial information about a limited company. Briefly state what these are.

1	
2	

The most important users and their needs

The *Conceptual Framework* explains that although financial statements may be used by a wide range of different groups of people, they are **primarily prepared to meet the needs of two specific groups**:

- Existing and potential investors
- Existing and potential lenders and other creditors

These are the people who **provide capital** (finance) to an entity, either in the form of share capital (equity) as owners, or in the form of loans.

Existing and potential investors need to make decisions that involve buying, selling or holding equity (shares) or debt instruments (loan stock and debentures). They need information about the returns that they expect from an investment (dividends, interest, repayment of the principal amount of a debt instrument or market price increases).

Existing and potential lenders and other creditors need to make decisions about providing or settling loans and other forms of credit. They need information about the returns they can expect from lending (interest payments and the eventual repayment of the principal amount of the loan).

Consequently, investors and lenders need information about the amount, timing and uncertainty of future net cash inflows to the entity. This in turn means that they need information about:

- the resources of an entity (assets)

- the claims against an entity (liabilities); and

- how efficiently and effectively the entity's management have discharged their responsibilities to use the entity's resources (stewardship).

For example, management may have a responsibility to protect the entity's resources from the unfavourable effects of economic factors such as price changes. Management may also have to make sure that the entity complies with applicable laws and other regulations. Users need information about the way in which management has carried out its responsibilities so that they can make decisions such as how to vote at company meetings or whether to reappoint or replace management.

Many investors, lenders and other users cannot require the entity to provide them with the information that they need as they are **external** to the entity. **They have to rely on the published financial statements.**

(This is an important reason why accounting regulations such as the Companies Act and IFRSs are necessary: to make sure that published financial statements meet the information needs of owners and lenders.)

The *Conceptual Framework* makes one other important point. General purpose financial reports (published financial statements) cannot provide all of the information that users need. They may also need to consider relevant information from other sources, for example, general economic conditions and expectations, political events and information about the industry in which the company operates.

Limitations of financial reports

The *Conceptual Framework* identifies the limitations of general purpose financial reports:

- **They are not designed to show the value of a reporting entity.** However, they provide information that may help users to estimate its value.

  Financial statements show an entity's equity and reserves, which is the **total amount of its assets less its liabilities**. This is **not the same as the market value of the company's shares**. Many assets and liabilities are measured at their original cost to the company, rather than their market value. In addition, companies may have many important and valuable assets that are not recognised in the statement of financial position, such as goodwill and human resources.

- **They may not meet the needs of every individual user.** Individual investors, lenders and other creditors (primary users) may have different information needs and these may conflict. The reporting entity may include additional information where this is most useful to particular users.

- **They are prepared primarily for existing and potential investors, lenders and other creditors**. Other groups of people, such as regulators and members of the public, may be interested in financial information about an entity. These groups may find general purpose financial reports useful, but they are **not primarily directed towards these other groups**. **Management** also needs financial information, but **can obtain the information that it needs internally.**

- **They are based on estimates, judgements and models rather than exact depictions.** The *Conceptual Framework* establishes the concepts that underlie those estimates, judgements and models.

Information about an entity's economic resources, claims and changes in resources and claims

General purpose financial reports provide information about the **financial position** of a reporting entity:

- Its **economic resources**; and
- the **claims** against it.

Economic resources (assets) and claims (liabilities)

General purpose financial reports also provide information about the effects of transactions and other events that **change** a reporting entity's economic resources and claims.

Both types of information are useful in making decisions about providing resources to an entity.

Information about the nature and amounts of a reporting entity's economic resources and claims can help users to assess:

- the reporting entity's liquidity and solvency (its ability to meet its liabilities as they fall due)

- its needs for additional finance and

- how successful it is likely to be in obtaining finance.

Changes in economic resources and claims

Changes in an entity's economic resources (its assets) and claims (its liabilities) result mainly from its **financial performance** (its profit or loss for the year and other gains or losses).

Information about a reporting entity's financial performance helps users to understand the return that the entity has produced on its economic resources. This is an indication of how efficiently and effectively management has used the resources of the entity and is helpful in predicting the entity's future returns on its economic resources.

Changes in an entity's economic resources and claims **may also result from other transactions and events**, such as issuing additional ownership (equity) shares. Users also need information about this type of change.

Accrual accounting

The *Conceptual Framework* explains that financial information should be prepared using ACCRUAL ACCOUNTING. (You should already be familiar with the accruals concept from your earlier studies.)

Accrual accounting shows the effects of transactions and other events on a reporting entity's economic resources and claims in the periods in which those

effects occur, even if the resulting cash receipts and payments occur in a different period.

Information about an entity's economic resources and claims and changes in these during a period is more useful in assessing an entity's past and future performance than information based solely on cash receipts and payments during that period.

Cash flow information

Information about a reporting entity's **cash flows** during a period also helps users to assess the entity's ability to generate cash in the future.

It also shows how the reporting entity obtains and spends cash, including information about its borrowing and repayment of debt. Cash flow information helps users to understand a reporting entity's operations and its financing and investing activities.

The statement of cash flows and the usefulness of the information it provides is covered in Chapter 5.

WHAT MAKES FINANCIAL INFORMATION USEFUL?

The **qualitative characteristics** of useful financial information identify the types of information that are likely to be most useful when making decisions about an entity on the basis of the financial statements.

If information in the financial statements is to be useful, it must possess certain fundamental qualities. It must:

- be relevant; and
- must faithfully represent what it purports to represent

These qualities are known as the **fundamental qualitative characteristics** of useful financial information.

Relevance

Information is relevant if it is **capable of making a difference** in the decisions made by users.

Information may be capable of making a difference in a decision even if some users choose not to use it or are already aware of it from other sources (for example, the press).

Financial information is capable of making a difference in decisions if it has **predictive value**, **confirmatory value** or both.

Financial statements show how an entity has performed in the past, but this is often used as a basis for **predicting what might happen in the future.**

For example, if the statement of financial position shows that a business has plenty of cash or other resources now, users know that it will probably be able to take advantage of any opportunities to expand in future (perhaps by buying another business or recruiting extra staff). It will probably also be able to react if there are unexpected losses in future (perhaps by having assets that it can sell for cash in order to meet its debts and carry on trading).

Users often use financial statements to predict:

- Future dividend and wage payments
- Movements in the market price of the entity's shares (if it is listed)
- The entity's ability to meet its liabilities as they fall due

Financial information is also used to **confirm** (or change) users past conclusions about an entity's financial performance or financial position.

Information can have both predictive value and confirmatory value. For example, revenue for the current year can be used to predict revenue for next year. Actual revenue for the current year can also be compared with expected revenue that was predicted using last year's financial statements.

MATERIALITY is an important aspect of relevance. Information is only relevant if it is material.

Materiality

Information is **material** if omitting it or misstating it could influence decisions that users make on the basis of financial information about a specific reporting entity.

The *Conceptual Framework* explains that materiality is entity-specific. It depends on the nature or size (or both) of items taken in the context of an individual entity's financial statements.

In practice, materiality is often judged in relation to a cut-off point (for example, an error is material if it exceeds 1% of sales revenue). Whether an item is material can depend on its nature and on the circumstances, as well as on its size. For example, limited companies are required by law to disclose certain information about directors' earnings. This information must be exact, even though the amounts involved might be relatively small in relation to the accounts as a whole.

If information is not material it is not useful. Including it may obscure the overall picture given by the financial statements or distract users from information that is genuinely significant.

Accounting standards need not be applied to immaterial items.

Task 2

A company has sales revenue of £1 million, net profit of £20,000 and net assets of £500,000. Which of these errors is likely to be material?

    (a)   Revenue is overstated by £1,000. The cost of sales figure is not affected.

    (b)   Plant and equipment is understated by £30,000 because an item has been incorrectly treated as an expense.

Neither of them	
(a) only	
(b) only	
Both of them	

Faithful representation

Financial statements must faithfully represent the economic phenomena (for example, transactions and events) that they purport to represent. A perfectly faithful representation is:

- complete
- neutral
- free from error.

In practice, this means that:

- The financial statements should include all information necessary for a user to understand what is being depicted, including all necessary descriptions and explanations.

- The information in the financial statements should be selected and presented without bias. It should not be slanted, weighted, emphasised, de-emphasised or manipulated to increase the probability that the information will be received favourably or unfavourably by users.

- There must be no errors or omissions in the description of the item (phenomenon) reported. The process used to produce the reported information should be selected and applied with no errors in the process.

'Free from error' does not mean perfectly accurate in all respects. For example, financial statements use estimates. An estimate does not always turn out to be correct. However, when estimates are used they should be clearly described as estimates and there must be no errors in selecting and applying the process for making the estimate.

A faithful representation, by itself, does not necessarily result in useful information. Suppose that an entity receives a government grant to purchase an asset. The cost of the asset to the entity is nil. If the entity records the cost of the

asset as nil in its financial statements, this is a faithful representation of its cost, but users may then not be aware that the entity has the asset. They have been deprived of useful and relevant information.

Substance over form is the principle that financial statements should report the commercial and economic substance of a transaction, rather than its strict legal form. Substance over form is sometimes described as an aspect of faithful representation.

In most cases, the substance of a transaction and its legal form are the same, but some transactions are more complex. When substance and form are different, reporting the substance of the transaction rather than the legal form can have a dramatic effect on the financial statements. During the 1980s some entities began to devise complicated transactions so as to control assets and incur liabilities without having to include them in the statement of financial position. As a result, this form of 'creative accounting' (known as **off balance sheet financing**) became common.

CREATIVE ACCOUNTING is a term used to describe accounting treatments which are technically within the law and accounting standards but which give a biased impression of a company's performance.

The enhancing qualitative characteristics of financial information

There are four characteristics that enhance, or improve, the usefulness of information that is relevant and faithfully represented. These are:

- comparability
- verifiability
- timeliness
- understandability

Comparability

Users need to be able to compare:

- The financial statements of an entity through time
- The financial statements of different entities

Consistency helps to achieve comparability. Consistency is the use of the same methods for the same items from one period to the next and in a single period, the use of the same methods across entities.

In practice, accounting standards and other regulations normally require that:

- Similar items must be treated in the same way
- Items must normally be treated in the same way from one accounting period to the next

- Entities must disclose the accounting policies adopted in the financial statements
- Financial statements must show corresponding information (comparative figures) for preceding periods

Comparability does not mean uniformity. For information to be comparable, like things must look alike and different things must look different.

Comparability is reduced if accounting standards allow alternative methods for the same item. (Over the years the IASB has reduced the number of instances in which an entity has a choice of accounting treatment. However, there are still a few areas in which IFRSs allow alternatives, for example, in measuring non-current assets. This will be covered in later chapters.)

Verifiability

Verifiability helps to assure users that information faithfully represents the economic data that it purports to represent.

If information is verifiable, it means that different knowledgeable and independent observers could reach a consensus (broad agreement but not necessarily complete agreement) that a particular way of presenting an item is a faithful representation.

Verification can be direct (for example, through an observation, such as counting cash). It can also be indirect (for example, through checking the quantities and costs used in calculating the value of closing inventories and checking the calculation itself). However, not all information can be verified. For example, forecasts of future periods cannot be verified until that future period occurs. In this case the entity should disclose the assumptions it has made in making the forecasts.

Timeliness

To be useful, information must be available to decision makers in time to be capable of influencing their decisions.

Generally, the older the information is, the less useful it is. For example, the latest set of financial statements is normally the most relevant for decision-making. However, older financial information may still be useful for identifying and assessing trends (for example, growth in profits over a number of years).

Understandability

Classifying, characterising and presenting information clearly and concisely makes it understandable.

However, some information is complex and cannot be made easier to understand. Excluding this information from the financial statements would make them more understandable, but they would also be incomplete and potentially misleading.

Financial reports are prepared for users who have a reasonable knowledge of business and economic activities and who review and analyse the information diligently. Users may sometimes need help from an adviser in order to understand complex financial information.

A 'fair presentation' or a 'true and fair view'

The accounts of UK limited companies are required by law to show 'a true and fair view' of their profit or loss (financial performance) during the accounting period and their state of affairs (financial position) at the period end. Where financial statements follow IFRS, they are required to give a 'fair presentation' or to 'present fairly' the information.

Financial information cannot be useful to users unless it gives a fair presentation of an entity's performance and position or represents a true and fair view. But what does a 'fair presentation' or a 'true and fair' view mean?

There is no definition of 'true and fair' and the *Conceptual Framework* does not discuss the meaning of 'fair presentation', but the following points are relevant:

- 'True and fair' is a legal concept and in extreme cases its meaning may be decided by the courts.

- Financial statements prepared in accordance with all applicable regulations will normally give a true and fair view/fair presentation.

- The meaning of 'true and fair' and 'fair presentation' evolve over time and in accordance with changes in the business environment and in generally accepted accounting practice.

THE UNDERLYING ASSUMPTION

The IASB believes that the GOING CONCERN concept is fundamental to the preparation of accounts. This concept is so generally accepted that users can assume it has been followed unless the financial statements state otherwise. In the *Conceptual Framework* going concern is described as an **underlying assumption.**

Financial statements are normally prepared on the assumption that the entity will continue to operate for the foreseeable future. This means that its management do not intend or need to liquidate or curtail the scale of its operations materially. For example, if an entity is a going concern there should be no need to sell off any significant part of the business or restrict any of its normal trading activities.

This assumption is reflected in the way that the income statement and the statement of financial position are drawn up.

This is important because it affects the information that users need about the entity's assets and liabilities:

- If the entity is a going concern, users will be more interested in its ability to use its assets to generate cash and profits than in the amount that the assets would be worth on the open market. Therefore non-current assets are stated at cost (or current value) less depreciation.

- If the entity is not a going concern, the information that is relevant to users is the amount that can be realised from selling off its assets. Therefore non-current assets are stated at the amount that they are worth if they are sold separately on the open market immediately ('break-up values').

THE ELEMENTS OF FINANCIAL STATEMENTS

In your earlier studies you will have learned that financial statements are made up of a number of different items, for example: income; expenses; assets; liabilities; capital.

The IASB's *Conceptual Framework for Financial Reporting* defines five elements of financial statements. These are:

- Assets
- Liabilities
- Equity
- Income
- Expenses

Assets

In simple terms, an **asset** is a resource that a business owns or is able to use.

Assets are classified as either NON-CURRENT ASSETS or CURRENT ASSETS. Non-current assets are sometimes called **fixed assets**.

- A **non-current asset** is an asset that a business intends to hold for some time (usually more than one year) in order to use it to generate income.

- A **current asset** is an asset that a business holds for the short term, for conversion into cash in the course of trading.

Task 3

Give three examples of each of the following:

(a)   Non-current assets

1	
2	
3	

(b)   Current assets

1	
2	
3	

The *Conceptual Framework* gives a more formal definition:

An ASSET is a resource controlled by the entity as a result of past events and from which future economic benefits are expected to flow to the entity.

This definition is very wide and there are two important things to note:

- An entity often owns its assets, but this need not be the case as long as it controls them. A business may lease a motor vehicle, and thus has the right to use the vehicle throughout its useful life, even though it never legally owns it. The vehicle is an asset of the business because the business controls the motor vehicle.

- An asset is something that provides future economic benefit. This means that it should eventually result in an inflow of cash. For example, a factory is used to produce goods that will be sold for cash.

Liabilities

In simple terms, a liability is something which a business owes to somebody else.

Examples of liabilities:

- Amounts owing to suppliers
- Accruals for services
- Advance payments received from customers
- Bank overdraft
- Loans

Like assets, liabilities are classified into current liabilities and long-term (non-current) liabilities.

- CURRENT LIABILITIES are payable within one year.

- NON-CURRENT (LONG-TERM) LIABILITIES are payable after more than one year.

The definition in the *Conceptual Framework* is as follows:

A LIABILITY is a present obligation of the entity arising from past events, the settlement of which is expected to result in an outflow of resources embodying economic benefits from the entity.

There are three important things to note:

- There must be an obligation, in other words, an entity only has a liability if it cannot avoid an outflow of economic benefit.

- An outflow of economic benefits normally means incurring expenditure or paying cash to somebody, but this is not always the case. An entity might have a liability to provide goods or services in return for cash or another benefit.

- If an entity recognises a liability in its statement of financial position, the transaction or event giving rise to the liability must have happened before the year-end.

Equity

EQUITY is the owners' residual interest in the assets of the entity after deducting all its liabilities.

Equity is sometimes known as **ownership interest**. In other words, equity is what the entity 'owes' to its owners. This is reported in the entity's statement of financial position and in the accounts of a sole trader or a partnership, it is called **capital**.

Income and expenses

An entity's **income** normally comes from sales of goods or services, but can come from fees, interest received, dividends received or rent. This kind of income is known as **revenue** and it arises as a result of the ordinary business activities of an entity. Income can also come from **gains**, for example, profits on the disposal of non-current assets.

Expenses include items which arise in the normal course of business, such as cost of sales, wages and depreciation. They also include **losses**, for example, the destruction of assets in a fire or flood, or a loss on disposal of a non-current asset.

Profit is the amount by which a business's income exceeds its expenditure. A business makes a loss if its expenditure exceeds its income.

The *Conceptual Framework* defines income and expenses as follows:

INCOME is increases in economic benefits during the accounting period in the form of inflows or enhancement of assets or decreases of liabilities that result in increases in equity, other than those relating to contributions from owners.

Income increases assets or decreases liabilities. For example, a sale increases cash or amounts receivable (debtors).

CONTRIBUTIONS FROM OWNERS are increases in equity (ownership interest) resulting from transfers from owners in their capacity as owners.

Increases in share capital are contributions from owners.

EXPENSES are decreases in economic benefits during the accounting period in the form of outflows or depletions of assets or incurrences of liabilities that result in decreases in equity, other than those relating to distributions to owners.

Expenses decrease assets or increase liabilities. For example, the payment of wages decreases cash.

DISTRIBUTIONS TO OWNERS are decreases in equity (ownership interest) resulting from transfers to owners in their capacity as owners.

Dividend payments are the most common distribution to owners.

The elements and the accounting equation

The relationship between the elements is shown below:

- ASSETS – LIABILITIES = EQUITY
- EQUITY = CONTRIBUTIONS FROM OWNERS + INCOME – EXPENSES – DISTRIBUTIONS TO OWNERS

This is simply a restatement of the basic accounting equation that you have learned in your earlier studies:

- ASSETS – LIABILITIES = CAPITAL
- CAPITAL = OPENING NET ASSETS + PROFIT – DRAWINGS

You may have noticed that income and expenses (and therefore profits and losses) are defined only in relation to changes in assets and liabilities. In other words:

- An increase in net assets results in income or a gain (a profit)
- A decrease in net assets results in an expense or a loss

RECOGNISING THE ELEMENTS OF FINANCIAL STATEMENTS

The IASB's *Conceptual Framework* provides rules as to when items (assets and liabilities, income and expenses) should be recognised in the financial statements.

IASs and IFRSs use the terms RECOGNITION and DERECOGNITION.

- When an item is included in the financial statements it is said to be **recognised**.

- When an item is removed from the financial statements it is **derecognised**.

The recognition criteria

An item that meets the definition of an element (eg, an asset or a liability) should be recognised if:

- It is **probable** that any future economic benefit associated with the item will flow to or from the entity
- The item has a cost or value that can be measured with **reliability**

Suppose that an entity buys a machine. The machine exists in a physical sense; the entity intends to use it to make goods for resale, so it is probable that economic benefits (sales revenue) will flow to the entity (cash will eventually be received). The cost of the machine to the entity is a matter of fact and there is documentation to prove it (it can be measured with reliability).

Contrast this with internally generated goodwill. (You will have learned about goodwill when you learned how to prepare partnership accounts during your earlier studies.) Most businesses generate some goodwill and this gives rise to future economic benefits. Therefore goodwill meets the definition of an asset. However, it fails to meet both recognition criteria: it is very difficult to prove that internally generated goodwill really exists and it is impossible to value it objectively. This is why internally generated goodwill and similar intangible assets are not normally recognised in the financial statements.

Many accounting standards incorporate these recognition principles, for example:

- IAS 16 *Property, Plant and Equipment*
- IAS 38 *Intangible Assets*
- IAS 37 *Provisions, Contingent Liabilities and Contingent Assets*

These Standards will be covered in later chapters.

Task 4

A company spends £100,000 on an advertising campaign to promote its products. The company should recognise an asset.

Is this statement True or False?

True	
False	

Recognising gains and losses

Income (or gains) and expenses (or losses) are defined in relation to changes in assets and liabilities. This means that (assuming that there are no contributions from owners or distributions from owners):

- If a transaction increases net assets, income or a gain is recognised

- If a transaction reduces or eliminates net assets, an expense or a loss is recognised

In other words:

- CLOSING NET ASSETS – OPENING NET ASSETS = PROFIT/LOSS FOR THE PERIOD

MEASURING THE ELEMENTS OF FINANCIAL STATEMENTS

Measurement is the process of determining the monetary amounts at which items are recognised and carried in the financial statements.

An entity must select a basis on which to measure items, particularly assets.

The IASB *Conceptual Framework* describes four possible measurement bases:

- Historic cost
- Current cost
- Realisable value
- Present value

Historical cost

Assets are recorded at the amount of cash paid or the fair value of the consideration given to acquire them at the time of the acquisition.

Liabilities are normally recorded at the amounts of cash expected to be paid to satisfy the liability in the normal course of business.

For example, a company buys a machine for £10,000. The historic cost of the machine is £10,000.

Current cost

Assets are carried at the amount of cash that would have to be paid if the same or a similar asset was acquired currently.

Liabilities are carried at the amount of cash that would be required to settle the obligation currently.

For example, a company purchased a machine five years ago for £10,000. An identical machine can now be purchased for £30,000.

The historic cost of the machine is £10,000. The current cost of the machine is £30,000.

Realisable value

Assets are carried at the amount of cash that could currently be obtained by selling the asset.

Liabilities are carried at the amounts of cash expected to be paid to satisfy the liabilities in the normal course of business (sometimes known as settlement value).

For example, a company purchased a machine for £10,000 (its historic cost). This machine could be sold for £20,000.

The realisable value of the machine is £20,000.

Present value

Assets are carried at the present discounted value of the future net cash inflows that the item is expected to generate in the normal course of business.

Liabilities are carried at the present discounted value of the future net cash outflows that are expected to be required to settle the liabilities in the normal course of business.

When cash flows are discounted, they are adjusted to take account of the time value of money.

For example, a company buys a machine for £10,000. The machine will be used to produce goods for sale. It is expected to generate discounted net cash flows (sales revenue less the costs of running the machine) of £5,000 per year for five years.

The present value of the machine is £25,000 (5 × £5,000).

Measurement bases

Historic cost is the most common way of measuring items. In practice, many entities combine historic cost with the other bases:

- Inventories are carried at the lower of cost and net realisable value. (Net realisable value is the amount that could be obtained by selling an asset, less any costs of selling it.)

- Some types of investment (securities) are carried at market value.

- Current cost accounting may be used to deal with the effects of inflation (this is very rare in the UK).

Many IASs and IFRSs allow or require a further measurement basis that is **not** discussed in the *Conceptual Framework*: fair value.

FAIR VALUE is the amount for which an asset could be exchanged between knowledgeable, willing parties in an arm's length transaction.

The fair value of an item is normally its market value.

Many companies adopt modified historic cost accounting: some assets (usually land and buildings) are included in the statement of financial position at current value or fair value while the remaining assets are included at historic cost.

CHAPTER OVERVIEW

- Financial information must be presented fairly if it is to be useful. This normally means that it must comply with all applicable regulations

- Regulation ensures that:
  - Users are able to compare the financial statements of different companies and of the same company over time
  - Users are not deliberately misled by the financial statements
  - Financial statements provide the information that users need

- The most important sources of regulation in the UK are:
  - The Companies Act 2006
  - Accounting Standards

- International Accounting Standards (IASs) and International Financial Reporting Standards (IFRSs) are issued by the International Accounting Standards Board (IASB)

- The Companies Act 2006 states that the directors of a limited company must file annual accounts with the Registrar of Companies

- Every shareholder in a limited company is entitled to receive a copy of the company's annual accounts

- These can be either 'Companies Act accounts' or 'IAS accounts'

- Published IAS accounts consist of:
  - A statement of financial position
  - A statement of comprehensive income
  - A statement of changes in equity
  - A statement of cash flows
  - Notes

- Directors have a legal duty to keep proper accounting records

- The published accounts must show a true and fair view/fair presentation: they must comply with the requirements of the Companies Acts and applicable accounting standards

- The *Conceptual Framework for Financial Reporting* sets out the principles and concepts that the IASB believes should underlie the preparation and presentation of financial statements

CHAPTER OVERVIEW CONTINUED

- The objective of general purpose financial reporting is to provide financial information about the reporting entity that is useful to existing and potential investors, lenders and other creditors in making decisions about providing resources to the entity.

- Useful financial information has two fundamental qualitative characteristics:

    - Relevance
    - Faithful representation

- The enhancing qualitative characteristics of useful financial information are:

    - Comparability
    - Verifiability
    - Timeliness
    - Understandability

- Going concern is regarded as a fundamental accounting concept/underlying assumption

- The elements of financial statements are:

    - Assets
    - Liabilities
    - Equity
    - Income
    - Expenses

- The elements restate the accounting equation:

    - Assets – Liabilities = Equity

    - Equity = Contributions from owners + Income – Expenses – Distributions to owners

- An item that meets the definition of an element should be recognised if:

    - It is probable that any future economic benefit associated with the item will flow to or from the entity; and

    - The item has a cost or value that can be measured with reliability

- A number of different measurement bases are used in financial statements:

    - Historical cost
    - Current cost
    - Realisable value
    - Present value

- Historic cost is the most commonly used, but this may be combined with other bases (eg, some assets may be carried at current cost)

Keywords

Accounting Standards – authoritative statements of how particular types of transactions and other events should be reflected in financial statements

Published accounts/financial statements – the financial statements of limited companies that are circulated to shareholders and filed with the Registrar of Companies (also referred to as **statutory accounts**)

Companies Act accounts – published accounts that comply with the accounting rules in the Companies Act 2006 and with the requirements of UK accounting standards

IAS accounts – published accounts that comply with the requirements of IASs/IFRSs

Conceptual framework – a set of concepts and principles that underpin the preparation of financial statements

Accrual accounting – financial statements show the effects of transactions and other events on a reporting entity's economic resources and claims in the periods in which those effects occur, even if the resulting cash receipts and payments occur in a different period.

Going concern – financial statements are prepared on the basis that an entity will continue in operational existence for the foreseeable future

Materiality – information is material if omitting it or misstating it could influence decisions that users make on the basis of financial information about a specific reporting entity

Substance over form – the financial statements must report the commercial and economic substance of a transaction, rather than its strict legal form, if these are different

Creative accounting – accounting treatments which are technically within the law and accounting standards but which give a biased impression of a company's performance

Asset – resource controlled by an entity as a result of a past event from which future economic benefits are expected to flow to the entity

Non-current assets – assets that a business intends to hold for some time (usually more than one year)

Current assets – assets that a business holds for the short term, for conversion into cash in the course of trading

Liability – a present obligation of an entity arising from past events, the settlement of which is expected to result in an outflow of economic benefits

Current liabilities – liabilities that are payable within one year

Non-current liabilities (long-term liabilities) – liabilities that are payable after more than one year

Equity – the residual amount found by deducting all of an entity's liabilities from all of an entity's assets

Income – increases in economic benefits in the form of increases of assets or decreases of liabilities that result in increases in equity other than contributions from owners

Expenses – decreases in economic benefits during the accounting period in the form of decreases of assets or increases of liabilities that result in decreases in equity other than distributions to owners

Contributions from owners – increases in ownership interest resulting from transfers from owners in their capacity as owners

Distributions to owners – decreases in ownership interest resulting from transfers to owners in their capacity as owners

Recognition – including an item in the financial statements

Derecognition – removing an item from the financial statements

Historic cost – assets are recorded at the amount of cash paid or the fair value of the consideration given to acquire them at the time of the acquisition

Current cost – assets are carried at the amount of cash that would have to be paid if the same or a similar asset was acquired currently

Realisable value – assets are carried at the amount of cash that could currently be obtained by selling the asset

Present value – assets are carried at the present discounted value of the future net cash inflows that the item is expected to generate in the normal course of business

Fair value – the amount for which an asset could be exchanged between knowledgeable, willing parties in an arm's length transaction

TEST YOUR LEARNING

Test 1

List the four bodies that form part of the international standard-setting structure.

Test 2

The IASB's Conceptual Framework for Financial Reporting is an accounting standard.

Is this statement True or False?

True	
False	

Test 3

State the objective of general purpose financial reporting.

Test 4

According to the IASB's *Conceptual Framework*, who are the most important users of financial statements? Choose TWO

Employees	
Government	
Investors	
Lenders	

Test 5

According to the IASB's *Conceptual Framework*, which ONE of the following items is the most important assumption underlying financial statements?

Accruals	
Consistency	
Going concern	
Reliability	

Test 6

According to the IASB's *Conceptual Framework*, which ONE of the following is a **fundamental** qualitative characteristic of useful financial information?

Consistency	
Going concern	
Relevance	
Timeliness	

Test 7

List the elements that appear in financial statements according to the *Conceptual Framework for Financial Reporting*.

Test 8

A business has signed a contract to pay its managing director £200,000 per year for the next five years. He has agreed to work full-time for the business over that period.

The business should recognise a liability in respect of the contract.

Is this statement True or False?

True	✓
False	

chapter 3:
THE STATEMENT OF FINANCIAL POSITION

chapter coverage 📖

In Chapter 1 we introduced the limited company income statement and statement of financial position. In the next three chapters we look at the financial statements in more depth. This chapter explains the general requirements of IAS 1 *Presentation of Financial Statements*. It then focuses on the statement of financial position: the required format and the information that must be disclosed. The best way to master the drafting of financial statements for limited companies is to practise on as many questions and past assessment tasks as possible. The topics covered are:

✍ Presentation of financial statements

✍ The statement of financial position

✍ Accounting for share issues

PRESENTATION OF FINANCIAL STATEMENTS

In the assessment, you will be expected to prepare IAS accounts. IAS 1 *Presentation of Financial Statements* sets out general requirements for the presentation of financial statements.

The purpose of financial statements

The objective of financial statements is to provide information about the financial position, financial performance and cash flows of an entity that is useful to a wide range of users in making economic decisions.

Financial statements also show the results of management's stewardship of the resources entrusted to it.

Note that this is very similar to the objective of financial statements set out in the *Conceptual Framework*.

Components of financial statements

IAS 1 states that a complete set of financial statements comprises:

- A **statement of financial position** as at the end of the period
- A **statement of comprehensive income** for the period (see Chapter 4)
- A **statement of changes in equity** for the period (see Chapter 4)
- A **statement of cash flows** for the period (see Chapter 5)
- **Notes**, comprising a summary of significant accounting policies and other explanatory information

IAS 1 allows the use of other titles for the statements. For example, the statement of financial position can be called a 'balance sheet'. However, in your assessment you will be expected to use the titles set out above.

IAS 1 also states that an entity should present all the financial statements with equal prominence.

Identification of the financial statements

An entity should clearly identify each of the financial statements and the notes and should distinguish them from other information published in the same document.

In many cases, a company annual report contains material other than the financial statements. IFRSs only apply to the financial statements and the notes, not to any other material presented with them. Users need to be able to distinguish between these items.

In addition, the following information must be displayed prominently:

- The name of the reporting entity
- Whether the financial statements are for a single entity or a group
- The date at the end of the reporting period, or the period covered
- The currency in which the financial statements are presented (eg, £)
- The level of rounding used (eg, £'000, or £million)

Other reports and statements

These can include:

- A financial review (sometimes called Operating and Financial Review, Management Commentary or Business Review)
- A director's report
- Environmental and social reports

Unlike the financial statements themselves, which provide mainly numerical information, these other reports consist mainly of narrative information.

Financial review

This provides additional information and explanations about the entity's financial performance and financial position. It normally describes the business, its objectives and activities and the principal uncertainties and risks that it faces. It may also describe:

- The main factors that influence financial performance (for example, changes in the business environment such as economic downturn and how these affect the entity)
- The entity's sources of finance (for example, the proportion of debt to equity)
- Resources that the entity has but which are not recognised in the statement of financial position (for example, internally developed brand names or technical expertise).

The directors' report

Under the Companies Act 2006 limited companies must prepare a directors' report for each financial year.

The directors are required to disclose specific information, including:

- The names of persons who were directors at any time during the financial year
- The principal activities of the company during the year
- The amount (if any) that the directors recommend should be paid as dividends

Unless the company is a small company, the directors' report must also contain a business review. This is similar to a financial review and must include:

- A fair review of the company's business
- A description of the principal risks and uncertainties facing the company

Environmental and social reports

Environmental reports provide details of the impact of an entity's operations on the natural environment and of the action it is taking or will take to protect the environment. They may be combined with social reports, which explain the way in which the entity affects the wider community (for example, as a major employer or through charitable activities).

Most large and quoted companies publish some sort of environmental report, either as part of the published annual financial statements or as a separate document. However, companies do not have to publish an environmental report and neither the Companies Act nor IASs and IFRSs contain any specific requirements about the information to be disclosed. Therefore companies can publish as much or as little information as they choose.

Fair presentation

IAS 1 states that:

- Financial statements shall **present fairly** the financial position, financial performance and cash flows of an entity

Like 'true and fair view', 'present fairly' is not defined, but the Standard goes on to say that:

- Fair presentation requires the faithful representation of the effects of transactions, other events and conditions in accordance with the definitions and recognition criteria for assets, liabilities, income and expenses set out in the *Conceptual Framework*

- Fair presentation can normally be achieved if financial statements comply with IFRSs

- IFRSs includes all standards and interpretations adopted by the IASB:

    - International Financial Reporting Standards (IFRSs)

    - International Accounting Standards (IASs)

    - Interpretations issued by the IFRS Interpretations Committee (IFRICs) or by its predecessor, the Standing Interpretations Committee (SIC)

    (You do not need to know the content of any Interpretations for your assessment.)

Complying with IFRSs

- Where financial statements comply with IFRSs this must be stated explicitly in the notes.

- Financial statements must not be described as complying with IFRSs unless they comply with **all** the requirements of IFRSs (an entity cannot comply with some Standards and not others, or some requirements of a Standard and not others).

- There is an exception to this last rule. In **extremely rare circumstances**, complying with a particular requirement in a Standard may result in financial statements that are so misleading that they do not provide useful information. In this situation, an entity departs from that requirement and adopts a different accounting treatment which does present the information fairly.

    The notes to the financial statements then disclose:

    - That management has concluded that the financial statements present fairly the entity's financial position, financial performance and cash flows;

    - That it has complied with applicable standards, except that it has departed from a particular requirement to achieve a fair presentation;

    - The title of the relevant Standard and information about the departure: the treatment that the Standard would normally require; the reason why this treatment would be misleading in the circumstances; and the treatment actually adopted; and

    - The financial impact of the departure on each item affected, for each period presented.

Accounting principles

Going concern

Financial statements must be prepared on a going concern basis, unless the entity is not a going concern:

- Management must make an assessment of the entity's ability to continue as a going concern

- Any material uncertainties about the entity's ability to continue as a going concern must be disclosed

- If financial statements are not prepared on a going concern basis, this must be disclosed, together with the reason why the entity is not regarded as a going concern

The *Conceptual Framework* explains that going concern is the **underlying assumption** when financial statements are prepared.

Accruals

Financial statements must be prepared on the accruals basis, except for cash flow information.

Under the **accruals** (or matching) concept, revenue and costs are recognised in the financial statements for the accounting period in which the transactions and events that give rise to them occur, rather than in the period in which the cash is received or paid.

Task 1

Give two examples of the use of the accruals concept in accounts.

1	
2	

Materiality and aggregation

Financial statements cannot report every single aspect of every relevant transaction and event, because this would obscure the overall picture. Individual items are aggregated (added together) so that significant totals are shown, rather than individual figures.

This has to be done in such a way that the information is helpful to users, rather than misleading. IAS 1 states that:

- Each material class of similar items must be presented separately in the financial statements

- Items that are dissimilar must be presented separately. They cannot be aggregated unless they are individually immaterial

Information is **material** if omitting it or misstating it could influence decisions that users make on the basis of financial information about a specific reporting entity.

For example, inventories, receivables and cash are all shown as separate classes of items in the statement of financial position, grouped together under the heading of current assets.

Offset

Assets and liabilities, and income and expenses, should not be offset (netted-off against each other) unless this is required or permitted by a standard.

For example, a company may have two bank accounts, one of which is overdrawn. The bank account which is not overdrawn is shown in current assets; the bank overdraft is shown in current liabilities. The two accounts cannot be netted-off against each other.

Frequency of reporting

Financial statements should be prepared at least annually.

If the end of the reporting period (year-end) changes so that the financial statements are prepared for a different period, the entity should disclose:

- The reason for the change
- The fact that the comparative figures are not entirely comparable

Comparative information

Comparative figures must be disclosed for the previous period for all amounts reported in the financial statements, unless another Standard permits or requires otherwise.

Comparative information must be included for narrative and descriptive information where it is necessary in order to help users understand the current period's financial statements.

It is very unlikely that you will be asked to provide comparative figures in the assessment.

Consistency of presentation

An entity must present and classify items in the financial statements in the same way from one period to the next unless:

- There has been a significant change in the entity's operations which means that a different presentation is now more appropriate; or

- A new IFRS requires a different presentation.

THE STATEMENT OF FINANCIAL POSITION

The format for the statement of financial position is shown below. It is very similar to the one that you met in the previous chapter.

IAS 1 does not actually require specific formats, but it *does* provide illustrations of formats that meet its requirements. The format shown below has been adapted from these illustrations.

You will be expected to follow this format in the assessment.

Format of the statement of financial position

Statement of financial position as at...

	£'000
Assets	
Non-current assets	
Intangible assets	X
Property, plant and equipment	X̲
	X̲
Current assets	
Inventories	X
Trade and other receivables	X
Cash and cash equivalents	X̲
	X̲
Total assets	X̲
Equity and liabilities	
Equity	
Share capital	X
Share premium	X
Revaluation reserve	X
Retained earnings	X̲
Total equity	X̲
Non-current liabilities	
Bank loans	X
Long-term provisions	X̲
	X̲
Current liabilities	
Trade and other payables	X
Tax payable	X
Bank overdrafts and loans	X̲
	X̲
Total liabilities	X̲
Total equity and liabilities	X̲

The statement of financial position only shows total amounts. The analysis of the totals is given in the notes.

Information to be presented in the statement of financial position

The statement of financial position must include line items that present the following amounts for the period:

- Intangible assets (see Chapter 7)

- Property, plant and equipment (see Chapter 6)

- Investment property (see Chapter 6)

- Inventories (see Chapter 7)

- Trade and other receivables

- Cash and cash equivalents

- Non-current assets held for sale (see Chapter 6)

- Trade and other payables

- Provisions (see Chapter 8)

- Financial liabilities (eg loan stock and other loans)

- Liabilities and assets for current tax (see Chapter 8)

- Liabilities and assets for deferred tax (see Chapter 8)

- Investments accounted for using the equity method (see Chapter 11)

- Non-controlling interests, presented within equity (see Chapter 10)

- Issued capital and reserves attributable to owners (equity shareholders) of the parent

This is the **minimum** level of disclosure. IAS 1 states that an entity should present additional line items, headings and subtotals when this helps users to understand the information in the statement of financial position.

Current and non-current assets and liabilities

The statement of financial position must classify assets and liabilities as either current or non-current and present these categories separately.

An asset is current if:

- The entity expects to realise it (receive it as cash or another asset) or sell or consume it in its normal operating cycle (eg within the time that would normally pass between the purchase of inventories and the receipt of cash from their sale as finished goods)

- It is held primarily for trading

- It is expected to be realised (received) within 12 months after the reporting period

- It is cash or a cash equivalent (a short-term investment or deposit that can be easily converted into cash)

A liability is current if:

- The entity expects to settle it in its normal operating cycle

- It is held primarily for trading

- It is due to be settled (paid) within 12 months after the reporting period

- The entity does not have the unconditional right to delay settling it for at least 12 months after the reporting period

All other assets and liabilities are non-current.

Further analysis of items in the statement of financial position

The line items shown in the statement of financial position should be analysed further, where this is necessary.

- The analysis can be shown either in the statement of financial position or in the notes

- Line items should be subclassified in a manner appropriate to the entity's operations

Examples:

- Property, plant and equipment is analysed (disaggregated) into classes, for example: land and buildings, plant and machinery, motor vehicles

- Receivables are analysed into trade receivables, other receivables and prepayments

- Inventories are analysed between raw materials, work in progress and goods for resale

- Equity capital and reserves are analysed between various classes, such as share capital, share premium and reserves

Share capital and reserves

The following must be disclosed, either in the statement of financial position or in the statement of changes in equity (see Chapter 4) or (normally) in the notes:

- The number of shares authorised

- The number of shares issued and fully paid

- The par (nominal) value per share

- A description of the nature and purpose of each reserve within equity

- A reconciliation of the number of shares outstanding at the beginning and at the end of the period

Illustration

Notes to the financial statements: Share capital

Share capital consists of 2,000,000 ordinary shares with a par value of 50p each.

Task 2

Indicate whether the following statements are True or False:

	True	False
Intangible assets are current assets		
Long-term provisions are a current liability		
Share premium is part of equity		
Tax payable is a current liability		

HOW IT WORKS

In your assessment you may be asked to draft either a statement of comprehensive income and/or a statement of financial position in the correct format from a trial balance or an extended trial balance.

The trial balance of Thetford Ltd as at 31 March 20X3 is as follows.

Thetford plc

Trial balance as at 31 March 20X3

	Debit £'000	Credit £'000
Trade payables		3,230
Sales		29,956
Cash at bank	259	
Interest	280	
Trade receivables	4,990	
Land and buildings – cost	11,512	
Fixtures and fittings – cost	4,335	
Motor vehicles – cost	6,453	
Dividend paid	630	
Ordinary share capital		4,000
Accruals		189
8% bank loan repayable 20X8		7,000
Administrative expenses	4,715	
Retained earnings		7,476
Prepayments	129	
Share premium		2,000
Buildings – accumulated depreciation		588
Fixtures and fittings – accumulated depreciation		1,593
Motor vehicles – accumulated depreciation		2,820
Inventories as at 1 April 20X2	6,322	
Purchases	19,377	
Allowance for doubtful debts		150
	59,002	59,002

Further information

(a) The inventories at the close of business on 31 March 20X3 were valued at cost at £7,484,000.

(b) The corporation tax charge for the year has been calculated as £2,062,000.

(c) Administrative expenses of £58,000 relating to February 20X3 have not been included in the trial balance.

(d) In June 20X2 the company paid £28,000 insurance costs, which covered the period from 1 July 20X2 to 30 June 20X3. This amount was included in the administrative expenses in the trial balance.

(e) Interest on the bank loan for the last six months of the year has not been included in the accounts in the trial balance.

Required

Draft the statement of financial position for Thetford Ltd as at 31 March 20X3.

The adjustments

Taking each of the items of further information in turn:

(a) Closing inventories:

DEBIT	Inventories (statement of financial position)	£7,484,000	
CREDIT	Inventories (income statement)		£7,484,000

(b) Corporation tax:

DEBIT	Tax expense (income statement)	£2,062,000	
CREDIT	Tax payable (statement of financial position)		£2,062,000

(c) Accruals:

DEBIT	Administrative expenses	£58,000	
CREDIT	Accruals		£58,000

(d) Prepayments:

This is the expense for the three months ended 30 June 20X3: 3/12 × 28,000

DEBIT	Prepayments	£7,000	
CREDIT	Administrative expenses		£7,000

(e) Loan interest:

This is the interest for the second six months of the year: $7,000,000 \times 8\% \times 6/12$

DEBIT	Interest payable (income statement)	£280,000	
CREDIT	Accruals (statement of financial position)		£280,000

The profit for the year

In this example, the statement of comprehensive income is not required, but we can calculate the profit for the year by taking the relevant figures from the trial balance and then making the adjustments drawn up above.

	£'000	£'000
Sales		29,956
Opening inventories	6,322	
Purchases	19,377	
Closing inventories (adjustment (a))	(7,484)	
Cost of sales		(18,215)
Administrative expenses per TB	4,715	
Adjustment (c) (accrual)	58	
Adjustment (d) (prepayment)	(7)	
		(4,766)
Interest per TB	280	
Adjustment (e) (accrual)	280	
		(560)
Tax (adjustment (b))		(2,062)
		4,353

Workings

Some of the figures in the statement of financial position (in this case cash and cash equivalents, share capital, share premium and the bank loan) can be taken directly from the trial balance. Notice that in this example the bank loan is a non-current liability, because it is repayable after more than 12 months.

The figure for inventories is the debit side of adjustment (a): the figure at the year-end.

The figure for tax payable is the credit side of adjustment (b): the amount of corporation tax payable for the year.

The remaining figures must be built up from workings.

1   Property, plant and equipment

	Cost	Acc dep'n	
	£'000	£'000	£'000
Land and buildings	11,512	588	10,924
Fixtures and fittings	4,335	1,593	2,742
Motor vehicles	6,453	2,820	3,633
	22,300	5,001	17,299

2   Trade and other receivables

	£'000
Trade receivables	4,990
Less allowance for doubtful debts	(150)
	4,840
Prepayments per TB	129
Insurance (adjustment (d))	7
	4,976

3   Retained earnings

	£'000
At 1 April 20X2	7,476
Profit for the year (calculated above)	4,353
Dividend paid (from TB)	(630)
At 31 March 20X3	11,199

4   Trade and other payables

	£'000	£'000
Trade payables		3,230
Accruals: per TB	189	
administrative expenses (adjustment (c))	58	
interest (adjustment (e))	280	
		527
		3,757

Note: In the Assessment you will be given workings to complete for the more complicated figures (such as property, plant and equipment and retained earnings). You are not required to use them, but the data from the workings will be taken into account if you make errors in the statement itself.

We can now draw up the statement of financial position.

In the Assessment, you will be given a pro-forma statement to complete. The pro-forma will show the main headings (in **bold** below). You will be asked to select the other line items from a 'pick list' (sometimes called a 'drop-down list'). IAS 1 does not prescribe the exact wording of the line items, so they **may** change very slightly from task to task. For example, the liability for corporation tax may appear as 'tax payable' (as in this example) or 'tax liability'.

Thetford Ltd: Statement of financial position as at 31 March 20X3

	£'000
Assets	
Non-current assets:	
Property, plant and equipment (W1)	17,299
Current assets:	
Inventories	7,484
Trade and other receivables (W2)	4,976
Cash and cash equivalents	259
	12,719
Total assets	30,018
Equity and liabilities	
Equity:	
Share capital	4,000
Share premium	2,000
Retained earnings (W3)	11,199
Total equity	17,199
Non-current liabilities	
8% bank loan	7,000
Current liabilities	
Trade and other payables (W4)	3,757
Tax payable	2,062
	5,819
Total liabilities	12,819
Total equity and liabilities	30,018

Task 3

Given below is the trial balance of Sawyer Ltd as at 31 July 20X2.

Trial balance as at 31 July 20X2

	Dr £'000	Cr £'000
Ordinary share capital		5,800
Share premium		3,120
Revaluation reserve		840
Trade receivables	6,870	
Trade payables		1,930
Retained earnings at 31 July 20X2		7,460
Tax payable		2,333
Cash at bank		765
Inventories at 31 July 20X2	4,898	
Land and buildings at cost	12,350	
Plant and machinery at cost	9,980	
Accumulated depreciation		
Buildings		1,370
Plant and machinery		4,480
7% loan stock repayable 20X9		6,000
	34,098	34,098

Draft the statement of financial position as at 31 July 20X2.

(Complete the left hand column by writing in the correct line items from the list provided.)

Sawyer Ltd: Statement of financial position as at 31 July 20X2

	£'000
Assets	
Non-current assets:	
▼	
Current assets:	
▼	
▼	
Total assets	

	£'000
Equity and liabilities	
Equity:	
▼	
▼	
▼	
▼	
Total equity	
Non-current liabilities	
▼	
Current liabilities	
▼	
▼	
▼	
Total liabilities	
Total equity and liabilities	

Picklist for line items:

Bank overdraft

Inventories

Property, plant and equipment

Loan stock

Retained earnings

Revaluation reserve

Share capital

Share premium

Tax payable

Trade and other payables

Trade and other receivables

Workings

(Complete the left hand column by writing in the correct narrative from the list provided.)

Property, plant and equipment		£'000
	▼	
	▼	
	▼	
	▼	

Picklist:

Buildings accumulated depreciation

Land and buildings at cost

Plant and machinery accumulated depreciations

Plant and machinery at cost

ACCOUNTING FOR SHARE ISSUES

In the assessment, you may be asked to adjust a trial balance to record an issue of share capital.

To issue shares, a company can make:

- A normal issue at par (nominal value)
- A normal issue at a premium (above nominal value)
- A bonus issue — costs o.
- A rights issue

Task 4

Benton Ltd issues 250,000 50p ordinary shares at par. The shares are fully paid at the time of issue.

Show the double entry to record the share issue.

Journal

Account name	Debit	Credit
	£	£

Share premium

A company may issue shares at a premium, in other words, at above the nominal value of the shares. The premium is the difference between the nominal value of the shares and their market price.

When this happens, the Companies Act requires that a sum equal to the premium is transferred to a SHARE PREMIUM account. The share premium account is a non-distributable reserve. In other words, it cannot be used to pay dividends to shareholders.

Setting up a share premium reserve protects the company's creditors. It ensures that the total amount invested by shareholders remains available to meet the company's liabilities should the need arise.

HOW IT WORKS

A company issues 150,000 50p ordinary shares at 75p each. The shares are fully paid in cash at the time of issue.

For each share purchased, the shareholders have paid the nominal value of 50p and a premium of 25p. The total amount received by the company is:

	£
Nominal value (150,000 × 50p)	75,000
Premium (150,000 × 25p)	37,500
	112,500

The double entry to record the share issue is:

DEBIT	Bank	£112,500	
CREDIT	Share capital		£75,000
CREDIT	Share premium		£37,500

In the statement of financial position, the shares will appear as follows:

Equity:

	£
Share capital	75,000
Share premium	37,500

Bonus issues

A BONUS ISSUE is the issue of extra shares to existing shareholders at no cost. Bonus issues are made to shareholders in proportion to their existing shareholdings. A bonus issue is sometimes known as a SCRIP ISSUE.

For example, suppose that A holds 1,000 ordinary shares in X plc. The directors of X plc declare a bonus issue of 1 for 5 new ordinary shares. A receives one bonus share for every five shares that she currently holds, so she receives 200 new shares in total. She does not have to pay anything for these shares.

A bonus issue does not raise any additional finance for the company. It is simply a means of reclassifying reserves as share capital. A company may wish to do this in order to increase the capital base of the company or to encourage investment by making shares appear cheaper (because the market price of the shares will fall).

Any reserve can be used to make a bonus issue, but the share premium account is the reserve most commonly used as it is non-distributable. This is one of the few legally permitted uses of the share premium account.

HOW IT WORKS

A company has the following equity:

	£
Share capital (£1 ordinary shares)	100,000
Share premium	50,000
Retained earnings	350,000
	500,000

It makes a 1 for 4 bonus issue, using the share premium account.

The total number of new shares issued is 25,000 (100,000 ÷ 4).

The double entry to record the bonus issue is:

DEBIT	Share premium	£25,000	
CREDIT	Share capital		£25,000

Equity now appears as follows:

	£
Share capital (£1 ordinary shares)	125,000
Share premium	25,000
Retained earnings	350,000
	500,000

Rights issues

A RIGHTS ISSUE is an issue of shares to existing shareholders at below market value. The shares are offered to shareholders in proportion to their existing shareholdings. The shareholders can choose whether or not to take the shares offered to them.

A rights issue is a relatively cheap and convenient way of raising extra capital. It has the further advantage that existing shareholders retain control of the company.

HOW IT WORKS

A company has the following equity:

	£
Share capital (£1 ordinary shares)	50,000
Share premium	10,000
Retained earnings	90,000
	150,000

It makes a 1 for 5 rights issue at £1.10 per share. All the existing shareholders take up the new shares for cash.

The total number of new shares issued is 10,000 (50,000 ÷ 5).

The double entry to record the rights issue is:

DEBIT	Bank (10,000 × £1.10)	£11,000	
CREDIT	Share capital		£10,000
CREDIT	Share premium		£1,000

Equity now appears as follows:

	£
Share capital (£1 ordinary shares)	60,000
Share premium	11,000
Retained earnings	90,000
	161,000

Task 5

Hemsell Ltd has the following share capital and reserves:

	£
Share capital (25p ordinary shares)	100,000
Share premium	30,000
Retained earnings	170,000
	300,000

It makes a rights issue of one new share for every five existing shares at a price of 40p per share. All the existing shareholders take up the rights issue for cash. It then makes a bonus issue of one new share for every eight existing shares, using non-distributable reserves.

Show how equity appears after both of these issues have been made.

	£
Share capital (25p ordinary shares)	
Share premium	
Retained earnings	

CHAPTER OVERVIEW

- Financial statements must comply with all the requirements of IFRSs that apply

- Where complying with a particular requirement results in financial statements that are misleading, an entity departs from that requirement and discloses information about the departure (extremely rare)

- Financial statements must be prepared on a going concern basis and on the accruals basis

- Each material class of similar items must be presented separately in the financial statements

- Assets and liabilities, and income and expenses, should not be offset

- Financial statements should be prepared at least annually

- An entity must present and classify items consistently from one period to the next

- IAS 1 sets out the line items which should be disclosed in the statement of financial position

- The statement of financial position classifies assets and liabilities as either current or non-current

- An asset or a liability is normally current if: it is held primarily for the purpose of being traded; it is expected to be received or paid within 12 months after the end of the reporting period

- If a company issues shares at a premium (above their nominal value), a sum equal to the premium is transferred to a share premium account

Keywords

Share premium – a non-distributable reserve consisting of the difference between consideration received for shares and the nominal value of the shares issued

Bonus issue (scrip issue) – an issue of extra shares to existing shareholders at no cost, made to shareholders in proportion to their existing shareholdings

Rights issue – an issue of shares to existing shareholders at below market value, offered to shareholders in proportion to their existing shareholdings

TEST YOUR LEARNING

Test 1

A company cannot change its reporting date (its year end).

Is this statement True or False?

True	
False	

Test 2

List the items that appear in the statement of financial position under 'Current assets'.

Test 3

Which ONE of the following items need NOT be disclosed as a separate line item in the statement of financial position?

Financial liabilities	
Investment properties	
Prepayments	
Trade and other payables	

Test 4

You are provided with the following balances relating to a company:

	£'000	£'000
Trade receivables	4,294	
Bank overdraft		474
Retained earnings		4,503
Allowance for doubtful debts		171
Land and buildings: cost	7,724	
Plant and machinery: cost	6,961	
Inventories	3,061	
Trade payables		1,206
Tax payable		1,458
Buildings: accumulated depreciation		468
Plant and machinery: accumulated depreciation		2,810
Prepayments	94	
Accruals		169
Bank loan		5,400
Ordinary share capital		3,000
Share premium		1,950
Revaluation reserve		525
	22,134	22,134

Draft a statement of financial position in accordance with the requirements of IAS 1.

(Complete the left hand column by writing in the correct line items from the list provided.)

Statement of financial position as at...

	£'000
Assets	
Non-current assets:	
▼	
Current assets:	
▼	
▼	
Total assets	
Equity and liabilities	
Equity:	
▼	
▼	
▼	
▼	
Total equity	
Non-current liabilities	
▼	
Current liabilities	
▼	
▼	
▼	
Total liabilities	
Total equity and liabilities	

Picklist for line items:

Bank loan
Bank overdraft
Inventories
Property, plant and equipment
Retained earnings
Revaluation reserve
Share capital
Share premium
Tax payable
Trade and other payables
Trade and other receivables

Workings

(Complete the left hand column of each working by writing in the correct narrative from the list provided.)

(1) Property, plant and equipment

	£'000
▼	
▼	
▼	
▼	

Picklist:

Accumulated depreciation: Buildings
Accumulated depreciation: Plant and machinery
Land and buildings: Cost
Plant and machinery: Cost

(2) Trade and other receivables

	£'000
▼	
▼	
▼	

Picklist:

Accruals
Allowance for doubtful debts
Prepayments
Trade payables
Trade receivables

(3) Trade and other payables

		£'000
	▼	
	▼	

Picklist:

Accruals
Allowance for doubtful debts
Prepayments
Trade payables
Trade receivables

Test 5

Knave Ltd issues 200,000 50p ordinary shares at a market price of 80p. All shares are fully paid in cash as soon as they are issued.

Show the double entry to record the share issue.

Journal

Account name	Debit £	Credit £

chapter 4:
THE STATEMENTS OF FINANCIAL PERFORMANCE

chapter coverage 📖

In this chapter we concentrate on an entity's performance and the way in which it is presented in the financial statements. In particular, we look at the statement of total comprehensive income and at the statement of changes in equity. We also explain the requirements of an important accounting standard: IAS 8 *Accounting Policies, Changes in Accounting Estimates and Errors*.

The topics covered are:

✍ Assessing financial performance

✍ The statement of comprehensive income

✍ Profit or loss

✍ Other comprehensive income

✍ The statement of changes in equity

✍ Notes to the financial statements

✍ Summary of the financial statements

✍ Accounting policies

ASSESSING FINANCIAL PERFORMANCE

What is performance?

Shareholders and other users of the financial statements need information about the financial performance of an entity.

But what exactly is financial performance? The simple view is that it is the amount that is available for distribution to the shareholders, in other words, profit before dividends, or profit after tax.

An alternative view is that financial performance is wider than profit. It is the total return that an entity obtains on the resources that it controls. It includes all gains and losses, whether or not they have actually been received (realised) in the form of cash or are likely to be received in the near future. It can be expressed using the accounting equation:

PERFORMANCE (INCOME – EXPENSES) =

CLOSING EQUITY – OPENING EQUITY; or

NET GAINS/(LOSSES) =

CHANGE IN NET ASSETS IN THE ACCOUNTING PERIOD.

The IASB has adopted this second, wider view of performance.

The statement of comprehensive income required by IAS 1 shows TOTAL COMPREHENSIVE INCOME. IAS 1 defines this as

- The change in equity during a period resulting from transactions and other events, other than those changes resulting from transactions with owners in their capacity as owners.

An entity's total comprehensive income is:

- Its profit or loss for the period; plus
- Its other comprehensive income.

Task 1

A company has revalued one of its buildings during the year, resulting in a significant gain.

Are the following statements True or False?

	True	False
The gain is part of the company's performance		✓
The gain should be recognised in profit or loss	✓	

THE STATEMENT OF COMPREHENSIVE INCOME

IAS 1 requires a **statement of comprehensive income**. An entity's TOTAL COMPREHENSIVE INCOME consists of:

- its profit or loss; and
- other comprehensive income.

PROFIT OR LOSS is income less expenses.

OTHER COMPREHENSIVE INCOME is items of income and expense that are not recognised in profit or loss. For example, when a non-current asset is revalued, the difference between its original cost less depreciation and its fair or market value is not included in profit or loss for the period. Instead, it is recognised as part of other comprehensive income.

IAS 1 allows the statement of comprehensive income to be presented as either a single statement, or as two separate statements:

- An income statement (showing income less expenses to give the profit or loss for the period); and ·

- A statement of comprehensive income (showing profit or loss and items such as gains and losses where non-current assets are revalued).

In the assessment you will be asked to draft a single statement of comprehensive income.

Where an IAS or an IFRS states that an item should be recognised 'in profit or loss', this means that it is included in the income statement section of the statement of comprehensive income or in the separate income statement (if two statements are prepared).

Format of the statement of comprehensive income (a single statement including profit or loss)

Statement of comprehensive income for the year ended...

Continuing operations	£'000
Revenue	X
Cost of sales	(X)
Gross profit	X
Distribution costs	(X)
Administrative expenses	(X)
Profit/(loss) from operations	X
Finance costs	(X)
Profit/(loss) before tax	X
Tax	(X)
Profit/(loss) for the period from continuing operations	X
Discontinued operations	
Profit/(loss) for the period from discontinued operations	(X)
Profit/(loss) for the period	X
Other comprehensive income for the period:	
Gains on property revaluation	X
Total comprehensive income for the period	X

Example of an income statement and a statement of comprehensive income (two statements)

Income statement for the year ended...

Continuing operations	£'000
Revenue	X
Cost of sales	(X)
Gross profit	X
Distribution costs	(X)
Administrative expenses	(X)
Profit/(loss) from operations	X
Finance costs	(X)
Profit/(loss) before tax	X
Tax	(X)
Profit/(loss) for the period from continuing operations	X
Discontinued operations	
Profit/(loss) for the period from discontinued operations	(X)
Profit/(loss) for the period	X

Statement of comprehensive income for the year ended...

	£'000
Profit/(loss) for the period	X
Other comprehensive income for the period:	
Gains on property revaluation	X
Total comprehensive income for the period	X

PROFIT OR LOSS

Analysis of expenses

There are two methods of analysing expenses within profit or loss based on:

- the nature of the expenses
- their function within the entity

IAS 1 states that an entity should choose the method that provides information that is reliable and more relevant. This depends on the type of industry, the nature of the entity and on the methods previously used (because financial statements must be comparable over time if they are to be useful).

The statement of comprehensive income shown above analyses expenses based on their function within the entity. Expense items (or account balances) are not listed out individually, but must be analysed under the various headings.

Distribution costs are the costs of selling and delivering items to customers. They may include:

- sales force's salaries and commissions
- depreciation of sales force's cars
- delivery costs
- advertising

Administrative expenses are expenses other than direct costs of production and distribution costs. They may include:

- rent and rates
- light and heat
- office salaries
- postage and telephone
- directors' remuneration
- depreciation on office equipment, fixtures and fittings

A statement of comprehensive income that analysed expenses based on their nature would show material costs, depreciation and staff costs rather than cost of sales, distribution costs and administrative expenses. The advantage of using this format is that expenses do not have to be allocated to functional categories such as distribution costs and administrative expenses, which can be subjective.

Most entities use the function of expense method.

Example of a statement of comprehensive income showing the classification of expenses by nature

Statement of comprehensive income for the year ended...

Continuing operations	£'000
Revenue	X
Other income	X
Changes in inventories of finished goods and work in progress	(X)
Raw materials and consumables used	(X)
Employee benefits expense	(X)
Depreciation and amortisation expense	(X)
Other expenses	(X)
Finance costs	(X)
Profit/(loss) before tax	X
Tax	(X)
Profit/(loss) for the period from continuing operations	X
Discontinued operations	
Profit/(loss) for the period from discontinued operations	(X)
Profit/(loss) for the period	X

You will not be asked to prepare this form of statement in the assessment.

Information to be presented in the statement of comprehensive income/ income statement

- All items of income and expense recognised in a period must be included in profit or loss unless an accounting standard requires or permits otherwise

- The profit or loss section of the statement of comprehensive income must include line items that present the following amounts for the period:

  - Revenue

  - Finance costs

  - Share of the profit or loss of associates accounted for using the equity method (see Chapter 11)

  - Tax expense

  - The post-tax profit or loss of discontinued operations

  - Profit or loss

  Discontinued operations are discussed later in this chapter.

- An entity should present additional line items, headings and subtotals in the statement of comprehensive income when this is helpful to users in understanding its financial performance.

Unusual items

In theory, there are two types of unusual item that might need to be disclosed separately in the statement of comprehensive income:

- EXTRAORDINARY ITEMS are material items possessing a high degree of abnormality which arise from events or transactions that fall **outside the ordinary activities** of an entity and which are not expected to recur.

- **Other material items** which arise from events or transactions that fall within the **ordinary activities** of an entity. These items are sometimes called **exceptional items**.

IAS 1 states that an entity must not present any item of income and expense as an extraordinary item, either in the statement of comprehensive income or in the notes.

Why IAS 1 prohibits extraordinary items

Extraordinary items are **not** part of an entity's profit on ordinary activities. Therefore, in theory, they can be presented below profit after tax. This is illustrated below.

Extract from the statement of comprehensive income for the year ended...

	£m
Profit from operations	X
Material (exceptional) items	X
Finance costs	(X)
Profit on ordinary activities before tax	X
Tax on profit on ordinary activities	(X)
Profit on ordinary activities after tax	X
Extraordinary items	(X)
Profit for the period	X

Investors and their advisers normally take profit after tax as the starting point for their analysis of an entity's performance for the year. Before extraordinary items were prohibited, preparers of financial statements could and often did manipulate the profit figure by treating unusual gains as ordinary material items ('above the line') and treating unusual losses as extraordinary items ('below the line'). This made the entity's performance appear much better than it actually was.

Material items

Material items of income and expense should be disclosed separately. If they are very material, they may need to be disclosed as a separate line item in the statement of comprehensive income, otherwise they are disclosed in the notes to the financial statements.

Examples of items that might need to be disclosed separately:

- Losses where inventories or property, plant and equipment are written-down

- Expenses of restructuring the activities of an entity

- Gains or losses on disposal of items of property, plant and equipment

- Income from insurance claims or the settlement of legal proceedings

Information about the nature and amount of material items is relevant to users, because it helps them to predict an entity's future performance from its performance for the current year. For example, suppose that an entity's profit for the year is exceptionally large because it has made a gain on disposal of some property. Users need to be made aware that the entity's results have been improved by an unusual event which will probably not be repeated.

HOW IT WORKS

The example below takes you through a task very similar to the ones that you will be asked to perform in the assessment: drafting a statement of comprehensive income and a statement of financial position from an extended trial balance, in a form suitable for publication.

The extended trial balance of Cottage Ltd as at 31 December 20X1 is set out below.

You have been given the following further information:

(a) The corporation tax charge for the year has been calculated as £581,000.

(b) The company has paid an interim dividend during the year. It has also proposed a final dividend of 8p per share.

(c) Interest on the 8% bank loan has been paid for the first six months of the year only.

Description	Trial balance Debit £'000	Trial balance Credit £'000	Adjustments Debit £'000	Adjustments Credit £'000	Statement of comprehensive income Debit £'000	Statement of comprehensive income Credit £'000	Statement of financial position Debit £'000	Statement of financial position Credit £'000
Cash at bank	253						253	
8% bank loan		2,700						2,700
Trade receivables	2,709						2,709	
Allowance for doubtful debts		100		35				135
Sales		16,253				16,253		
Purchases	9,533				9,533			
Land and buildings: cost	2,991						2,991	
Fixtures and fittings: cost	1,441						1,441	
Motor vehicles: cost	1,429						1,429	
Inventories	3,602		4,195	4,195	3,602	4,195	4,195	
Accruals				95				95
Prepayments			45				45	
Land and buildings: accumulated deprecation		330		172				502
Fixtures and fittings: accumulated depreciation		359		334				693
Motor vehicles: accumulated depreciation		389		333				722
Interim dividend paid	192						192	
Trade payables		1,628						1,628
Interest	108				108			
Distribution costs	2,571		434		3,005			
Administrative expenses	1,895		490		2,385			
Intangible assets	3,208						3,208	
Share capital		3,500						3,500
Retained earnings		3,273						3,273
Share premium		1,400						1,400
Profit for the year					1,815			1,815
	29,932	29,932	5,164	5,164	20,448	20,448	16,463	16,463

The adjustments

Taking each of the items of further information in turn:

(a) Tax expense:

DEBIT   Tax expense (profit or loss)   £581,000

CREDIT   Tax payable (statement of financial position)   £581,000

Being the tax charge for the year ended 31 December 20X1.

(b) No adjustment required.

As well as declaring an ordinary dividend at the year-end, companies may pay an interim dividend part way through the year. In this case, the company has already paid an interim dividend of £192,000 and is now declaring a final dividend of 8p per ordinary share.

The final dividend has been proposed after the year-end. It is not a liability because the company had no obligation to pay it at the year-end (see the definition of a liability in Chapter 2). Therefore no adjustment is needed.

(c) Interest:

DEBIT   Interest payable (profit or loss)   £108,000

CREDIT   Accruals (statement of financial position)   £108,000

Being the bank loan interest for the second six months of the year ended 31 December 20X1 ($2,700,000 \times 8\% \times 6/12$).

The statement of comprehensive income

The figures for revenue, distribution costs and administrative expenses are taken straight from the ETB. The others must be built up using workings.

(1) Cost of sales

	£'000
Opening inventories	3,602
Purchases	9,533
	13,135
Closing inventories	(4,195)
	8,940

(2) Finance costs

This is the interest of £216,000 (2,700,000 × 8%) (adjustment (c)).

(3) Tax

This is the tax charge of £581,000 (adjustment (a))

We can now draft the statement of comprehensive income. Notice that in this example there are no items of other comprehensive income; all income and expenses are included in profit or loss.

Cottage Ltd: Statement of comprehensive income for the year ended 31 December 20X1

	£'000
Continuing operations	
Revenue	16,253
Cost of sales (W1)	(8,940)
Gross profit	7,313
Distribution costs	(3,005)
Administrative expenses	(2,385)
Profit from operations	1,923
Finance costs (W2)	(216)
Profit before tax	1,707
Tax (W3)	(581)
Profit for the period from continuing operations	1,126

The statement of financial position

Again, some of the figures can be taken directly from the ETB, but most of them must be built up from workings.

(1) Property, plant and equipment

	Cost	Acc dep'n	
	£'000	£'000	£'000
Land and buildings	2,991	502	2,489
Fixtures and fittings	1,441	693	748
Motor vehicles	1,429	722	707
	5,861	1,917	3,944

(2) Trade and other receivables

	£'000
Trade receivables	2,709
Less: allowance for doubtful debts	(135)
	2,574
Prepayments	45
	2,619

(3) Retained earnings

	£'000
At 1 January 20X1	3,273
Profit for the year	1,126
Dividend paid (from ETB)	(192)
At 31 December 20X1	4,207

(4) Trade and other payables

	£'000	£'000
Trade payables		1,628
Accruals: per ETB	95	
Interest (adjustment (c))	108	
		203
		1,831

We can now draft the statement of financial position.

Cottage Ltd: Statement of financial position as at 31 December 20X1

Assets	£'000
Non-current assets:	
Intangible assets	3,208
Property, plant and equipment (W1)	3,944
	7,152
Current assets:	
Inventories	4,195
Trade and other receivables (W2)	2,619
Cash and cash equivalents	253
	7,067
Total assets	14,219
Equity and liabilities	
Equity:	
Share capital	3,500
Share premium	1,400
Retained earnings (W3)	4,207
Total equity	9,107
Non-current liabilities	
8% bank loan	2,700
Current liabilities	
Trade and other payables (W4)	1,831
Tax payable	581
	2,412
Total liabilities	5,112
Total equity and liabilities	14,219

Task 2

The following balances have been extracted from the trial balance of Triton Ltd, a wholesaler.

	£'000
Sales	3,534
Opening inventories	228
Purchases	2,623
Closing inventories	264
Directors' salaries	32
Wages and salaries:	
sales staff	131
office staff	197
Advertising and marketing costs	16
Office expenses	128
Light and heat	16
Depreciation:	
freehold buildings	2
fixtures and fittings	36
delivery vans	10
Audit fees	5
Interest on bank loan	24
Tax expense	105

Draft the statement of comprehensive income, in a format suitable for publication.

Triton Ltd: Statement of comprehensive income for the year ended

	£'000
Continuing operations	
Revenue	
Cost of sales	
Gross profit	
Distribution costs	
Administrative expenses	
Profit from operations	
Finance costs	
Profit before tax	
Tax	
Profit for the period from continuing operations	

Workings

Cost of sales	£'000

Distribution costs	£'000

Administrative expenses	£'000

Discontinued operations

A DISCONTINUED OPERATION is a component of an entity that has either been disposed of or is held for sale and:

- Represents a separate major line of business or geographical area of operations; or

- Is part of a single co-ordinated plan to dispose of a separate major line of business or geographical area of operations.

If an operation or an asset is classified as held for sale, it should be available for immediate sale and the sale should be highly probable. Management should be committed to the sale (taking active steps to find a buyer) and the sale must be expected to take place within the next 12 months.

- A discontinued operation can be a department or division within a single company or (in some cases) a separate company within a group.

- A **component of an entity** is an operation and its cash flows that can be clearly distinguished, operationally and for financial reporting purposes, from the rest of the entity.

CONTINUING OPERATIONS are operations that are not discontinued.

Both IAS 1 *Presentation of financial statements* and IFRS 5 *Non-current Assets Held for Sale and Discontinued Operations* require the post-tax profit or loss of discontinued operations to be disclosed in the statement of comprehensive income. This is presented as a single line item and is the total of:

- The post-tax profit or loss of the discontinued operation; and
- The post-tax gain or loss on the disposal of the discontinued operation.

Presenting the results of discontinued operations separately enables users to predict the future performance of an entity. Users are made aware that profits or losses relating to a discontinued operation will not occur in future periods.

Task 3

During the year ended 31 December 20X4, Cable Ltd sold one of its four divisions. This division satisfies the definition of a discontinued operation.

The discontinued operation made a loss for the year of £80,000.

The profit on disposal of the discontinued operation was £95,000.

An extract from the statement of comprehensive income for the year is shown below:

Statement of comprehensive income for the year ended 31 December 20X4 (extract)

	£'000
Profit for the year from continuing operations	1,140
Discontinued operations	
Profit for the year from discontinued operations	95
Profit for the year attributable to equity holders	1,235

The amounts shown above are correct.

Is this statement True or False?

True	
False	

OTHER COMPREHENSIVE INCOME

IAS 1 states that all items of income and expense recognised in a period should be included in profit or loss (the income statement section of the statement of comprehensive income) for that period, unless another Standard requires otherwise.

An entity may have items of income and expense that are not recognised in profit or loss. Examples are:

- Gains and losses on revaluation of non-current assets (normally property, plant and equipment)
- Some types of foreign currency translation differences

Because these items are part of total comprehensive income, they are recognised as **other comprehensive income**. They are shown either in a single statement of comprehensive income, below profit or loss, or in a separate statement of comprehensive income, after the income statement.

The statement of comprehensive income provides users of the financial statements with useful information by bringing together all the income and expenses of an entity for an accounting period. It provides users with useful information about the different components of an entity's performance and highlights the effect of items such as revaluation gains.

You may have to deal with revaluation gains and losses in the assessment. You will not be asked to deal with any other items recognised in other comprehensive income.

Illustration: other comprehensive income

Statement of comprehensive income for the year ended...(extract)

	£'000
Profit/(loss) for the period	X
Other comprehensive income for the period:	
Gains on property revaluation	<u>X</u>
Total comprehensive income for the period	<u>X</u>

IAS 1 states that as a minimum, the statement of comprehensive income must include line items that present the following amounts for the period:

- Each component of other comprehensive income classified by nature
- Total comprehensive income

THE STATEMENT OF CHANGES IN EQUITY

IAS 1 requires an entity to present a statement of changes in equity. This can be thought of as a 'bridge' between the statement of comprehensive income and the statement of financial position.

What the statement shows

IAS 1 requires the following items to be shown in the statement of changes in equity:

- Total comprehensive income for the period (from the statement of comprehensive income)

- The effects of changes in accounting policies (retrospective application) for each component of equity (ie for share capital and each reserve)

- The effects of correcting prior period errors (retrospective restatement) for each component of equity

- The amounts of transactions with owners in their capacity as owners (share issues and the payment of dividends)

- A reconciliation between the amounts at the beginning and the end of the period for each component of equity. Each change must be separately disclosed

IAS 1 also requires disclosure of the amount of dividends recognised as distributions to owners during the period and the amount per share. This can be presented either in the statement of changes in equity or in the notes.

Changes in accounting policies and the correction of errors are covered later in this chapter.

Example of a statement of changes in equity

Statement of changes in equity for the year ended...

	Share capital £'000	Other reserves £'000	Retained earnings £'000	Total equity £'000
Balance at beginning of year	X	X	X	X
Changes in accounting policy			(X)	(X)
Restated balance	X	X	X	X
Changes in equity for the year				
Total comprehensive income		X	X	X
Dividends			(X)	(X)
Issue of share capital	X	X		X
Balance at end of year	X	X	X	X

Task 4

Chickpea Ltd made a profit of £609,000 for the year ended 31 December 20X3.

During the year:

(a)   Freehold properties were revalued, resulting in a gain of £125,000

(b)   The company issued 200,000 new £1 ordinary shares at a price of £1.50 each

(c)   A dividend of £100,000 was paid to equity shareholders

Total equity at 1 January 20X3 was £2,020,000.

Draft a statement of comprehensive income (starting from 'profit for the year') and a statement of changes in equity (total column only) for the year ended 31 December 20X3.

Statement of comprehensive income for the year ended 31 December 20X3 (extract)

	£'000
Profit for the year	
Other comprehensive income for the year	
Total comprehensive income for the year	

Statement of changes in equity for the year ended 31 December 20X3 (extract)

	£'000
Balance at 1 January 20X3	
Changes in equity for 20X3	
Balance at 31 December 20X3	

NOTES TO THE FINANCIAL STATEMENTS

Notes provide or disclose information that is not presented in the statement of financial position, the statement of comprehensive income, statement of changes in equity or statement of cash flows:

- Where it is required by other IFRSs

- Where additional information is relevant to an understanding of any of the financial statements

They should also present information about the basis of presentation of the financial statements and the accounting policies used.

Notes should be presented in a systematic manner. Each item in the main statements should be cross-referenced to any related information in the notes.

Typically, many of the notes provide further analysis of the totals shown in the main financial statements. For example, the notes to the statement of financial position normally include an analysis of trade and other receivables into trade receivables, prepayments and other receivables.

Accounting policies

The notes should disclose a summary of significant accounting policies adopted by the entity:

- The measurement basis (or bases) used (for example, historic cost, fair value, net realisable value)

- Other accounting policies that are relevant to an understanding of the financial statements

Example

Notes to the financial statements: Accounting policies (extract)

Property, plant and equipment

Items of property, plant and equipment are measured at cost less accumulated depreciation.

Depreciation is charged so as to allocate the cost of assets less their residual values over their estimated useful lives, using the straight-line method. The following annual rates are used for the depreciation of property, plant and equipment:

Buildings	2%
Plant and machinery	25%

Inventories

Inventories are measured at the lower of cost and net realisable value. Cost is calculated using the first-in, first-out (FIFO) method.

Dividends proposed

The notes should disclose:

- The amount of any dividends proposed or declared before the financial statements were authorised for issue

- The amount of dividend per share

This disclosure is necessary because dividends proposed after the end of the reporting period are not recognised in the financial statements.

Expenses

Where an entity prepares the usual form of statement of comprehensive income that classifies expenses by function (showing cost of sales, distribution costs and administrative expenses), IAS 1 requires additional information on the nature of expenses, including:

- Depreciation and amortisation expense
- Employee benefits expense

SUMMARY OF THE FINANCIAL STATEMENTS

This diagram summarises the way that the main financial statements and the elements of the financial statements interrelate.

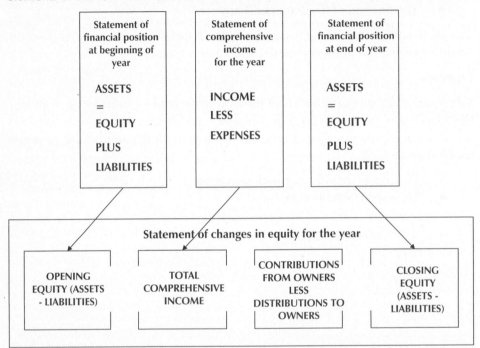

ACCOUNTING POLICIES

Preparers of accounts need to decide how they will treat particular items in the financial statements. For example, they may need to decide how to value a particular item of property, plant and equipment. All preparers of financial statements must select and apply **accounting policies**.

ACCOUNTING POLICIES are the specific principles, bases, conventions, rules and practices applied by an entity in preparing and presenting financial statements.

Examples of accounting policies:

- Property, plant and equipment is stated at fair value less accumulated depreciation

- Inventories are valued using the first-in first-out method

As well as selecting accounting policies, preparers of accounts have to make accounting estimates to arrive at amounts for items such as irrecoverable debts

and useful lives of assets. There are accepted techniques for making estimates, for example:

- Methods of depreciation (such as straight line and reducing balance)
- Methods of estimating allowances for doubtful debts

These methods and techniques are **not** accounting policies.

In simple terms, an accounting policy determines:

- How and when an item is recognised
- How (the basis) on which an item is measured
- How an item is presented

Selecting accounting policies

IAS 8 *Accounting Policies, Changes in Accounting Estimates and Errors* describes the way in which accounting policies should be selected. It states that:

- Where a specific IAS or IFRS applies to a transaction or event, this should be followed.

- Where there is no Standard that specifically applies, management must use judgement. The accounting policy selected must result in information that is:

  - Relevant to the economic decision-making needs of users
  - Reliable, so that the financial statements:

    - represent faithfully the financial position, financial performance and cash flows of the entity

    - reflect the economic substance of transactions, other events and conditions, and not merely the legal form

    - are neutral (free from bias)

    - are prudent (prepared using a degree of caution where there is uncertainty); and

    - are complete in all material respects

- When judging what is the most appropriate accounting policy, management should refer to the following sources of guidance:

  - Standards dealing with similar and related issues; then

  - The definitions, recognition criteria and measurement concepts for assets, liabilities, income and expenses in the *Conceptual Framework*. (See Chapter 2).

- Management may also consider recent pronouncements of other standard-setting bodies (eg the UK Accounting Standards Board) and accepted industry practices, if these do not conflict with international standards and the *Conceptual Framework*.

Consistency

An entity should select and apply its accounting policies consistently for similar transactions, other events and conditions, unless a Standard requires otherwise.

Changes in accounting policy

A company should only change an accounting policy if the change:

- Is required by a Standard
- Results in the financial statements providing reliable and more relevant information.

The following are **not** changes in accounting policy:

- The introduction of an accounting policy where there are transactions or events that are clearly different in substance from those previously occurring
- A change in an accounting estimate

It can sometimes be difficult to tell the difference between a change in an accounting policy and a change in an accounting estimate. A change in accounting policy results in a change to the way in which an item is:

- Recognised
- Presented
- Measured

Task 5

An entity has previously depreciated vehicles using the reducing balance method at 40% per year. It now uses the straight line method over a period of five years.

This is a change in accounting policy.

Is this statement True or False?

True	
False	

Applying changes in accounting policies

An accounting policy may have to be changed because a new Standard has been introduced. Most new Standards contain transitional arrangements, which explain how the change should be dealt with. Any transitional arrangements must be followed.

There are two possible ways of dealing with a change in accounting policy:

- **Retrospective application**: adjusting the financial statements so that they appear as if the new accounting policy has always been followed.

- **Prospective application**: adjusting the financial statements so that the new policy is followed from the date of the change; the full effect of the change is included in the profit or loss for the current period.

IAS 8 states that where there are no transitional arrangements in a new Standard, or where the entity has chosen to change an accounting policy, the change must be applied **retrospectively**.

This involves:

- Restating the comparative figures for the preceding period in the statement of comprehensive income and statement of financial position and the notes; and

- Adjusting the opening balance of retained earnings.

This process is often called making a **prior period adjustment** or making a prior year adjustment.

In addition, the entity must also present a statement of financial position at the beginning of the earliest comparative period.

This means that if, for example, an entity changed an accounting policy during the year ended 31 December 20X9, it would present **three** statements of financial position at:

- 31 December 20X7 (the beginning of the earliest comparative period)
- 31 December 20X8 (the end of the comparative period)
- 31 December 20X9 (the end of the current period)

HOW IT WORKS

Changeable Ltd was incorporated on 1 January 20X1. In the first two years' accounts it did not charge depreciation on certain freehold properties. The directors then decided that starting with the year ended 31 December 20X3, it should depreciate all property, plant and equipment.

Depreciation that would have been charged if the new policy had been applied from incorporation:

Year	£'000
20X1	30
20X2	60

The accounts for the year ended 31 December 20X2 showed the following movements on retained earnings.

	£'000
Retained earnings at 1 January 20X2	1,470
Retained earnings for the year	910
Retained earnings at 31 December 20X2	2,380

Profit for the year ended 31 December 20X3 (applying the new policy) is £915,000.

The prior period adjustment is the difference between retained earnings as reported and opening retained earnings as they would have been if the new policy had always been applied. This is £90,000 (£30,000 + £60,000).

Movements on the retained earnings reserve are as follows:

	20X3 £'000	20X2 £'000
Retained earnings at the beginning of the year	2,380	1,470
Change in accounting policy	(90)	(30)
Restated balance	2,290	1,440
Retained earnings for the year	915	850
Retained earnings at the end of the year	3,205	2,290

Changes in accounting estimates

Where there is a change in accounting estimate, the change must be recognised **prospectively**.

The effect is included in profit or loss only in the period of the change. There is no prior period adjustment.

Errors

Sometimes errors are made in preparing financial statements and these are not discovered until the following year, or even later. When they are discovered they must be corrected.

IAS 8 defines PRIOR PERIOD ERRORS as omissions from, and misstatements in, an entity's financial statements for one or more prior periods.

They arise from a failure to use reliable information that:

- Was available when the financial statements were authorised for issue; and

- Could reasonably be expected to have been obtained and taken into account.

They can include:

- Mathematical mistakes
- Mistakes in applying accounting policies
- Oversights
- Misinterpretations of facts
- Fraud

Task 6

In its financial statements for the year ended 31 December 20X3, a company makes an allowance of £30,000 for doubtful debts (based on a percentage of all trade receivables outstanding at the year-end date). After the financial statements have been published, it is discovered that the actual amount of debts not recovered is £50,000.

This is a prior period error.

Is this statement True or False?

True	
False	

IAS 8 states that **material** prior period errors must be corrected **retrospectively**. The financial statements must be restated as if the error had never occurred.

The method is the same as for a change in accounting policy: restate the comparative figures for the preceding period and adjust the opening balance of retained earnings.

In addition, the entity must present a statement of financial position at the beginning of the earliest comparative period.

CHAPTER OVERVIEW

- Users of the financial statements need information about the financial performance of an entity

- Financial performance (income – expenses) = closing equity – opening equity (change in net assets in the accounting period)

- The statement of comprehensive income shows the profit or loss for the year and items such as revaluation gains and losses which are not recognised in profit or loss

- IAS 1 sets out the line items which should be disclosed in the statement of comprehensive income

- All items of income and expense recognised in a period must be included in profit or loss unless a Standard requires otherwise

- The post-tax profit or loss of discontinued operations should be disclosed in the statement of comprehensive income

- The statement of changes in equity shows the movements in share capital and in each reserve for the year:

  - Changes in accounting policies
  - Correction of prior period errors
  - Total comprehensive income for the year
  - Issues of share capital
  - Dividends paid

- Selecting an accounting policy:

  - Follow any applicable IAS/IFRS

  - If none, management uses judgement

  - The policy selected must result in information that is relevant and reliable

- An entity should select and apply its accounting policies consistently for similar transactions, other events and conditions, unless a Standard requires otherwise

- A company should only change an accounting policy if the change is required by a Standard; or results in reliable and more relevant information

CHAPTER OVERVIEW CONTINUED

■ Changes in accounting policy are normally applied retrospectively. This involves:

– Restating the comparative figures for the preceding period in the statement of comprehensive income and statement of financial position and the notes; and

– Adjusting the opening balance of retained earnings

■ Changes in accounting estimates are recognised prospectively; the effect is included in profit or loss only in the period of the change

■ Material prior period errors must be corrected retrospectively; so that the financial statements appear as if the error had never occurred

Keywords

Total comprehensive income – the change in equity during a period resulting from transactions and other events, other than those changes resulting from transactions with owners in their capacity as owners

Profit or loss – income less expenses

Other comprehensive income – items of income and expense that are not recognised in profit or loss

Extraordinary items – material items possessing a high degree of abnormality which arise from events or transactions that fall outside the ordinary activities of an entity and which are not expected to recur

Discontinued operation – a component of an entity that has either been disposed of or is held for sale and represents a separate major line of business or geographical area of operations

Continuing operations – operations that are not discontinued

Accounting policies – the specific principles, bases, conventions, rules and practices applied by an entity in preparing and presenting financial statements

Prior period errors – omissions from, and misstatements in, an entity's financial statements for one or more prior periods

TEST YOUR LEARNING

Test 1

A gain on revaluation of non-current assets must always be included in profit or loss.

Is this statement True or False?

True	
False	

Test 2

During the year ended 31 December 20X6 Sycamore Ltd incurred general administrative expenses of £155,000. Depreciation of office furniture was £76,000.

Included in general administrative expenses was a payment for rent of £24,000 for the three months from 1 November 20X6 to 31 January 20X7.

What are total administrative expenses for the year ended 31 December 20X6?

£147,000	
£215,000	
£223,000	
£239,000	

Test 3

The directors of Tarragona plc have asked you to draft a statement of comprehensive income for the year ended 30 September 20X3.

They have given you the trial balance of the company which is set out below.

Tarragona plc: Trial balance as at 30 September 20X3

	Debit £'000	Credit £'000
Property, plant and equipment at cost	24,492	
Accumulated depreciation on property, plant and equipment		7,604
Trade receivables	4,150	
Long-term loan		3,780
Distribution costs	6,165	
Administration expenses	3,386	
Ordinary share capital		5,400
Share premium		1,800
Loss on disposal of discontinued operation	238	
Sales		33,202
Inventories as at 1 October 20X2	8,570	
Cash at bank	256	
Accruals		97
Interest	279	
Trade payables		2,435
Purchases	19,480	
Retained earnings		12,698
	67,016	67,016

Further information:

- The company is proposing a final dividend of 20 pence per share. No interim dividend was paid during the year.

- The inventories at the close of business on 30 September 20X3 were valued at cost at £10,262,000.

- The corporation tax charge for the year has been estimated at £1,333,000.

- Land that had cost £4,800,000 has been revalued by professional valuers at £5,800,000. No adjustment has yet been made to the trial balance. The revaluation is to be included in the financial statements for the year ended 30 September 20X3.

- During the year the company discontinued part of its operations. The results of the discontinued operation for the year have already been analysed by the company accountant. All of these results are included in the figures in the trial balance. The analysed results are set out below.

	Discontinued operation £'000
Revenue	748
Cost of sales	411
Gross profit	337
Distribution costs	165
Administrative expenses	146
	26

Draft a statement of comprehensive income for Tarragona plc for the year ended 30 September 20X3.

Tarragona plc

Statement of comprehensive income for the year ended 30 September 20X3

	£'000
Continuing operations	
Revenue	
Cost of sales	
Gross profit	
Distribution costs	
Administrative expenses	
Profit from operations	
Finance costs	
Profit before tax	
Tax	
Profit for the period from continuing operations	
Discontinued operations	
Profit/(loss) for the period from discontinued operations	
Profit for the period	
Other comprehensive income	
Gain on revaluation of land	
Total comprehensive income for the period	

Working

Cost of sales	£'000

Test 4

Complete the sentence below by writing in the appropriate words.

I. A. S.	are the specific principles, bases, conventions,

rules and practices applied by an entity in preparing and presenting financial statements.

Test 5

Prepare brief notes to answer the following question.

Under what circumstances does IAS 8 *Accounting Policies, Changes in Accounting Estimates and Errors* allow an entity to change an accounting policy?

Test 6

Changes in accounting policy are always applied retrospectively.

Is this statement True or False?

True	
False	

Test 7

Below are two statements about prior period errors.

1 All prior period errors must be corrected.

2 The correction of a prior period error affects the opening balance of retained earnings.

Which of the statements is correct?

1 only	
2 only	
Both statements	
Neither statement	

Test 8

The following information relates to Light Ltd:

Equity at 1 January 20X5

	£'000
Share capital (£1 ordinary shares)	1,000
Share premium	300
Retained earnings	700
	2,000

The following transactions and events took place during the year:

On 31 December 20X5 a freehold property was revalued to £500,000 and this valuation was incorporated into the financial statements. The property had previously been carried at historic cost less depreciation and had a carrying amount (net book value) of £350,000 immediately before the revaluation.

On 1 July 20X5 the company issued a further 100,000 £1 ordinary shares at a market price of £1.20.

On 31 December 20X5 the company paid a dividend of £50,000.

Profit for the year ended 31 December 20X5 was £300,000.

Draft a statement of changes in equity for Light Ltd for the year ended 31 December 20X5.

Statement of changes in equity for the year ended 31 December 20X5

	Share capital	Share premium	Revaluation reserve	Retained earnings	Total equity
	£'000	£'000	£'000	£'000	£'000
Balance at 1 January 20X5					
Changes in equity for 20X5					
Total comprehensive income					
Dividends					
Issue of shares					
Balance at 31 December 20X5					

chapter 5:
THE STATEMENT OF CASH FLOWS

chapter coverage 📖

In this chapter we introduce the statement of cash flows (sometimes called the cash flow statement). The statement of comprehensive income and the statement of financial position provide information about an entity's performance and financial position. The statement of cash flows, as its name suggests, shows the way in which an entity has generated and spent cash. IAS 7 *Statement of Cash Flows* requires companies to include a statement of cash flows in their financial statements and sets out the way in which the statement should be prepared and presented.

The topics covered are:

- ✍ The importance of cash
- ✍ IAS 7 *Statement of Cash Flows*
- ✍ Classifying cash flows
- ✍ Calculating net cash from operating activities
- ✍ Preparing the statement of cash flows: indirect method
- ✍ Preparing the statement of cash flows: direct method
- ✍ How useful is the statement of cash flows?
- ✍ Interpreting the statement of cash flows

THE IMPORTANCE OF CASH

However profitable a business may appear to be, it will not survive without adequate cash. Businesses need cash to pay suppliers and employees, to pay dividends to shareholders, to repay debt to lenders and to purchase property, plant, equipment and inventories to enable them to go on producing goods or providing services.

The needs of users

Users of the financial statements can get information about an entity's performance from the statement of comprehensive income. The statement of financial position shows the financial position (state of affairs) of the entity. Users also need information about the liquidity and solvency of an entity; the cash resources that it has and its ability to pay its debts as they fall due. They need information about **financial adaptability**: an entity's ability to take effective action to alter the amount and timing of its cash flows in order to respond to unexpected needs or opportunities.

Why profit is not the same as cash flow

The statement of comprehensive income and statement of financial position are drawn up on an accruals basis. Income and expenditure are recognised in the period in which the transactions giving rise to them occur, rather than the period in which the cash is received or paid. These can be very different. The period in which an item is recognised in the statement of comprehensive income and statement of financial position may depend on:

- The accounting policies adopted and the estimates used by the entity
- The judgement of management (where estimates have to be made)

Cash flow is a matter of fact (it can be verified by looking at the entity's bank statement). It is difficult to manipulate and is less likely to be distorted by 'creative accounting'.

IAS 7 STATEMENT OF CASH FLOWS

IAS 7 requires all companies to include a statement of cash flows in their published financial statements.

A STATEMENT OF CASH FLOWS summarises all movements of cash into and out of a business during the accounting period. Its purpose is to provide users with information about the historical changes in cash and cash equivalents of an entity from operating, investing and financing activities.

Cash flow information provides users with a means of assessing the ability of an entity to generate cash and the needs of the entity to use cash. Users need to be able to evaluate the ability of an entity to generate cash and the timing and certainty of its generation, in order to make economic decisions.

Basic format of the statement of cash flows

IAS 7 requires entities to classify their cash inflows and outflows under three standard headings. These are:

- Operating activities
- Investing activities
- Financing activities

The total cash flows for each heading are totalled to give the net inflow or outflow of cash and cash equivalents for the period.

Cash and cash equivalents

CASH FLOWS are inflows and outflows of cash and cash equivalents.

For most entities, 'cash' is made up of several different items: cash in hand, bank current accounts, deposits and loans. IAS 7 defines CASH as:

- Cash in hand (bank current accounts and petty cash)
- Demand deposits (ie deposits repayable on demand)

In practice, cash also includes bank overdrafts if (as is usual) they are repayable on demand.

Many entities may use short-term investments in order to manage their cash flow. Surplus cash is put into deposit accounts or used to buy investments in order to generate additional cash flow from interest or dividends.

CASH EQUIVALENTS are short-term, highly liquid investments that are readily convertible to known amounts of cash and which are subject to an insignificant risk of changes in value.

IAS 7 suggests that an investment is normally a cash equivalent if it matures within three months of the date of acquisition.

By basing the statement of cash flows on cash and cash equivalents, rather than simply on bank accounts and petty cash, IAS 7 enables users of the statement of cash flows to appreciate the way in which entities manage cash flow in practice. There is a potential problem because it can be difficult to decide whether or not a current asset investment is actually a cash equivalent; the classification can be subjective.

In the assessment it will be made clear if a current asset investment is a cash equivalent.

CLASSIFYING CASH FLOWS

Operating activities

IAS 7 defines OPERATING ACTIVITIES as the principal revenue producing activities of the entity and other activities that are not investing or financing activities.

Cash flows from operating activities consist of:

- Cash received from customers (receipts from the sale of goods or the rendering of services)
- Cash paid to suppliers for goods and services
- Cash paid to and on behalf of employees

In other words, the net cash flow from operating activities can be thought of as profit from operations adjusted for non-cash items.

Cash flows from operating activities also include payments and refunds of income tax unless they can be specifically identified with investing or financing activities. Corporation tax payments relate to profits from operations and so they are a cash flow from operating activities.

Investing activities

INVESTING ACTIVITIES are the acquisition and disposal of long-term assets and other investments not included in cash equivalents.

Cash flows from investing activities include:

- Payments to acquire property, plant or equipment and other long-term assets
- Receipts from sales of property, plant and equipment and other long-term assets
- Payments to acquire investments other than cash equivalents
- Receipts from sales of investments other than cash equivalents
- Cash advances and loans made to other parties and receipts from their repayment

Cash flows from investing activities also include cash flows from sales and purchases of investments in subsidiaries (other companies that the investor controls) and other businesses. These are unlikely to feature in your assessment because you will not be asked to prepare a statement of cash flows for a group of companies.

Cash flows from acquisitions and disposals of subsidiaries and other businesses should be presented separately in the statement of cash flows.

Financing activities

FINANCING ACTIVITIES are activities that result in changes in the size and composition of the contributed equity (share capital) and borrowings of the entity.

The main cash flows included under this heading are:

- Proceeds from issuing shares

- Proceeds from issuing debentures and other loans, (including bank loans)

- Repayment of amounts borrowed

Interest and dividends

IAS 7 does not assign cash flows relating to interest and dividends to a specific heading.

For example, interest paid is often shown under operating activities because it is deducted in arriving at the profit for the period. It could also be shown under financing activities, because it is a cost of obtaining finance.

Interest and dividends received are normally shown under investing activities because they are returns on investments but, in some cases, it might be possible to justify a different treatment. For example, a financial institution such as a bank would probably classify them as operating cash flows.

Dividends paid can be shown either under cash flows from operating activities or (normally) under cash flows from financing activities.

IAS 7 states that interest and dividends received and paid should be disclosed separately and that they must be classified in a consistent manner from period to period.

In the Assessment, you will be expected to include interest and dividends under the following headings:

- Interest paid under **operating activities**
- Dividends and interest received under **investing activities**
- Dividends paid under **financing activities**

Task 1

Which of the following items is **always** included in the statement of cash flows under the heading 'cash flows from financing activities'?

Cash received from the sale of property, plant and equipment	
Dividends paid	
Interest received	
Repayment of loans	

Net cash flows and gross cash flows

The total cash flow reported under each of the standard headings may be made up of several different items. For example, the net cash outflow for investing activities may be cash paid to purchase property, plant and equipment less cash received from the disposal of property, plant and equipment.

The total cash flows are the NET CASH FLOWS. The individual cash flows are GROSS CASH FLOWS. Major classes of gross cash receipts and gross cash payments arising from investing and financing activities must be disclosed separately.

CALCULATING NET CASH FROM OPERATING ACTIVITIES

There are two methods of arriving at this figure:

- List and total the actual cash flows: cash received from customers less cash paid to suppliers and cash paid to and on behalf of employees. This is known as the **direct method**.

- Adjust profit from operations or profit before tax for non-cash items such as depreciation, movements in working capital (normally inventories, receivables and payables) and any items that relate to investing or financing activities. This is known as the **indirect method**.

IAS 7 allows either method and you could be asked to use either in the assessment.

The indirect method

Using this method, the first part of the statement of cash flows is a reconciliation of profit from operations or profit before tax to net cash from operating activities:

	£'000
Profit from operations	X
Depreciation	X
(Gain)/loss on disposal of property, plant and equipment	(X)/X
(Increase)/decrease in inventories	(X)/X
(Increase)/decrease in receivables	(X)/X
Increase/(decrease) in payables	X/(X)
Cash generated from operations	X
Interest paid	(X)
Tax paid	(X)
	X

HOW IT WORKS

A company has a profit from operations of £20,500 for the year ended 31 December 20X2. The depreciation charge for the year is £4,000. Profit from operations also includes a loss on disposal of £500 on an item of plant.

Extracts from the statement of financial position are shown below:

	20X2	20X1
	£	£
Inventories	17,400	16,100
Receivables	21,500	20,500
Trade payables	18,400	17,600

Ignore interest and tax.

The company's profit is adjusted for non-cash items in order to arrive at cash generated from operations.

Step 1   Add back depreciation

Depreciation has been charged in arriving at profit from operations, but it does not involve the movement of cash. Therefore it is added back to profit from operations.

Step 2   Adjust for any profits or losses on the disposal of assets

The cash received from the sale of an asset is not a cash flow from operating activities. The profit or loss on sale must be removed from profit from operations:

- A profit on disposal is deducted
- A loss on disposal is added back

Step 3 Adjust for changes in working capital (inventories, receivables and payables)

The movements in working capital represent the differences between sales and cash received and purchases and cash paid.

Suppose that sales for the year were £100,000. Opening receivables were £20,500 and closing receivables were £21,500. Therefore cash received was £99,000: £1,000 less than the sales figure. The difference between sales and cash inflow is the difference between opening receivables and closing receivables: £1,000.

Suppose that total expenses were £75,000:

■ Opening inventories were £16,100 and closing inventories were £17,400. This means that total purchases were £76,300 (75,000 + 17,400 – 16,100).

■ Opening payables were £17,600 and closing payables were £18,400. Therefore cash paid was £75,500 (76,300 + 17,600 – 18,400).

■ The difference between operating expenses and cash inflow is £500, which is the difference between opening and closing inventories (£1,300 increase) less the difference between opening and closing payables (£800 increase).

In practice, we simply adjust profit for the differences between the opening and closing amounts:

■ Increase in inventories: deduct £1,300 (cash outflow)
■ Increase in receivables: deduct £1,000 (cash outflow)
■ Increase in trade payables: add £800 (cash inflow)

We can now draw up a reconciliation of profit from operations to cash generated from operations:

	£
Profit from operations	20,500
Depreciation	4,000
Loss on disposal of property, plant & equipment	500
Increase in inventories	(1,300)
Increase in receivables	(1,000)
Decrease in payables	800
Cash generated from operations	23,500

Interest paid and tax paid (not given in this example) are then deducted from cash generated from operations to give the net cash from operating activities.

This reconciliation helps users of the financial statements to understand the difference between profit and cash flow. It also shows the movements on the individual items within working capital. This enables users to see how successful or otherwise the entity has been in managing inventories, receivables and payables in order to generate cash.

Most companies use the indirect method.

The direct method

An entity may choose to show the net cash from operating activities using the direct method. This summarises the actual cash flows as follows:

	£'000	£'000
Cash received from customers	X	
Cash paid to suppliers and employees	(X)	
Cash generated from operations		X
Interest paid		(X)
Tax paid		(X)
Net cash from operating activities		X

The advantage of the direct method is that by showing the actual cash flows it enables users to see how the company generates and uses cash.

HOW IT WORKS

A company has profit from operations of £20,500 for the year ended 31 December 20X2. This was made up as follows:

	£
Revenue	100,000
Cost of sales	(59,700)
Gross profit	40,300
Operating expenses (including depreciation of £4,000 and loss on disposal of £500)	(19,800)
Profit from operations	20,500

Extracts from the statement of financial position are shown below:

	20X2	20X1
	£	£
Inventories	17,400	16,100
Receivables	21,500	20,500
Trade payables	18,400	17,600

Ignore interest and tax.

Step 1   Calculate cash received from customers by reconstructing the receivables account:

	£
Opening balance (statement of financial position)	20,500
Sales (statement of comprehensive income)	100,000
Closing balance (statement of financial position)	(21,500)
Cash received (balancing figure)	99,000

Or:

Receivables

	£		£
Balance b/f	20,500	**Cash received (bal fig)**	99,000
Sales	100,000	Balance c/f	21,500
	120,500		120,500

Step 2   Calculate purchases:

	£
Cost of sales (statement of comprehensive income)	59,700
Add: closing inventories (statement of financial position)	17,400
Less: opening inventories (statement of financial position)	(16,100)
	61,000
Operating expenses (statement of comprehensive income)	19,800
Less: depreciation and loss on disposal	(4,500)
	76,300

Remember that depreciation and losses on disposal do not involve the movement of cash. They must be deducted from cost of sales and/or other operating expenses.

Step 3 Calculate cash paid to suppliers and employees by reconstructing the trade payables account:

	£
Opening balance (statement of financial position)	17,600
Purchases (Step 2)	76,300
Closing balance (statement of financial position)	(18,400)
Cash paid (balancing figure)	75,500

Or:

Trade payables

	£		£
Cash paid (bal fig)	75,500	Balance b/f	17,600
Balance	18,400	Purchases	76,300
	93,900		93,900

Step 4 Calculate cash generated from operations

	£
Cash received from customers	99,000
Cash paid to suppliers and employees	(75,500)
Cash generated from operations	23,500

As with the indirect method, interest paid and tax paid (not given in this example) are then deducted from cash generated from operations to give the net cash from operating activities.

Task 2

Extracts from the statement of financial position of Barking Ltd are shown below:

	20X6	20X5	
	£	£	
Inventories	5,100	5,800	1200
Trade and other receivables	7,500	7,000	
Trade and other payables	5,700	6,000	

Profit from operations and depreciation for the year ended 30 June 20X6 were £20,000 and £5,000 respectively.

What is cash generated from operations for the year ended 30 June 20X6?

£14,900	
£15,100	
£24,500	
£24,900	

PREPARING THE STATEMENT OF CASH FLOWS: INDIRECT METHOD

The format of the statement of cash flows

In the assessment, the statement of cash flows is normally drafted in two parts:

- A reconciliation of profit from operations to net cash flow from operating activities; this shows the cash flows from operating activities using the indirect method

- A statement of cash flows showing cash flows from investing activities, cash flows from financing activities and the net movement in cash and cash equivalents for the period

In practice, different formats are possible. For example, the illustration in IAS 7 *Statement of Cash Flows* shows a single statement starting with profit before tax and with the reconciliation section headed 'Cash flows from operating activities'. All the formats show the same information, presented slightly differently.

The illustration below shows the format that you will use in the assessment.

Illustration

Reconciliation of profit from operations to net cash inflow from operating activities for the year ended 31 December 20X2

	£'000
Profit from operations	3,350
Adjustments for:	
Depreciation	490
Gain on disposal of property, plant and equipment	(100)
Decrease in inventories	1,050
Increase in trade and other receivables	(500)
Decrease in trade payables	(1,740)
Cash generated from operations	2,550
Interest paid	(270)
Tax paid	(900)
Net cash from operating activities	1,380

Statement of cash flows for the year ended 31 December 20X2

	£'000	£'000
Net cash from operating activities		1,380
Investing activities		
Purchase of property, plant and equipment	(900)	
Proceeds on disposal of property, plant and equipment	20	
Interest received	200	
Dividends received	200	
Net cash used in investing activities		(480)
Financing activities		
Proceeds of share issue	250	
Increase in bank loans	160	
Dividends paid	(1,200)	
Net cash used in financing activities		(790)
Net increase in cash and cash equivalents		110
Cash and cash equivalents at beginning of year (note)		120
Cash and cash equivalents at end of year (note)		230

Note: Cash and cash equivalents	**20X2**	**20X1**
	£'000	£'000
Cash on hand and balances with banks	40	25
Short-term investments	190	95
	230	120

IAS 7 requires this note, which discloses the components of cash and cash equivalents and reconciles the amounts in the statement of cash flows with the equivalent items reported in the statement of financial position.

This note is not often required in the assessment. The Assessor will ask you to draft the note, if it **is** required.

Task 3

Draft the statement of cash flows from the information provided below:

Cash flows	£'000
Cash and cash equivalents at the beginning of the period	7,000
Dividends paid	8,000
Dividends received	4,000
Increase in cash and cash equivalents for the period	10,000
Net cash from operating activities	39,000
Proceeds of share issue	50,000
Proceeds on disposal of property, plant and equipment	10,000
Purchase of property, plant and equipment	65,000
Repayment of long-term loan	20,000

Statement of cash flows for the year ended...

	£	£
Net cash from operating activities		39,000
Investing activities:		
Dividends received	4,000	
	(65,000)	
	10,000	
Net cash used in investing activities		(51,000)
Financing activities:		
	(20,000)	
Proceeds Share issue	50,000	
Dividend paid	(8,000)	
Net cash from financing activities		22,000
Net increase (decrease) in cash and cash equivalents for the year		10,000
Cash and cash equivalents at the beginning of the year		7,000
Cash and cash equivalents at the end of the year		17,000

HOW IT WORKS

The statement of financial position of Flow Ltd as at 31 December 20X7 is shown below, together with comparative figures.

	20X7		20X6	
	£'000	£'000	£'000	£'000
Assets:				
Property, plant and equipment		480		330
Current assets:				
Inventories	130		110	
Trade and other receivables	180		110	
Cash and cash equivalents	–		30	
		310		250
Total assets		790		580
Equity and liabilities				
Equity:				
Share capital		70		60
Share premium		30		20
Retained earnings		320		250
		420		330
Non-current liabilities:				
Bank loans		210		150
Current liabilities:				
Trade payables	80		50	
Tax liability	50		40	
Accruals	10		10	
Bank overdraft	20		–	
		160		100
Total liabilities		370		250
Total equity and liabilities		790		580

The summarised statement of comprehensive income for the year ended 31 December 20X7 is shown below:

	£'000
Profit from operations	170
Finance costs	(20)
Profit before tax	150
Tax	(40)
Profit for the year	110

Further information

The total depreciation charge for the year was £110,000.

During the year the company sold items of property, plant and equipment which had originally cost £50,000 and which had a carrying amount (net book value) of £30,000.

Profit from operations includes a loss on disposal of property, plant and equipment of £10,000 and a dividend received of £30,000.

A dividend of £40,000 was paid during the year.

Step 1   Calculate cash generated from operations

Add back depreciation and loss on disposal of assets to profit from operations. Loss on disposal of assets is a non-cash item and also it relates to investing activities. Then adjust for movements in inventories, receivables, trade payables and accruals.

Deduct the dividend received. This is a cash item, but it relates to investing activities.

Inventories have increased, so cash has been used to pay for the extra goods. Receivables and payables have both increased, meaning that less cash has been collected from customers and less cash has been paid to suppliers than in previous periods. The increase in inventories and receivables is deducted from profit (cash outflow) and the increase in payables is added to profit (cash inflow).

	£'000
Profit from operations	170
Adjustments for:	
Depreciation	110
Dividends received	(30)
Loss on sale of property, plant and equipment	10
Increase in inventories (130 – 110)	(20)
Increase in receivables (180 – 110)	(70)
Increase in payables (90 – 60)	30
Cash generated from operations	200

Step 2   Interest and tax

There are no accruals for interest payable. Therefore the figure is taken directly from the statement of comprehensive income.

The corporation tax expense shown in the statement of comprehensive income is usually an **estimate** of the tax payable for the year and is paid after the year-end. If:

- the figure in the statement of comprehensive income is the same as the closing liability in the statement of financial position; then

- the cash paid in the period is equal to the opening liability in the statement of financial position.

In this case, the figure in the statement of comprehensive income is **different** from the closing liability. We can calculate the cash outflow:

	£'000
Opening balance (statement of financial position)	40
Charge for the year (statement of comprehensive income)	40
Less: Closing balance (statement of financial position)	(50)
Cash paid (balancing figure)	30

Another way of doing this calculation would be to draw up a 'T'-account.

Tax

	£'000		£'000
Cash paid (bal fig)	30	Balance b/f	40
Balance c/f	50	Profit or loss	40
	80		80

We can now complete the reconciliation of profit from operations to net cash from operating activities.

	£'000
Cash generated from operations	200
Interest paid	(20)
Tax paid	(30)
Net cash from operating activities	150

Step 3 **Property, plant and equipment**

We need to calculate two amounts:

- Cash paid to acquire property, plant and equipment during the year (non-current asset additions); and

- Cash received from asset disposals during the year

To calculate the cash outflow/asset additions we use the opening and closing balances from the statement of financial position, the depreciation figure and the carrying amount (net book value) of assets disposed. The cash outflow is the balancing figure.

	£'000
Opening balance (statement of financial position)	330
Depreciation (normally given in question)	(110)
Disposals (at carrying amount)	(30)
Closing balance (statement of financial position)	(480)
Cash paid/Additions (balancing figure)	(290)

Again, another way of doing this would be to draw up a 'T'-account.

Property, plant and equipment

	£'000		£'000
Balance b/f	330	Disposals	30
		Depreciation	110
Additions: cash paid	290	Balance c/f	480
(balancing figure)			
	620		620

However, the pro-forma working you will be given in the assessment will be very similar to the columnar working above.

To calculate the cash received from disposals, deduct the loss on disposal from the carrying amount of the assets sold. (A gain on disposal is added to the carrying amount.)

	£'000
Carrying amount of assets sold	30
Loss on disposal	(10)
Cash received	20

Step 4 **Other investing and financing cash flows**

We have now calculated the additions of property, plant and equipment and the proceeds of sale of non-current assets so these figures can be entered straight into the statement of cash flows.

Dividends received can also be entered into the statement, under investing activities.

Most of the financing cash flows are simply the differences between the opening and closing figures in the statement of financial position.

The cash inflow from the issue of shares is made up of an increase in share capital of £10,000 (£70,000 – £60,000) plus an increase in share premium of £10,000 (£30,000 – £20,000). This is reported under financing activities.

Bank loans have increased in the year and therefore there is a cash inflow of £60,000 (£210,000 – £150,000) also reported under financing activities.

Dividends paid are also included in financing activities.

Step 5 **Cash and cash equivalents**

We need figures for cash and cash equivalents at the beginning and end of the year. The difference between these figures is the net increase or decrease in cash for the year, which should be the same as the total of the individual cash flows from operating, investing and financing activities.

	At 1 Jan 20X7	Cash flows	At 31 Dec 20X7
	£'000	£'000	£'000
Cash	30	(30)	–
Bank overdraft	–	(20)	(20)
	30	(50)	(20)

We are now able to complete the statement of cash flows.

Step 6 **Draft the completed statement of cash flows**

Reconciliation of profit from operations to net cash from operating activities for the year ended 31 December 20X7

	£'000
Profit from operations	170
Adjustments for:	
Depreciation	110
Dividends received	(30)
Loss on sale of property, plant and equipment	10
Increase in inventories (130 – 110)	(20)
Increase in receivables (180 – 110)	(70)
Increase in payables (90 – 60)	30
Cash generated from operations	200
Interest paid	(20)
Tax paid	(30)
Net cash from operating activities	150

Statement of cash flows for the year ended 31 December 20X7

	£'000	£'000
Net cash from operating activities		150
Investing activities:		
Purchase of property, plant and equipment	(290)	
Proceeds on disposal of property, plant and equipment	20	
Dividends received	30	
Net cash used in investing activities		(240)
Financing activities:		
Proceeds of share issue	20	
Increase in bank loans	60	
Dividends paid	(40)	
Net cash from financing activities		40
Net decrease in cash and cash equivalents		(50)
Cash and cash equivalents at 1 January 20X7		30
Cash and cash equivalents at 31 December 20X7		(20)

Calculating cash flows: the basic principle

The example above is typical of the tasks that you may be asked to complete in the assessment. However, it is possible that you could be asked to calculate other amounts, such as the depreciation charge for the year, or dividends paid during the year.

In the example above, we used the opening and closing statement of financial position and the statement of comprehensive income for the year to arrive at a balancing figure: the cash flow for the year. We can use the same method to find any cash flow amount or 'missing figure'. (This is similar to the technique that you may have used to find the 'missing' figures where there are incomplete records, earlier in your studies.)

HOW IT WORKS

The facts are as in the example above, except that this time the additional information is as follows:

- During the year the company purchased items of property, plant and equipment for £290,000. It sold items of property, plant and equipment which had originally cost £50,000 and which had a carrying amount (net book value) of £30,000.

We do not know the depreciation charge for the year. This is needed to complete the reconciliation of profit from operations to net cash flow from operating activities.

As before, we reconstruct the account for property, plant and equipment. If we know the opening and closing balances, plus the additions and disposals, the depreciation charge is the balancing figure.

	£'000
Opening balance (statement of financial position)	330
Additions	290
Disposals (at carrying amount)	(30)
Closing balance (statement of financial position)	(480)
Depreciation for the year (balancing figure)	110

This working is another way of reconstructing the 'T'-account.

Property, plant and equipment

	£'000		£'000
Balance b/f	330	Disposals	30
		Depreciation (balancing figure)	110
Additions: cash paid	290	Balance c/f	480
	620		620

HOW IT WORKS

Again, the facts are as in the example above, but this time the further information does not include the amount of dividends paid in the year.

We can calculate the amount by looking at the movement in the retained earnings reserve. If closing retained earnings is less than opening retained earnings plus the profit for the year, the difference is dividends paid.

	£'000
Opening balance (statement of financial position)	250
Profit for the year	110
Closing balance (statement of financial position)	(320)
Dividends (cash) paid (balancing figure)	40

Retained earnings

	£'000		£'000
Dividends paid (bal fig)	40	Balance b/f	250
Balance c/f	320	Profit for the year	110
	360		360

Task 4

Extracts from the statement of financial position of Dulwich Ltd are shown below:

	20X9 £'000	20X8 £'000
Bank overdraft	–	300
Loan stock	1,500	1,000
Share capital	2,000	1,500
Share premium	200	100

What is the cash from financing activities for the year ended 31 December 20X9?

£100,000	
£1,000,000	
£1,100,000	✓
£1,400,000	

PREPARING THE STATEMENT OF CASH FLOWS: DIRECT METHOD

The format of the statement of cash flows

Instead of the reconciliation of profit from operations to net cash flow from operating activities, the first part of the statement of cash flows lists and totals the actual cash flows.

You may be given these or you may be asked to calculate them from information in the statement of comprehensive income and statement of financial position.

If you are asked to calculate the cash flows, use the steps and the workings explained earlier in the chapter, in the section on calculating net cash from operating activities:

- Calculate cash received from customers by reconstructing the trade receivables account

- Calculate the figure for purchases (remembering to exclude depreciation and any gains or losses on disposal of assets)

- Calculate cash paid to suppliers and employees by reconstructing the trade payables account.

Then draw up the first part of the statement as shown below.

Statement of cash flows for the year ended 31 December 20X2 (extract)

	£'000
Operating activities	
Cash receipts from customers	30,150
Cash payments to suppliers and employees	(27,600)
Cash generated from operations	2,550
Interest paid	(270)
Tax paid	(900)
Net cash from operating activities	1,380

The remainder of the statement, that is, the sections headed 'investing activities' and 'financing activities' are prepared and presented in exactly the same way as under the indirect method.

HOW USEFUL IS THE STATEMENT OF CASH FLOWS?

Useful information provided by a statement of cash flows

Most people agree that the statement of cash flows provides useful information. It alerts users to possible liquidity problems by highlighting inflows and outflows of cash.

IAS 7 explains that a statement of cash flows, used together with the rest of the financial statements, can help users to assess:

- The changes in an entity's net assets and its liquidity and solvency
- An entity's ability to generate cash and cash equivalents and to affect the amounts and timing of cash flows in order to adapt to changing circumstances

There are other advantages of presenting a statement of cash flows:

- It shows an entity's ability to turn profit into cash (by allowing users to compare profit with cash flows from operating activities)
- Cash flow is a matter of fact and is difficult to manipulate
- Cash flow information is not affected by an entity's choice of accounting policies or by judgement
- The statement may help users to predict future cash flows
- Cash flow is easier to understand than profit
- The standard format enables users to compare the cash flows of different entities

Limitations of the statement of cash flows

There are some important limits to the usefulness of the statement of cash flows:

- Cash balances are measured at a point in time and therefore they can be manipulated. For example, customers may be offered prompt payment discounts or other incentives to make early payment, or an entity may delay paying suppliers until after the year-end. These are legitimate ways of managing cash flow (which is part of stewardship), but users may not be aware that this is being done, and may believe that the entity's position is better than it actually is.

- A high bank balance is not necessarily a sign of good cash management. Entities sometimes have to sacrifice cash flow in the short term to generate profits in the longer term, for example, by purchasing new plant and equipment. A business must have cash if it is to survive in the short term, but if it is to survive in the longer term it must also make a profit. Focusing on cash may mean that an entity has a healthy bank balance but makes a loss.

- The statement of cash flows is based on historical information and therefore it is not necessarily a reliable indicator of future cash flows.

Neither the statement of comprehensive income nor the statement of cash flows provides a complete picture of an entity's performance or position by itself.

INTERPRETING THE STATEMENT OF CASH FLOWS

You may be asked to interpret a statement of cash flows in the assessment. This can be done by simple observation.

Look at the net cash flow for the period and then at each category of cash flows in turn.

Net cash flow for the period

- Has cash increased or decreased in the period?

- How material is the increase/decrease in cash compared with the entity's cash balances?

- Does the entity have a positive cash balance or an overdraft?

A decrease in cash is not always a bad sign, particularly if the entity has used the cash to finance capital expenditure or has used surplus cash to purchase liquid resources.

Operating activities

Have inventories, receivables and payables increased or decreased?

A material increase in working capital is a worrying sign, particularly if the entity has a cash outflow from operating activities.

Interest, tax and dividends

Is there enough cash to cover:

- Interest payments?
- Taxation?
- Dividends?

As well as looking at the current period's cash outflows, look at the liabilities in the statement of financial position, if this information is available; these are the next period's cash outflows.

Remember that interest and corporation tax have to be paid when they are due, but the entity can delay payment of equity dividends until the cash is available.

Investing activities

A cash outflow to purchase assets is usually a good sign, because the assets will generate profits (and cash inflows) in future periods.

If there has been capital expenditure, where has the cash come from? Usually it will have come from several sources: operations; issuing shares or loan stock; taking out a loan; taking out an overdraft.

If the entity has taken out or increased an overdraft, this is usually a worrying sign. In theory, a bank overdraft is repayable on demand.

Financing activities

Ask the following questions:

- Is debt increasing or decreasing?
- Will the entity be able to pay its debt interest?
- Will the entity be able to repay the debt (if it falls due in the near future)?
- Is the entity likely to need additional long-term finance? (This might be the case if the bank overdraft is rapidly increasing or nearing its limit, or if the entity has plans to expand in the near future.)

CHAPTER OVERVIEW

- Businesses need cash in order to survive

- Users of the financial statements need information about the liquidity, solvency and financial adaptability of an entity: this is provided by a statement of cash flows

- IAS 7 requires all companies to include a statement of cash flows in their published financial statements

- Cash inflows and outflows must be presented under standard headings:

  - Cash flows from operating activities
  - Cash flows from investing activities
  - Cash flows from financing activities

- IAS 7 also requires a note analysing changes in cash and cash equivalents

- There are two methods of calculating net cash flow from operating activities:

  - List and total the actual cash flows: the direct method
  - Adjust profit for non-cash items: the indirect method

- IAS 7 allows either method

- Main advantages of cash flow information:

  - It shows an entity's liquidity, solvency and financial adaptability

  - It allows users to compare profit with net cash flow from operating activities

  - Cash flow is difficult to manipulate

  - It is not affected by accounting policies or by estimates

- Limitations of cash flow information:

  - Cash balances can be manipulated

  - Businesses need to make profits as well as to generate cash: short-term cash management may affect profit in the longer term

  - It is based on historical information

- To interpret a statement of cash flows: use simple observation; look at the net cash flow for the period; and at each category of cash flows in turn

Keywords

Statement of cash flows – primary statement that summarises all movements of cash into and out of a business during the reporting period

Cash flows – inflows and outflows of cash and cash equivalents

Cash – cash in hand and demand deposits (normally) less overdrafts repayable on demand

Cash equivalents – short-term, highly liquid investments that are readily convertible to known amounts of cash and which are subject to an insignificant risk of changes in value

Operating activities – the principal revenue producing activities of the entity and other activities that are not investing or financing activities

Investing activities – the acquisition and disposal of long-term assets and other investments not included in cash equivalents

Financing activities – activities that result in changes in the size and composition of the contributed equity (share capital) and borrowings of the entity

Net cash flows – the total cash flows reported under each of the standard headings in the statement of cash flows

Gross cash flows – the individual cash flows that make up the net cash flows reported under each of the headings in the statement of cash flows

TEST YOUR LEARNING

Test 1

IAS 7 requires all companies to present a statement of cash flows.

Is this statement True or False?

True	
False	

Test 2

Which of the following items does **not** meet the IAS 7 definition of cash?

Bank current account in foreign currency	
Bank overdraft	
Petty cash float	
Short-term deposit	

Test 3

Listed below are four transactions that will result in cash inflows or outflows. Complete the table to show the way in which each of the cash flows should be classified in the statement of cash flows.

Transactions:

(a)   Increase in short-term deposits classified as cash equivalents ✓
(b)   Issue of ordinary share capital
(c)   Receipt from sale of property, plant and equipment
(d)   Tax paid

Classification	Items
Operating activities	
Investing activities	
Financing activities	
Increase/decrease in cash and cash equivalents	

Test 4

(a) Alexander plc has calculated net cash flow from operating activities by listing and totalling the actual cash flows as shown below:

	£'000
Cash receipts from customers	32,450
Cash paid to suppliers and employees	(26,500)
Cash generated from operations	5,950
Interest paid	(300)
Tax paid	(800)
Net cash from operating activities	4,850

This method of calculating and presenting net cash from operating activities is called:

The direct method	
The indirect method	

(b) IAS 7 does not allow the method illustrated above.

Is this statement True or False?

True	
False	

Test 5

The following information relates to the property, plant and equipment of Bromley Ltd:

	20X2	20X1
	£	£
Cost	480,000	400,000
Accumulated depreciation	(86,000)	(68,000)
Carrying amount at 31 December	394,000	332,000

During the year ended 31 December 20X2 an asset which had originally cost £20,000 and had a carrying amount (net book value) of £8,000 was sold for £5,600.

(a) What amount should be included in the statement of cash flows for the year ended 31 December 20X2 under the heading 'investing activities'?

Cash inflow of £5,600	
Cash outflow of £64,400	
Cash outflow of £94,400	
Cash outflow of £100,000	

(b) What amount of depreciation should be added back to profit from operations in the reconciliation of profit from operations to net cash from operating activities?

£6,000	
£18,000	
£26,000	
£30,000	

Test 6

The statement of financial position of Orion Ltd as at 30 June 20X5 is provided below, together with comparative figures:

	20X5		20X4	
	£'000	£'000	£'000	£'000
Assets				
Non-current assets:				
Property, plant and equipment		2,030		1,776
Current assets:				
Inventories	1,009		960	
Trade and other receivables	826		668	
Cash	25		100	
		1,860		1,728
Total assets		3,890		3,504
Equity and liabilities				
Equity				
Share capital		1,200		1,200
Share premium		200		200
Retained earnings		1,171		1,028
		2,571		2,428
Non-current liabilities:				
Long-term loan		610		460
Current liabilities				
Trade and other payables	641		563	
Tax liabilities	68		53	
		709		616
Total liabilities		1,319		1,076
Total equity and liabilities		3,890		3,504

Further information:

(a) No non-current assets were sold during the year. The depreciation charge for the year amounted to £305,000.

(b) The profit before tax for the year ended 30 June 20X5 was £270,000. Interest of £62,000 was charged in the year. The tax charge for the year was £68,000.

(c) A dividend of £59,000 was paid during the year.

Required

(a) Prepare a reconciliation of profit from operations to net cash from operating activities for Orion Ltd for the year ended 30 June 20X5.

(b) Prepare a statement of cash flows for Orion Ltd for the year ended 30 June 20X5.

(Complete the left hand columns by writing in the correct line item or narrative from the list provided.)

Reconciliation of profit from operations to net cash from operating activities for the year ended 30 June 20X5

		£'000
	▼	
	▼	
	▼	
	▼	
	▼	
Cash generated from operations		
	▼	
	▼	
Net cash from operating activities		

Picklist for line items:

Depreciation
Increase/decrease in inventories
Increase/decrease in receivables
Increase/decrease in trade payables
Interest paid
Profit from operations
Tax paid

Statement of cash flows for the year ended 30 June 20X5

	£'000	£'000
Net cash from operating activities		
Investing activities:		
▼		
Net cash used in investing activities		
Financing activities:		
▼		
▼		150
Net cash from financing activities		
Net increase/(decrease) in cash and cash equivalents for the year		
Cash and cash equivalents at the beginning of the year		
Cash and cash equivalents at the end of the year		

Picklist for line items:

Dividends paid
Increase/decrease in long term loan
Purchase of property, plant and equipment

Working

Property, plant and equipment		£'000
	▼	
	▼	
	▼	

Picklist for line items:

Depreciation
Property, plant and equipment at the beginning of the year
Property, plant and equipment at the end of the year

Test 7

The statement of cash flows of Keynes Ltd is shown below.

Reconciliation of profit from operating activities to net cash from operating activities for the year ended 31 December 20X5

	£'000
Profit from operations	4,214
Adjustments for:	
Depreciation	1,400
Decrease in inventories	280
Increase in receivables	(910)
Increase in trade payables	32
Cash generated from operations	5,016
Interest paid	(560)
Tax paid	(1,170)
Net cash from operating activities	3,286

Statement of cash flows for the year ended 31 December 20X5

	£'000	£'000
Net cash from operating activities		3,286
Investing activities		
Purchase of property, plant and equipment	(2,830)	
Proceeds on disposal of property, plant and equipment	96	
		(2,734)
Net cash used in investing activities		
Financing activities		
Repayment of loan stock	(310)	
Dividends paid	(480)	
Net cash used in financing activities		(790)
Net decrease in cash and cash equivalents for the year		(238)
Cash and cash equivalents at the beginning of the year		240
Cash and cash equivalents at the end of the year		2

Prepare brief notes to answer the questions below.

Do you think that the company is having problems in managing its cash flow? If not, can you explain why?

chapter 6:
TANGIBLE NON-CURRENT ASSETS

chapter coverage 📖

This is the first of four chapters that deal with the requirements of accounting standards. In this chapter we look at the accounting treatment of tangible non-current assets, as set out in:

- IAS 16: *Property, Plant and Equipment*

- IAS 23: *Borrowing Costs*

- IAS 40: *Investment Property*

- IFRS 5: *Non-current Assets Held for Sale and Discontinued Operations*

Although you may be asked to account for any of these items, for example, as an adjustment to the financial statements, you should remember that a more common type of assessment task is to explain the required accounting treatment, often to a non-accountant or someone with limited knowledge of accountancy. These topics are also popular subjects for objective test or short answer questions (for example, multiple-choice or true/false). This means that you must understand the requirements of accounting standards and be prepared to apply them to a practical situation.

The topics covered are:

- ✍ Recognising property, plant and equipment

- ✍ Measurement after recognition

- ✍ Depreciation

- ✍ Disposals

- ✍ Disclosures

- ✍ Borrowing costs

- ✍ Investment property

- ✍ Non-current assets held for sale

RECOGNISING PROPERTY, PLANT AND EQUIPMENT

IAS 16 Property, plant and equipment

IAS 16 sets out the way in which items of property, plant and equipment should be treated in the financial statements. It applies to all items of property, plant and equipment except:

- Items which are classified as held for sale, which are covered by IFRS 5; and

- Investment properties, which are covered by IAS 40.

PROPERTY, PLANT AND EQUIPMENT are tangible items that are:

- Held for use in the production or supply of goods or services, for rental to others, or for administrative purposes; and

- Expected to be used during more than one period.

In other words, property, plant and equipment includes all types of tangible non-current assets: land, buildings, machinery, computers, motor vehicles and office furniture.

Recognition

The cost of an item of property, plant and equipment is recognised as an asset if, and only if:

- It is probable that future economic benefits associated with the item will flow to the entity; and

- The cost of the item can be measured reliably.

This rule reflects the IASB's *Conceptual Framework for Financial Reporting*. This defines an asset as a resource from which future economic benefits are expected to flow to an entity.

Measurement at recognition

When it is first recognised, an item of property, plant and equipment is measured at its cost.

The COST OF AN ASSET is its purchase price, including import duties and non-refundable purchase taxes, less any trade discounts or rebates.

Cost also includes any further costs directly attributable to bringing the item to the location and condition necessary for it to be capable of operating in the manner intended by management.

BPP
LEARNING MEDIA

Directly attributable costs

Directly attributable costs may include:

- Acquisition costs (eg stamp duty, import duties)
- Wages and salaries paid to employees involved in constructing the item
- The cost of site preparation
- Delivery and handling costs
- Installation and assembly costs
- Costs of testing whether the asset is functioning properly
- Professional fees (eg legal fees, architects' fees)

The following should not be included in the cost of an item of property, plant and equipment:

- Costs of opening a new facility

- Costs of introducing a new product or service (eg advertising or similar costs)

- Costs of conducting business in a new location or with a new type of customer (eg staff training costs)

- Administrative or general overhead costs

Task 1

A company purchased a building and converted it into offices for its own use. It incurred the following costs:

	£'000
Building	300
Legal fees (relating to the purchase)	5
Alterations (labour and materials)	50

The cost of the alterations included £5,000 relating to general overheads.

Calculate the amount that should be capitalised in respect of the new offices.

£

Subsequent expenditure

During its life, an item of property, plant and equipment may need to be maintained, improved or upgraded.

- Subsequent expenditure that simply **services** the item should be recognised in profit or loss as it is incurred. Examples of this kind of expenditure are the cost of repairs, maintenance and small parts.

BPP
LEARNING MEDIA

- Subsequent expenditure should only be included in the cost of an item if it meets the recognition criteria above, ie, it will probably result in future economic benefits to the entity. This will be the case where the expenditure **improves the performance** of an asset. Examples:

  - The cost of modifying plant to increase its useful economic life or its capacity

  - The cost of upgrading machine parts to achieve a substantial improvement in the quality of output

MEASUREMENT AFTER RECOGNITION

The two measurement models in IAS 16

IAS 16 allows a choice after an item of property, plant and equipment is first recognised. An entity adopts one of two models:

- The **cost model**: an item is measured at (historic) cost less accumulated depreciation and any accumulated impairment losses.

- The **revaluation model**: an item is measured at fair value less any subsequent accumulated depreciation and subsequent accumulated impairment losses.

(Impairment losses are covered in Chapter 7.)

IAS 16 states that if an item is revalued, the entire class of property, plant and equipment to which that asset belongs must be revalued.

A CLASS OF ASSETS is a grouping of assets of a similar nature and use in the entity's operations. Examples of classes include: land; land and buildings; machinery; ships; aircraft; motor vehicles; furniture and fixtures; office equipment. For example, an entity could revalue all land and buildings or it could revalue land and leave all other assets at historic cost.

This means that similar items are treated consistently (as required by IAS 1). It also means that entities cannot revalue items selectively. For example, an entity cannot revalue only those items that have increased in value while keeping the items that have fallen in value at cost.

This ensures that the financial statements provide useful information.

Fair value

FAIR VALUE is the amount for which an asset could be exchanged between knowledgeable, willing parties in an arm's length transaction. The fair value of an item of property, plant and equipment is normally its market value.

An entity can only adopt the revaluation model if the fair value of an item can be measured reliably.

- The fair value of land and buildings or plant and equipment is usually market value. Valuation of land and buildings is normally carried out by professionally qualified valuers.

- Some specialised items can be difficult to value. Because of their specialised nature, they are rarely, if ever, sold on the open market for a continuation of their existing use. Therefore there may be no evidence of their market value. In this situation, fair value can be estimated using either depreciated replacement cost or the future income that the item will generate for the entity.

- Examples of specialised properties would include schools, universities, hospitals, oil refineries, power stations, museums.

Frequency of valuation

Using fair values provides users of the financial statements with relevant information. However, the information will not be useful if the valuations are not kept up-to-date.

IAS 16 does not require annual revaluations or set out a minimum time period between revaluations. It states that revaluations should be made with sufficient regularity to ensure that the carrying amount of an item does not differ materially from its actual fair value at the end of the reporting period.

An asset's CARRYING AMOUNT (sometimes called net book value) is its cost or valuation less any accumulated depreciation and accumulated impairment losses.

This means that to some extent the frequency of revaluation depends on the judgement of management. Some items need to be revalued annually because their fair value changes significantly and often. Other items may only need to be revalued every three or five years.

Accounting for a revaluation gain

Revaluation gains are not normally recognised in profit or loss, but must be taken directly to a separate revaluation reserve and reported as other comprehensive income.

The double entry to record a revaluation gain is:

DEBIT Property, plant and equipment: cost/valuation with the difference between fair value and historic cost/previous valuation

DEBIT Property, plant and equipment: accumulated depreciation with the total depreciation charged on the asset to date

CREDIT Revaluation reserve with the difference between the revalued amount and carrying amount at historic cost/previous valuation

IAS 16 states that a revaluation gain can **only** be recognised in profit or loss if it reverses a revaluation loss that has previously been recognised in profit or loss.

HOW IT WORKS

Upward Ltd purchased a freehold property for £400,000 on 1 January 20X1. At that date the property had a useful life of 50 years. On 31 December 20X3 the property was valued at £600,000 and the directors decided to incorporate this valuation in the financial statements for the year ended 31 December 20X3.

At 31 December 20X3, the carrying amount of the property (at historic cost) is:

	£'000
Cost	400
Less: accumulated depreciation (400 × 3/50)	(24)
	376

The double entry to record the revaluation is:

DEBIT	Freehold property: cost/valuation	£200,000
DEBIT	Freehold property: accumulated depreciation	£24,000
CREDIT	Revaluation reserve	£224,000

The note to the statement of financial position appears as follows:

	Freehold land and buildings £'000
Cost at 1 January 20X3	400
Revaluation	200
Valuation at 31 December 20X3	600
Accumulated depreciation at 1 January 20X3	16
Charge for the year (400 / 50)	8
Revaluation	(24)
Accumulated depreciation at 31 December 20X3	–
Net carrying amount at 31 December 20X3	600
Net carrying amount at 1 January 20X3	384

The revaluation surplus of £224,000 is recognised in the statement of comprehensive income as 'other comprehensive income' and in the statement of financial position as a revaluation reserve within equity.

Task 2

Walnut Ltd purchased a freehold property for £250,000 on 1 January 20X1. The useful life of the property was 40 years from that date. On 31 December 20X5 the property was revalued to £350,000.

Show the double entry to record the revaluation.

Journal

Account name	Debit £	Credit £

Revaluation losses

- If the asset was previously carried at historic cost, revaluation losses are recognised immediately in profit or loss.

- If the asset has previously been revalued upwards, revaluation losses are first set against the balance on the revaluation reserve relating to that asset. This means that losses are recognised in other comprehensive income until the carrying amount reaches depreciated historic cost. Any remaining loss is then recognised in profit or loss.

HOW IT WORKS

Downward Ltd purchased some land for £500,000 on 1 January 20X1. On 31 December 20X3 the land was valued at £750,000 and the directors decided to incorporate this valuation in the financial statements. On 31 December 20X5 the land was valued at £450,000.

Land is not depreciated, so the double entry to record the upward revaluation on 31 December 20X3 is:

DEBIT	Land: cost/valuation	£250,000	
CREDIT	Revaluation reserve		£250,000

A revaluation loss of £300,000 must be recognised in the financial statements for the year ended 31 December 20X5. The loss is first set against the balance of £250,000 on the revaluation reserve and recognised as a loss in other comprehensive income. The remaining £50,000 is recognised as a loss in profit or loss.

The double entry to record the downward revaluation is:

DEBIT	Revaluation reserve	£250,000	
DEBIT	Profit or loss	£50,000	
CREDIT	Land: cost/valuation		£300,000

DEPRECIATION

DEPRECIATION is the systematic allocation of the depreciable amount of an asset over its useful life.

The purpose of depreciation is to allocate the cost (or fair value) of an asset to the accounting periods expected to benefit from its use. It is an application of the accruals concept.

Depreciation is not:

- A way of reflecting the fall in value of an asset over its life. Even if an asset is measured under the revaluation model, its fair value less costs to sell (net realisable value) is not necessarily the same as its carrying amount.

- A means of ensuring that an asset can be replaced at the end of its life. The replacement cost of an asset normally exceeds the amount of depreciation provided, due to rising prices.

The basic principles

IAS 16 states that:

- The depreciation charge for each period should be recognised in profit or loss (ie, as an expense in the statement of comprehensive income).

- The depreciable amount of an asset should be allocated on a systematic basis over its useful life.

The DEPRECIABLE AMOUNT is the cost of an asset (or, where an asset is revalued, the revalued amount) less its residual value. For example, an item costing £10,000 with a residual value of £1,000 has a depreciable amount of £9,000.

RESIDUAL VALUE is the estimated amount that an entity would currently obtain from disposal of the asset at the end of its useful life.

The USEFUL LIFE of an asset is the period over which it is expected to be available for use by an entity.

Choosing a method

The depreciation method used should reflect the pattern in which the asset's future economic benefits are expected to be consumed by the entity.

IAS 16 does not prescribe a method of depreciation. The directors must exercise their judgement in selecting a method.

To calculate depreciation, an entity must determine the useful life and residual value of an asset and the depreciation method to be used. An entity needs to consider:

- The expected usage of the asset by the entity (this may depend on the asset's expected capacity or physical output).

- The expected physical wear and tear (this may depend on repairs and maintenance expenditure and the way in which the asset is operated).

- Technical or commercial obsolescence, for example arising from changes or improvements in production, or a change in the market demand for the product or service.

- Legal or similar limits on the use of the asset, such as expiry dates of related leases.

The most common methods of depreciation are:

- The straight line method. This is the simplest to apply and results in the same charge for each period of the asset's useful life. It is also the most suitable method where the pattern of consumption of an asset's economic benefits is uncertain.

- The reducing balance method (sometimes called the diminishing balance method). This is suitable where an asset provides greater economic benefits when new than when older. For example, a machine may be less capable of producing a high quality product towards the end of its life because it breaks down more often, or because it is less technologically advanced than the latest model. Repair and maintenance costs are likely to increase as this type of asset grows older; therefore there is a more even allocation of total costs (depreciation and maintenance) over the life of the asset.

- The unit of production method or machine hour method. These are suitable where an asset's economic benefits are consumed primarily through use, rather than over time.

Depreciating an asset with different parts

An asset may consist of different parts with different useful lives. For example:

- Some items of property, plant and equipment need to have parts replaced every few years. For example, a furnace may require relining every five years.

- Some items need regular major inspections as a condition of continuing to operate them. For example, safety regulations may require an aircraft to be overhauled every three years.

Provided that the general recognition criteria are met, these costs should be recognised as part of the cost of the item. The carrying amount of the parts that are replaced or of the previous inspection is derecognised (disposed or scrapped).

Where the cost of a separate part of an asset is significant in relation to the total cost of the asset, each part must be depreciated separately over its individual useful life.

HOW IT WORKS

A machine is purchased for £700,000. It has an estimated useful life of 12 years. Part of the machine needs to be replaced every four years at an additional cost of £100,000. Depreciation is charged on a straight line basis over the machine's useful life.

The part of the machine that needs to be replaced is depreciated over four years, while the rest of the machine is depreciated over 12 years. Annual depreciation is:

	£'000
Part (100 ÷ 4)	25
Remainder (600 ÷ 12)	50
	75

At the beginning of Year 5 the part is replaced and the cost of the replacement part is treated as an addition. The replacement part is then depreciated over four years as before.

Year	1 £'000	2 £'000	3 £'000	4 £'000	5 £'000	6 £'000
Cost						
B/f	700	700	700	700	700	700
Additions	–	–	–	–	100	–
Disposals	–	–	–	–	(100)	–
Cost c/f	700	700	700	700	700	700
Depreciation b/f	–	75	150	225	300	275
Charge	75	75	75	75	75	75
Disposals	–	–	–	–	(100)	–
Depreciation c/f	75	150	225	300	275	350
Carrying amount c/f	625	550	475	400	425	350

Changing the method of depreciation

The depreciation methods used should be reviewed at least at each year-end. If there has been a significant change in the expected pattern of consumption of the future economic benefits associated with the asset, the method should be changed to reflect the changed pattern.

As we saw in an earlier chapter, a change in the method of depreciation is a change in an accounting estimate, not a change in accounting policy. There is no prior period adjustment.

The carrying amount of the asset is depreciated using the new method over the asset's remaining useful life, beginning in the period in which the change is made.

Task 3

On 1 January 20X1 Hazel Ltd purchased a machine for £20,000. The machine was depreciated over ten years, using the straight line method.

On 1 January 20X3, the directors decided to change the method of depreciation, so that the machine was depreciated at 25% per annum on the reducing balance.

Calculate the depreciation charge for the year ended 31 December 20X3.

£ 4000

Review of useful life and residual value

The residual value and the useful life of an asset should be reviewed at least at each year-end. If expectations differ from previous estimates, the change is dealt with as a change in accounting estimate. It is not a change in accounting policy.

If a useful life is revised, the carrying amount of the asset at the date of revision should be depreciated over the revised remaining useful life.

A change in estimated residual value should be accounted for prospectively over the asset's remaining useful life.

Task 4

On 1 January 20X1 Hazel Ltd purchased a machine for £20,000. The machine was depreciated over ten years, using the straight line method.

On 1 January 20X3, the directors reviewed the useful life of the machine and came to the conclusion that it was only five years from that date.

Calculate the depreciation charge for the year ended 31 December 20X3.

£

Depreciation and revalued assets

IAS 16 states that all items of property, plant and equipment must be depreciated over their useful lives.

Where an asset has been revalued, the depreciation charge must be based on the **revalued amount**.

The only asset which should not be depreciated is land. This normally has an indefinite useful life (unless it is used for mining or similar activities).

Depreciation must be charged even where:

- The fair value of the asset exceeds its carrying amount; or
- The entity has repaired and maintained the asset so that its useful life has been extended.

In the past, many entities used one or both of these arguments to avoid charging depreciation on revalued buildings.

If the residual value of an asset is equal to or greater than the asset's carrying amount, the depreciation charge is zero.

DISPOSALS

The carrying amount of an item of property, plant and equipment is derecognised (removed from the financial statements):

- On disposal

- When no future economic benefits are expected from its use or disposal

The gain or loss on a derecognised asset is treated as follows:

- The gain or loss on derecognition of an item should be recognised in profit or loss (the statement of comprehensive income) of the period in which the derecognition occurs.

- If it is material it may need to be separately disclosed in the statement of comprehensive income.

- The gain or loss on the disposal (or derecognition) of an item is the difference between the net sale proceeds (if any) and the carrying amount (whether this is based on historical cost or on a valuation).

- Where there is a disposal of a revalued asset the gain or loss on revaluation has already been recognised in equity and in other comprehensive income (at the time of the revaluation). The gain or loss would be recognised twice if the gain or loss on disposal were based on the original cost of the asset.

- The gain is transferred from the revaluation reserve to retained earnings. The transfer does not pass through profit or loss (the statement of comprehensive income) for the current year.

Task 5

On 1 January 20X1 Cashew Ltd purchased a building for £300,000. The useful life of the building was 50 years from that date.

On 1 January 20X4, the building was revalued to £500,000. The useful life of the building was deemed to be 50 years from the date of valuation.

On 31 December 20X7, the building was sold for £700,000.

Calculate the gain on disposal.

£

DISCLOSURES

The following information should be disclosed for each class of property, plant and equipment:

- The measurement bases used for determining the gross carrying amount (ie, cost or fair value)

- The depreciation methods used

- The useful lives or the depreciation rates used

- Total depreciation charged for the period

- The gross carrying amount (cost or valuation) at the beginning of the period and at the end of the period

- The cumulative amount of accumulated depreciation or impairment at the beginning of the period and at the end of the period

- A reconciliation of the net carrying amount at the beginning of the period and at the end of the period, separately disclosing additions, disposals, revaluations, depreciation and impairment losses in the period

Management uses judgement to estimate the useful lives of assets and to select a depreciation method. Users of the financial statements need information about the accounting policies adopted, the amount of depreciation charged and accumulated depreciation at the end of the period in order to compare the financial position and performance of different entities.

The reconciliation note

This is an illustration of the way in which the reconciliation between amounts in the statement of financial position at the beginning and end of the year is normally presented. The separate classes of property, plant and equipment are shown in the column headings.

	Land and buildings	Plant and machinery	Motor vehicles	Fixtures and fittings	Total
	£'000	£'000	£'000	£'000	£'000
Cost (or valuation)					
At beginning of year	X	X	X	X	X
Additions	X	X	–	X	X
Revaluation	X	–	–	–	X
Disposals	(X)	(X)	(X)	(X)	(X)
At end of year	X	X	X	X	X
Depreciation					
At beginning of year	X	X	X	X	X
Charge for year	X	X	X	X	X
Revaluation	(X)	–	–	–	(X)
Disposals	(X)	(X)	(X)	(X)	(X)
At end of year	X	X	X	X	X
Net carrying amount					
At end of year	X	X	X	X	X
At beginning of year	X	X	X	X	X

BORROWING COSTS

Sometimes entities borrow money in order to finance the construction of an asset.

BORROWING COSTS are interest and other costs incurred by an entity in connection with the borrowing of funds.

Accounting treatments

IAS 23 *Borrowing Costs* states that where an entity incurs borrowing costs the following accounting treatment should be followed:

- Borrowing costs that are directly attributable to the acquisition, construction or production of a qualifying asset are capitalised as part of the cost of that asset.

- Other borrowing costs must be recognised as an expense in the period in which they are incurred.

A QUALIFYING ASSET is an asset that necessarily takes a substantial period of time to get ready for its intended use or sale.

- Examples of qualifying assets are manufacturing plants and investment properties. Inventories are not normally qualifying assets. Assets that are ready for their intended use or sale when they are acquired are not qualifying assets.

- Directly attributable finance costs are those that would have been avoided if there had been no expenditure on the asset.

The amount to be capitalised

- If an entity borrows funds specifically for the purpose of obtaining a qualifying asset, the amount capitalised is the actual costs incurred.

- If an entity borrows funds generally and uses these to obtain a qualifying asset, the amount capitalised is the expenditure on the asset multiplied by the interest rate applicable to the entity's total borrowings. (A weighted average interest rate is used where the borrowings come from more than one source.)

- An entity should start to capitalise borrowing costs on the date when it:

    – Incurs expenditures for the asset; and

    – Incurs borrowing costs; and

    – Undertakes activities that are necessary to get the asset ready for its intended use or sale.

- An entity should cease to capitalise borrowing costs when substantially all the activities necessary to prepare the asset for its intended use or sale are complete.

Task 6

On 1 January 20X7 Macadamia Ltd took out a bank loan of £750,000 to finance the construction of a new factory. Interest of 8% was payable on the loan.

Construction work began on 1 April 20X7 and was completed on 30 September 20X7. The loan was repaid on 31 December 20X7.

Finance costs of £30,000 should be recognised in profit or loss for the year ended 31 December 20X7.

Is this statement True or False?

True	
False	

INVESTMENT PROPERTY

As the name suggests, investment properties are held as investments, rather than for use in the entity's operating activities.

IAS 40 *Investment Property* sets out the way in which these assets should be treated and disclosed in the financial statements.

The definition

IAS 40 defines INVESTMENT PROPERTY as property (land or a building or both) held to earn rentals or for capital appreciation or for both, rather than for:

- Use in the production or supply of goods or services or for administrative purposes; or

- Sale in the ordinary course of business.

Examples of investment property:

- Land held for long-term capital appreciation rather than for short-term sale in the ordinary course of business

- Land held for a currently undetermined future use

- A building owned by the entity and leased out under an operating lease

- A building that is vacant but held to be leased out under an operating lease

- Property that is being constructed or developed for future use as an investment property

The following are not investment properties:

- Property intended for sale in the ordinary course of business
- Owner-occupied property (including property occupied by employees)

An operating lease is a lease that is similar to a rental agreement; the substance of the agreement is that the legal owner continues to control the property and obtain economic benefits from it. Leases are covered in Chapter 8.

Recognition

Investment property is recognised as an asset when, and only when:

- It is probable that the future economic benefits that are associated with the investment property will flow to the entity; and
- Its cost can be measured reliably.

When an investment property is first recognised it is measured at its cost. Transaction costs (for example, legal fees and property transfer taxes) are included in the initial cost of an investment property.

Accounting treatment after initial recognition

There is a choice between two accounting treatments:

- The cost model
- The fair value model

All investment properties must be treated in the same way; it is not possible to use the cost model for some and the revaluation model for others.

The cost model

Investment properties are measured at their original cost less accumulated depreciation and accumulated impairment losses. The treatment is exactly the same as under the cost model in IAS 16.

The fair value model

The reasoning behind the fair value model is that investment properties are not 'consumed' in the business. Therefore it is not appropriate to depreciate them. The most useful information about investment properties is their fair value and the changes in that fair value.

- All investment property is measured at fair value.
- Fair value is the price at which the property could be exchanged between knowledgeable, willing parties in an arm's length transaction (ie, normally open market value).
- Investment properties are not depreciated.

- Instead, properties are remeasured at each year-end. Gains and losses arising from changes in fair value are recognised in profit or loss for the period.

Notice the two important differences from the revaluation model for other property covered by IAS 16: under the fair value model the property is **not depreciated**; and the gain or loss on revaluation is recognised **in profit or loss**, not in other comprehensive income.

Task 7

On 1 January 20X5 Brazil Ltd purchased a building for £500,000. The useful life of the building was 50 years from that date.

The building meets the definition of an investment property and management has decided to adopt the fair value model in IAS 40 *Investment Property*.

At 31 December 20X5 the fair value of the building was £550,000. The useful life of the building was unchanged.

What are the amounts to be included in profit or loss and in other comprehensive income in respect of the property for the year ended 31 December 20X5?

Profit or loss	Other comprehensive income	
Expense of £10,000	Nil	
Net gain of £40,000	Nil	
Gain of £50,000	Nil	
Expense of £10,000	Gain of £60,000	

Disposals

An investment property is derecognised (removed from the statement of financial position) on disposal or when it is permanently withdrawn from use and no future economic benefits are expected from its disposal.

Gains and losses on disposal are calculated as the difference between the net disposal proceeds and the carrying amount of the asset. They are recognised in profit or loss in the period in which the disposal takes place.

Disclosures

An entity should disclose whether it applies the cost model or the fair value model.

NON-CURRENT ASSETS HELD FOR SALE

At the year-end, an entity may have items of property, plant and equipment or other types of non-current asset that it intends to sell shortly after the year end. IFRS 5 *Non-current Assets Held For Sale and Discontinued Operations* sets out the required accounting treatment for these items.

- An entity should classify a non-current asset as held for sale if its carrying amount will be recovered principally through a sale transaction rather than through continuing use. In other words, an asset is held for sale if the entity expects to obtain future income from the asset by selling it, rather than by continuing to use it in the business.

- An asset that is held for sale is measured at the lower of its carrying amount and its fair value less costs to sell. If fair value less costs to sell is lower than the carrying amount, the loss is treated as an impairment loss and recognised in profit or loss.

- An asset that is held for sale is not depreciated.

- Non-current assets held for sale are presented separately from other assets in the statement of financial position.

Example

Statement of financial position (extract) at...

Assets	£'000
Non-current assets	
Property, plant and equipment	<u>X</u>
	<u>X</u>
Current assets	
Inventories	X
Trade and other receivables	X
Cash and cash equivalents	<u>X</u>
	<u>X</u>
Non-current assets held for sale	<u>X</u>
	<u>X</u>
Total assets	<u>X</u>

In this way, users of the financial statements are made aware of any material disposals of assets that are about to take place.

CHAPTER OVERVIEW

- An item of property, plant and equipment is recognised if: it is probable that future economic benefits associated with the item will flow to the entity; the cost of the item can be measured reliably

- An item of property, plant and equipment is initially measured at its cost

- After an item of property, plant and equipment is first recognised, it is either carried at cost (the cost model) or at fair value (the revaluation model). If an item is revalued, all assets of the same class must be revalued. Valuations must be kept up-to-date

- Double entry to record a revaluation:

  Debit property, plant and equipment: cost/valuation with the difference between fair value and historic cost/previous valuation

  Debit property, plant and equipment: accumulated depreciation with the total depreciation charged on the asset to date

  Credit revaluation reserve with the difference between the revalued amount and carrying amount at historic cost/previous valuation

- Revaluation gains are reported in other comprehensive income and in equity (the revaluation reserve)

- The depreciable amount of an asset should be allocated on a systematic basis over its useful life

- Where an asset has been revalued, the depreciation charge must be based on the revalued amount

- The gain or loss on the disposal of an item of property, plant and equipment is the difference between the net sale proceeds and the carrying amount (whether this is based on historical cost or on a valuation)

- Borrowing costs that are directly attributable to the acquisition or construction of a qualifying asset should be capitalised as part of the cost of the asset

- Investment properties should be included in the statement of financial position either at cost (following the cost model in IAS 16) or at fair value (the fair value model)

- If the fair value model is adopted, changes in the fair value of investment properties are recognised in profit or loss

- Non-current assets held for sale are measured at the lower of carrying amount and fair value less costs to sell. They are separately disclosed in the statement of financial position

Keywords

Property, plant and equipment – tangible items that: are held for use in the production or supply of goods or services, for rental to others, or for administrative purposes; and are expected to be used during more than one period

Cost of an asset – purchase price, including import duties and non-refundable purchase taxes, less any trade discounts or rebates, plus any further costs directly attributable to bringing the item to the location and condition necessary for it to be capable of operating in the manner intended by management

A class of assets – a grouping of assets of a similar nature and use in the entity's operations

Fair value – the amount for which an asset could be exchanged between knowledgeable, willing parties in an arm's length transaction

Carrying amount – the amount at which an asset is recognised after deducting any accumulated depreciation (amortisation) and accumulated impairment losses

Depreciation – the systematic allocation of the depreciable amount of an asset over its useful life

Depreciable amount – the cost of an asset (or, where an asset is revalued, the revalued amount) less its residual value

Residual value – the estimated amount that an entity would currently obtain from disposal of the asset at the end of its useful life

Useful life – the period over which an asset is expected to be available for use by an entity

Borrowing costs – interest and other costs incurred by an entity in connection with the borrowing of funds

Qualifying asset – an asset that necessarily takes a substantial period of time to get ready for its intended use or sale

Investment property – property (land or a building or both) held to earn rentals or for capital appreciation or for both, rather than for: use in the production or supply of goods or services or for administrative purposes; or sale in the ordinary course of business

TEST YOUR LEARNING

Test 1

Tarragon Ltd purchases an item of plant. As well as the purchase price of the plant itself, Tarragon Ltd has to incur the cost of installing the plant and testing it once it has been installed.

This additional expenditure should be included in the statement of financial position as part of the cost of the plant.

Is this statement True or False?

True	
False	

Test 2

Sage Ltd incurs expenditure of £5,000 on repainting the outside of an office building.

This expenditure cannot be capitalised as part of the cost of the building.

Is this statement True or False?

True	
False	

Test 3

Basil Ltd owns three properties. Information about these properties is shown below:

	Cost	Accumulated depreciation	Fair value
	£'000	£'000	£'000
Property A	100	10	120
Property B	150	10	140
Property C	120	10	180

The properties are all currently carried in the company's statement of financial position at depreciated historic cost.

(a) Property A and Property C can be carried at fair value, while Property B can be carried at historic cost.

Is this statement True or False?

True	
False	

(b) Once the company has adopted a policy of revaluing property, plant and equipment, it must update the valuation annually.

Is this statement True or False?

True	
False	

(c) Show the journal entry needed to incorporate the revaluations in the financial statements of Basil Ltd.

Journal

Account name	Debit	Credit
	£	£

Test 4

IAS 16 *Property, Plant and Equipment* states that all entities should use the straight line method of depreciation.

Is this statement True or False?

True	
False	

Test 5

On 1 January 20X1 a freehold property was purchased for £500,000. Its estimated useful life was 25 years at that date. On 1 January 20X6 the property was revalued to £600,000 and this revaluation was recognised in the financial statements. The useful life of the property remained unchanged. The property is depreciated using the straight line method.

What is the depreciation charge for the year ended 31 December 20X6?

£20,000	
£24,000	
£30,000	

Test 6

IAS 23 *Borrowing costs* states that an entity should capitalise all borrowing costs incurred in the acquisition of non-current assets.

Is this statement True or False?

True	
False	

Test 7

The directors of Dill Ltd are about to purchase two new properties. They intend to use one of these as a hostel for their employees, who will pay rent. The other property will be let to other businesses.

Prepare brief notes for the directors of Dill Ltd to answer the following questions:

(a) What is meant by investment property according to IAS 40 *Investment Property?*

(b) Are these two properties likely to qualify as investment properties? If not, why not?

Test 8

The directors of Parsley Ltd are preparing the financial statements of the company for the year ended 31 December 20X6. Just after the year-end they sold a surplus factory building. The directors took the decision to sell the building in October 20X6 and were in negotiations with the buyer at the year-end.

Prepare brief notes for the directors of Parsley Ltd to answer the following questions:

(a) When should an asset be classified as held for sale according to IFRS 5 *Non-current Assets Held for Sale and Discontinued Operations?*

(b) If an asset is held for sale, how should it be measured and presented in the financial statements?

chapter 7:
INTANGIBLE ASSETS AND INVENTORIES

chapter coverage 📖

This chapter covers the accounting treatment of intangible assets, impairment (loss of value) of assets and inventories.

As with the accounting treatment of tangible non-current assets covered in the previous chapter, you must understand the requirements of the accounting standards and be prepared to explain them and apply them.

The topics covered are:

✎ Intangible assets

✎ Impairment of assets

✎ Accounting for inventories

INTANGIBLE ASSETS

Recognition

An INTANGIBLE ASSET is an identifiable non-monetary asset without physical substance.

If an asset is identifiable, it is either:

- Separable (capable of being separated or divided from the rest of the business and sold or otherwise disposed of); or

- It arises from contractual or other legal rights, whether or not these rights are themselves separable or transferable.

Examples of intangible assets:

- Brand names
- Market and technical knowledge
- Franchises
- Licences
- Patents
- Computer software
- Customer lists
- Publishing titles
- Trademarks

The basic principles are the same as for other non-current assets.

An intangible asset is recognised when, and only when:

- It is probable that the expected future economic benefits that are attributable to the asset will flow to the entity; and

- The cost of the asset can be measured reliably.

Most non-current assets generate economic benefits in the form of sales revenue from new products and services. An intangible asset can also generate economic benefits by reducing costs. For example, specialised technical knowledge can make a production process more efficient and lead to cost savings.

Task 1

A company that develops and markets scientific equipment has several extremely well qualified and talented members of staff. The company's success is undoubtedly the result of their work.

The company can recognise the staff or their expertise as an asset in the company's statement of financial position.

Is this statement True or False?

True	
False	

Initial measurement

When an intangible asset is first recognised it is measured at cost.

Goodwill

GOODWILL is the excess of the value of a business as a whole over the total value of its individual assets and liabilities.

You will already have met goodwill during your earlier studies. Goodwill is classified as an intangible asset.

For example, A Ltd buys an unincorporated business for £100,000. The fair values of its assets and liabilities are as follows:

	£'000
Property, plant and equipment	70
Net current assets	30
Long-term liabilities	(10)
	90

As well as acquiring the assets and liabilities of the business for £90,000, A Ltd has acquired goodwill worth £10,000. Goodwill may arise as a result of a number of factors, such as the reputation of the business, the quality of its products, or the skill of its management. It cannot exist independently of the business.

There are two kinds of goodwill:

- Internally generated goodwill (sometimes called inherent goodwill)
- Purchased goodwill

INTERNALLY GENERATED GOODWILL is the goodwill that a business generates over time. Almost all businesses have some internally generated goodwill.

PURCHASED GOODWILL is the difference between the cost of an acquired entity and the aggregate of the fair values of that entity's identifiable assets and liabilities.

In the example above, the business that A Ltd acquired has internally generated goodwill. In the accounts of A Ltd this goodwill is purchased goodwill.

How goodwill is treated

IAS 38 *Intangible assets* states that internally generated goodwill should never be recognised as an asset. This is because it cannot be measured reliably; all methods of valuing it are subjective.

Purchased goodwill is recognised as an asset because it has a cost to the business that has acquired it. It can be measured reliably because there has been a transaction which establishes its value as a fact at a particular point in time.

Purchased goodwill is outside the scope of IAS 38. It is covered in more detail in Chapters 10 and 11 on group accounts.

Research and development

Many companies spend large amounts on research and development projects. If these are successful, they result in new products or services that may provide significant income for many years to come.

Research and development expenditure may be an asset, rather than an expense, if it gives access to future economic benefits for the entity. There is an argument for treating it as an asset, capitalising it in the statement of financial position and matching it with the income that it produces in future accounting periods (applying the accruals concept).

On the other hand, it may be impossible to predict whether a project will give rise to future income or to precisely identify the future income if it is received. If this is the case the expenditure must be charged to profit or loss in the period in which it is incurred.

The research phase and the development phase

IAS 38 separates a research and development project into a **research phase** and a **development phase**.

- RESEARCH is original and planned investigation undertaken with the prospect of gaining new scientific or technical knowledge and understanding.

- DEVELOPMENT is the application of research findings or other knowledge to a plan or design for the production of new or substantially improved materials, devices, products, processes and systems before the start of commercial production or use.

How the expenditure is treated

Research phase

At this stage it is impossible to be certain that the project will generate any future economic benefit.

Therefore expenditure on research is treated as an expense and recognised in profit or loss when it is incurred. No intangible asset is recognised.

Development phase

Development expenditure may result in identifiable income (economic benefits) in future periods. It should not be recognised as an asset unless it is reasonably certain that this will be the case.

IAS 38 states that an intangible asset arising from development should be recognised if an entity can demonstrate all of the following:

- The **technical feasibility** of completing the intangible asset so that it will be available for use or sale

- Its **intention to complete** the intangible asset and use or sell it

- Its **ability to use or sell** the intangible asset

- **How** the intangible asset will **generate probable future economic benefits** (including the existence of a market for output of the asset or the asset itself; or, if it is to be used internally, the usefulness of the intangible asset)

- The **availability of adequate** technical, financial and other **resources** to complete the development and to use or sell the intangible asset

- Its ability to **measure reliably** the expenditure attributable to the intangible asset during its development

If any of these conditions are not met, the expenditure must be charged to profit or loss in the period in which it is incurred.

Task 2

A company has incurred expenditure of £50,000 in investigating a new process. It is hoped that the new process can eventually be adapted and used to manufacture Product Z more efficiently than at present, resulting in considerable cost savings. The project is at a very early stage and the outcome is uncertain.

In the financial statements, this expenditure should be:

Recognised as an intangible asset in the statement of financial position	
Recognised as an expense in profit or loss	✓

Other internally generated intangible assets

IAS 38 states that internally generated brands, mastheads, publishing titles, customer lists and items similar in substance should not be recognised as intangible assets.

Task 3

Fifteen years ago, a company developed a brand of self-raising flour. The brand has now become a household name and has captured a substantial share of the market. One of the directors has claimed that it is worth at least £10 million to the company.

The brand cannot be recognised as an intangible asset in the company's financial statements.

Is this statement True or False?

True	✓
False	

The cost of an internally generated intangible asset

The cost of an internally generated intangible asset includes all directly attributable costs necessary to create, produce and prepare the asset to be capable of operating in the manner intended by management.

Examples:

- Costs of materials and services

- Costs of employee benefits (eg wages and salaries)

- Fees to register a legal right

- Amortisation (depreciation) of patents and licences that are used to generate the intangible asset

The following should not be included in the cost of an internally generated intangible asset:

- Selling, administrative and other general overhead expenditure

- Inefficiencies and initial operating losses incurred before the asset achieves planned performance

- Expenditure on training staff to operate the asset

Measurement after recognition

This is similar to the measurement of property, plant and equipment. After an intangible asset is first recognised, there is a choice between the cost model and the revaluation model.

The cost model

The intangible asset is carried at its cost less any accumulated amortisation (depreciation) and any accumulated impairment losses.

IAS 38 defines cost and amortisation:

- The cost of an intangible asset is the amount of cash or cash equivalents paid or the fair value of other consideration given to acquire an asset at the time of its acquisition or construction.

- AMORTISATION is the systematic allocation of the depreciable amount of an intangible asset over its useful life.

The revaluation model

The intangible asset is carried at a revalued amount: its fair value at the date of revaluation less any subsequent accumulated amortisation and any subsequent accumulated impairment losses.

Fair value is the amount for which the asset could be exchanged between knowledgeable, willing parties in an arm's length transaction.

- **Fair value** is determined by reference to an active market

- An ACTIVE MARKET is a market in which all the following conditions exist:

  - The items traded are homogeneous (of the same kind)
  - Willing buyers and sellers can normally be found at any time
  - Prices are available to the public

- Revaluations should be made with such regularity that at the year-end the carrying amount of the asset is not materially different from its fair value

- If an intangible asset is revalued, all other assets in its class must also be revalued (unless there is no active market for those assets)

It is **rare** for an entity to adopt the revaluation model because for most types of intangible asset no active market exists.

Revaluation gains and losses

The accounting treatment is similar to the treatment for gains and losses relating to property, plant and equipment.

- A revaluation gain is recognised in other comprehensive income and credited to equity as a revaluation surplus. It is not included in profit or loss.

- A revaluation loss is normally recognised in profit or loss.

- If the intangible asset has previously been revalued upwards, a revaluation loss is debited to equity and set against the revaluation surplus relating to that asset. Any excess loss is recognised in profit or loss.

The useful life of an intangible asset

Management needs to assess the useful life of an intangible asset, which can be finite or indefinite.

- An intangible asset has an indefinite useful life when there is no foreseeable limit to the period over which the asset is expected to generate net cash inflows for the entity.

- All the relevant factors should be taken into account: expected usage; typical product life cycles; the likelihood of obsolescence; expected actions by competitors; whether the useful life of the asset is dependent on the useful life of other assets of the entity.

Where the useful life is finite

An intangible asset with a finite useful life is amortised on a systematic basis over its useful life.

- Amortisation begins when the asset is available for use (when it is in the location and condition necessary for it to be capable of operating in the manner intended by management).

- Amortisation ceases when the asset is derecognised (on disposal or where no future economic benefits are expected).

- The amortisation method used reflects the pattern in which the asset's future economic benefits are expected to be consumed. The straight line method is used if this pattern cannot be determined reliably.

- The amortisation charge for each period is included in profit or loss.

- The residual value of the asset is normally assumed to be zero.

- The amortisation period and the amortisation method are reviewed at least at each year-end. Any change is dealt with as a change in accounting estimate, not a change in accounting policy.

Where the useful life is indefinite

An intangible asset with an indefinite useful life is not amortised.

Instead it remains in the statement of financial position but is reviewed for impairment (loss in value):

- Annually; and
- Whenever there is an indication that it may be impaired.

Impairment is covered in the next section.

The useful life of the asset is also reviewed each period to determine whether events and circumstances continue to support the previous assessment of an indefinite useful life. If the asset is then assessed as having a finite useful life, the change is accounted for as a change in accounting estimate.

IMPAIRMENT OF ASSETS

Impairment

When an asset is impaired, it has suffered a loss in value.

IMPAIRMENT is a reduction in the recoverable amount of an asset below its carrying amount.

An IMPAIRMENT LOSS is the amount by which the carrying amount of an asset exceeds its recoverable amount.

IAS 36 *Impairment of Assets* applies to all assets, including investments in other companies, except:

- Inventories (see IAS 2)
- Investment property measured at fair value (see IAS 40)
- Non-current assets held for sale (see IFRS 5)

When an impairment review must be carried out

IAS 36 states that assets should be reviewed for impairment if there is some indication that impairment has occurred. Indicators that an asset has been impaired could be apparent from external or internal sources of information.

External sources of information

- A significant decline in an asset's market value during the period

- Significant changes with an adverse effect on the entity in the technological, market, economic or legal environment in which the entity operates or in the market to which an asset is dedicated. (These changes might include the entrance of a major competitor, an economic downturn or new regulations that affect the entity's business.)

- An increase in market interest rates or market rates of return on investments likely to affect the discount rate used in calculating value in use and decrease the asset's recoverable amount materially. (Value in use is explained later in this chapter.)

- The carrying amount of the net assets of the entity is more than its market capitalisation. (The market capitalisation of an entity is the total value of its shares.)

Indicators from internal sources of information

- Evidence that an asset is obsolete or has been physically damaged.

- Significant changes with an adverse effect on the entity have taken place in the way in which an asset is used or expected to be used. These changes include the asset becoming idle, plans to discontinue or restructure the operation to which an asset belongs, plans to dispose of an asset before the previously expected date, and reassessing the useful life of an asset as finite rather than indefinite.

- Evidence that the economic performance of an asset is, or will be, worse than expected. (For example, cash flows or operating profit generated by the asset are significantly worse than expected).

This list is not exhaustive. There might be other indications that an asset is impaired.

Certain assets must always be reviewed for impairment at least annually, even if there are no signs that the asset has become impaired:

- Intangible assets with an indefinite useful life
- Goodwill acquired in a business combination (see Chapter 10)

Carrying out an impairment review

To determine whether an asset is impaired, its carrying amount is compared with its recoverable amount.

- CARRYING AMOUNT is the amount at which an asset is recognised after deducting any accumulated depreciation (amortisation) and accumulated impairment losses.

- An asset's RECOVERABLE AMOUNT is the higher of fair value less costs to sell or value in use.

- FAIR VALUE LESS COSTS TO SELL is the amount obtainable from the sale of an asset in an arm's length transaction between knowledgeable, willing parties, less the costs of disposal.

- VALUE IN USE is the present value of the future cash flows expected to be obtained from an asset (as a result of continuing to use it in the business, normally to produce goods or provide services for sale to customers).

**As asset should be measured
at the lower of:**

Carrying amount   **Recoverable amount**

Higher of

**Fair value less
costs to sell**   **Value in use**

If an asset is impaired, the entity can either sell the asset, or continue to use it in the business. IAS 36 assumes that an entity will always choose the course of action that will result in the most cash.

If the carrying amount exceeds the recoverable amount, the asset or goodwill is impaired and should be written-down.

HOW IT WORKS

Cumin Ltd carries out impairment reviews on three assets, details of which are as follows:

	Carrying amount	Fair value less costs to sell	Value in use
	£'000	£'000	£'000
Asset A	20	18	25
Asset B	25	20	22
Asset C	30	40	38

Step 1   Determine recoverable amount (the higher of fair value less costs to sell and value in use)

- Asset A: £25,000 (value in use)

- Asset B: £22,000 (value in use)

- Asset C: £40,000 (fair value less costs to sell)

Step 2   Compare recoverable amount with carrying amount

- If recoverable amount is less than carrying amount, the asset is impaired

- Only Asset B is impaired; recoverable amount is £22,000, £3,000 less than carrying amount

Fair value less costs to sell

The best evidence of an asset's fair value less costs to sell is normally its market price in a binding sale agreement in an arm's length transaction. This is adjusted for any costs directly attributable to the disposal of the asset.

Examples of costs of disposal:

- Legal costs
- Stamp duty
- Cost of removing the asset
- Direct costs of bringing an asset into condition for sale

If there is no binding sale agreement, but the asset is traded in an active market, fair value less costs to sell is the asset's market price less the costs of disposal.

If there is no binding sale agreement or active market, fair value less costs to sell should be based on the best information available.

Value in use

Estimating the value in use of an asset involves two steps:

- Estimating the future cash inflows and outflows to be obtained from continuing use of the asset and from its ultimate disposal
- Applying the appropriate discount rate to those future cash flows

Estimates of the future cash flows should take into account any possible variations in their amount and their timing.

The discount rate used should reflect current market assessments of the time value of money and any risk (uncertainty) specific to the asset.

HOW IT WORKS

The idea behind the value in use calculation is that an asset generates income for an entity. The sooner the cash is received the more it is worth to the entity. Surplus cash can be invested to obtain interest. Using the cash to reduce a loan or an overdraft saves the entity interest. Discounting the cash flows adjusts them to reflect the time value of money.

It is extremely unlikely that you will be asked to perform this kind of calculation in the assessment, but you could be asked to explain the reasoning behind it.

Suppose that A Ltd has an item of plant. The plant produces goods for sale to customers. A Ltd estimates that sales income from these goods will be as follows:

Year 1	£20,000
Year 2	£20,000
Year 3	£15,000

The current market rate of bank interest is 10% per annum.

	Cash inflow	Discount rate (from tables)	£
Year 1	20,000	0.909	18,180
Year 2	20,000	0.826	16,520
Year 3	15,000	0.751	11,265
			45,965

The value in use of the plant is the present value (the discounted value) of the total cash inflows that can be obtained by using it: £45,965.

Accounting for impairment losses

Where the recoverable amount of an asset is less than its carrying amount, the asset is impaired. The carrying amount of the asset must be reduced to its recoverable amount. The reduction is an impairment loss.

- Impairment losses are recognised in profit or loss if the asset has not previously been revalued.

- Impairment losses are recognised in other comprehensive income if the asset has previously been revalued above cost. The impairment loss is treated as a downward revaluation. Any impairment below depreciated historical cost is recognised in profit or loss.

- When an impairment loss on an asset is recognised, the remaining useful life should be reviewed and revised if necessary. The revised carrying amount should be depreciated over the revised estimate of the remaining useful life.

HOW IT WORKS

Juniper Ltd bought a machine on 1 January 20X1. The machine cost £60,000 and had a useful life of six years. It was depreciated using the straight line method.

On 1 January 20X3 an impairment review was carried out, and the recoverable amount of the plant was estimated at £30,000. Its useful life was reviewed and was estimated to be two years at that date.

At 1 January 20X3 the carrying amount of the machine is:

	£
Cost	60,000
Less: accumulated depreciation (two years)	(20,000)
	40,000

The recoverable amount of the machine is £30,000 and so an impairment loss of £10,000 is recognised in profit or loss. The double entry is:

DEBIT	Impairment loss	£10,000
CREDIT	Plant and machinery: accumulated depreciation	£10,000

The remaining useful life of the machine is now two years and therefore the annual depreciation charge is now £15,000 (£30,000 ÷ 2).

The total charge to profit or loss for the year ended 31 December 20X3 is £25,000 (impairment loss of £10,000 and depreciation of £15,000).

If the impairment loss is material, it may need to be disclosed separately in a note to the financial statements.

Task 4

Coriander Ltd carries out an impairment review on a freehold property. You are provided with the following information:

	£'000
Carrying amount (based on a valuation)	150
Depreciated historic cost	100
Fair value less costs to sell	110
Value in use	90

The impairment loss to be recognised in profit or loss is:

£Nil	
£10,000	
£40,000	
£60,000	

Cash-generating units

Sometimes it is not possible to estimate the recoverable amount of an individual asset. Some assets, such as goodwill, do not generate cash inflows independently of other assets. This means that it is impossible to calculate value in use.

In this situation, assets are grouped together and the impairment review is carried out for each group of assets, or **cash-generating unit**.

A CASH-GENERATING UNIT is the smallest identifiable group of assets that generates cash inflows that are largely independent of the cash inflows from other assets or groups of assets.

A cash-generating unit is normally a department or a single company within a group of companies.

Testing goodwill

Goodwill has to be tested for impairment annually. Because goodwill does not generate cash flows by itself, it must be allocated to a cash-generating unit. The impairment test is then carried out for the cash-generating unit as a whole.

- The carrying amount of the unit is compared with the recoverable amount.

- If the recoverable amount of the unit is greater than the carrying amount, the unit and the goodwill are not impaired

- If the carrying amount is greater than the recoverable amount of the unit, the unit is impaired

Any impairment loss is then allocated between the assets in the cash-generating unit:

- First, to goodwill

- Then to the other assets in the unit on a pro rata basis based on carrying amount

HOW IT WORKS

The carrying amounts of the assets in a cash generating unit are as follows:

	£
Goodwill	20,000
Other intangible assets	50,000
Property plant and equipment	150,000
	220,000

The recoverable amount of the unit is £180,000. Therefore there is an impairment loss of £40,000. This is allocated as follows:

	Before impairment £	Impairment loss £	After impairment £
Goodwill	20,000	(20,000)	–
Other intangible assets	50,000	(5,000)	45,000
Property plant and equipment	150,000	(15,000)	135,000
	220,000	(40,000)	180,000

The impairment loss is first allocated to goodwill. The remaining loss of £20,000 is allocated to other intangibles and property, plant and equipment on a pro rata basis as follows:

Intangibles: 50,000/200,000 × £20,000 = £5,000

Property, plant and equipment: 150,000/200,000 × £20,000 = £15,000

Disclosure

The following information must be disclosed for each class of assets:

- The amount of impairment losses recognised in profit or loss for the period; and

- The line item of the statement of comprehensive income in which those impairment losses are included.

ACCOUNTING FOR INVENTORIES

The way in which closing inventories are valued can have a significant impact on the financial statements as a whole.

- It is normally material in the context of an entity's statement of financial position. Because inventory is part of an entity's working capital, over or understating the figure may affect users' views of the liquidity and solvency of the entity.

- Closing inventories are deducted from purchases to arrive at cost of sales and therefore inventory valuation directly affects profits.

IAS 2 Inventories

Inventories can consist of:

- Goods purchased for resale

- Consumable stores (for example stationery)

- Raw materials and components that will be used to manufacture products for sale

- Work in progress: products that are partly completed

- Amounts relating to long-term contracts

- Finished goods

IAS 2 defines INVENTORIES as assets:

- Held for sale in the ordinary course of business

- In the process of production for such sale

- In the form of materials or supplies to be consumed in the production process or in the rendering of services

IAS 2 contains a basic rule about inventories:

- Inventories should be measured at the lower of cost and net realisable value

Cost

The cost of inventories comprises all costs of purchase, costs of conversion and other costs incurred in bringing the inventories to their present location and condition.

- Cost of purchase is the purchase price. It also includes import duties, transport and handling costs and any other directly attributable costs, less trade discounts, rebates and subsidies.

- Costs of conversion include direct labour, direct expenses, and any production or other overheads that are attributable to bringing the product or service to its present location and condition.

The key point to notice is that cost includes expenditure that is attributable to bringing the product to its present location and condition. For example:

- Transport costs are included and therefore the cost of identical items may be different if they are in different locations

- Design costs are included if a product has to be specially designed for a particular customer

It follows that costs that have not been incurred directly in bringing the inventory to its present condition and location are not included in the cost of inventories. IAS 2 gives examples of costs that cannot be included:

- Abnormal amounts of wasted materials, labour or other production costs

- Storage costs, unless those costs are necessary in the production process before a further production stage

- Administrative overheads

- Selling costs

- Interest cost (unless the inventories are qualifying assets under IAS 23 *Borrowing costs*; this is rare)

These items must be recognised as expenses in the period in which they are incurred.

Net realisable value

NET REALISABLE VALUE is the estimated selling price in the ordinary course of business less:

- The estimated costs of completion; and
- The estimated costs necessary to make the sale.

Net realisable value is likely to be less than cost where:

- There is an increase in costs or a fall in selling price

- Inventories have deteriorated physically

- Products become obsolete

- It is part of the marketing strategy of the company to sell products at a loss

- There are errors in production or purchasing

IAS 2 states that:

- When inventories are sold, the carrying amount (cost or net realisable value) of those inventories is recognised as an expense in the period in which the related revenue is recognised.

Where inventory is written-down to net realisable value, the loss is recognised in profit or loss in the period in which it is incurred.

As we have seen, inventories should be stated at the lower of cost and net realisable value.

- Closing inventories have been purchased in the current accounting period, but will not be sold until the following accounting period. If inventories are valued at cost, the cost of purchasing the inventories is carried forward to be matched with the sales revenue when it arises in the following period. This is an application of the accruals (or matching) concept.

- If inventories were valued at selling price (net realisable value), the entity would normally be taking a profit on the inventories before they were actually sold and the profit made. This is not acceptable because it contravenes the matching concept. Also, the information is not reliable; the entity has not yet made the profit.

- The exception to this rule is where net realisable value is lower than cost, in other words, where the entity expects to make a loss. If inventories are written-down to net realisable value, the loss is an expense in the period in which it occurs. This is prudent, and means that closing inventories are not overstated.

Applying the lower of cost and net realisable value rule

The comparison between cost and net realisable value must be made for each individual item of inventory, or each group of similar items. It cannot be made for inventories as a whole.

Task 5

Lewis Ltd sells three products, A, B and C. At the year-end, inventories of these are as follows:

	Cost £	Selling price £	Selling costs £
A	2,880 ✓	3,600	180
B	5,500	5,400	366
C	3,310	3,350	165

What is the amount at which inventories should be valued for inclusion in the statement of financial position?

£11,099	
£11,590	
£11,639	
£11,690	

Methods of arriving at the cost of inventories

IAS 2 states that where items of inventory are not ordinarily interchangeable each individual item should be measured at its actual cost.

For example, an art dealer might have several unique works of art for sale. Each of these would be included in inventories at its actual cost.

However, businesses normally purchase large quantities of identical items at regular intervals throughout the year. It is very unlikely that management knows the actual cost of each individual item in inventories at the year-end.

There are a number of methods of arriving at the cost of closing inventory in this situation. The three most common are:

- FIRST IN FIRST OUT (FIFO): this assumes that items are used in the order in which they were received from suppliers; the items in inventory are the most recent purchases.

- LAST IN FIRST OUT (LIFO): this assumes that the most recent purchases are used first; the items in inventory are the earliest purchases.

- WEIGHTED AVERAGE COST (AVCO): after each purchase the weighted average cost of the inventory is calculated: the total cost of the items in inventory is divided by the total number of items in inventory; this average is taken as the cost of each item.

IAS 2 states that **either** the **first in first out (FIFO)** formula or the **weighted average cost** formula should be used.

- Last in first out (LIFO) is **not allowed**.

- The same method should be used for all inventories having a similar nature and use.

HOW IT WORKS

Rowling Ltd made the following purchases of inventory.

1 March	20 units @	£100 per unit
15 March	20 units @	£150 per unit

On 30 March it sold 30 units.

Value of closing inventories at 31 March:

FIFO

- The items sold are assumed to be the 20 units purchased on 1 March and ten units purchased on 15 March.

- Therefore the items in inventory are ten units purchased on 15 March.

- Value of inventories : £1,500 (10 × £150).

AVCO

- Total cost of items purchased in March is £5,000 (20 × 100 + 20 × 150).

- Cost per item is £125 (£5,000 ÷ 40).

- Value of inventories : £1,250 (10 × £125).

CHAPTER OVERVIEW

- If an intangible asset is identifiable, it is either: separable; or it arises from contractual or other legal rights

- The following internally generated intangible assets are never recognised: goodwill, brands, mastheads, publishing titles, customer lists and similar items

- Expenditure on research is recognised in profit or loss when it is incurred

- Development expenditure should be recognised as an asset if all the following can be demonstrated:

  - Technical feasibility of completing the asset
  - Intention and ability to complete the asset and to use or sell it
  - How it will generate future economic benefits
  - Availability of adequate resources
  - Ability to measure the expenditure reliably

- After initial recognition, intangible assets are carried either at cost (the cost model) or at fair value (the revaluation model). Revaluation gains are credited to equity

- If an intangible asset has a finite useful life, it should be amortised on a systematic basis over its useful life

- If an intangible asset has an indefinite useful life, it is not amortised. It is reviewed for impairment at least annually

- To determine whether an asset is impaired, its carrying amount is compared with its recoverable amount

- If recoverable amount is less than carrying amount, the asset is impaired and an impairment loss is recognised

- Impairment losses are recognised in profit or loss if the asset has not previously been revalued. Otherwise they are treated as downward revaluations

- Inventories should be stated at the lower of cost and net realisable value

- The comparison between cost and net realisable value must be made for each individual item of inventory, or each group of similar items

- Either FIFO or AVCO must be used to arrive at the cost of inventories

Keywords

Intangible asset – an identifiable non-monetary asset without physical substance

Goodwill – the excess of the value of a business as a whole over the total value of its individual assets and liabilities

Internally generated goodwill – the goodwill that a business generates over time

Purchased goodwill – the difference between the cost of an acquired entity and the aggregate of the fair values of that entity's identifiable assets and liabilities

Research – original and planned investigation undertaken with the prospect of gaining new scientific or technical knowledge and understanding

Development – the application of research findings or other knowledge to a plan or design for the production of new or substantially improved materials, devices, products, processes, systems before the start of commercial production or use

Amortisation – the systematic allocation of the depreciable amount of an intangible asset over its useful life

Active market – a market in which the items traded are of the same kind; where willing buyers and sellers can normally be found at any time; and where prices are available to the public

Impairment – a reduction in the recoverable amount of an asset below its carrying amount

Impairment loss – the amount by which the carrying amount of an asset exceeds its recoverable amount

Carrying amount – the amount at which an asset is recognised after deducting any accumulated depreciation (amortisation) and accumulated impairment losses

Recoverable amount – the higher of fair value less costs to sell or value in use

Fair value less costs to sell – the amount obtainable from the sale of an asset in an arm's length transaction between knowledgeable, willing parties, less the costs of disposal

Value in use – the present value of the future cash flows expected to be obtained from an asset as a result of continuing to use it in the business

Cash-generating unit – the smallest identifiable group of assets that generates cash inflows that are largely independent of the cash inflows from other assets or groups of assets

Inventories – assets: held for sale in the ordinary course of business; in the process of production for such sale; or in the form of materials or supplies to be consumed in the production process or in the rendering of services

Net realisable value – the estimated selling price in the ordinary course of business less: the estimated costs of completion; and the estimated costs necessary to make the sale

First in first out (FIFO) – a method of valuing inventories that assumes that items are used in the order in which they were received from suppliers

Last in first out (LIFO) – a method of valuing inventories that assumes that the most recent purchases are used first

Weighted average cost (AVCO) – a method of valuing inventories which divides the total cost of the items in inventory by the total number of items in inventory to arrive at the cost of each item

TEST YOUR LEARNING

Test 1

During the year ended 31 December 20X4, a company started two new research and development projects:

Project X: New adhesive. Expected to cost a total of £2,000,000 to complete. Future revenues from the sale of the product are expected to exceed £4,000,000. The completion date of the project is uncertain because external funding will have to be obtained before the work can be completed.

Project Y: New type of cloth. Expected to cost a total of £900,000 to develop. Expected total revenues £2,500,000 once work completed – completion date expected to be early 20X5. Most of the expenditure on the project has now been incurred and the company expects to be able to fund the remainder from its ongoing operations.

On the basis of this information, how should the expenditure on these projects be treated in the financial statements for the year ended 31 December 20X4?

Recognise expenditure on both projects in profit or loss	
Recognise expenditure on Project X in profit or loss Recognise expenditure on Project Y as an intangible asset	
Recognise expenditure on Project Y in profit or loss Recognise expenditure on Project X as an intangible asset	
Recognise expenditure on both projects as an intangible asset	

Test 2

Indicate which of the following statements are True or False.

	True	False
An intangible asset may have an indefinite useful life		
An intangible asset should always be amortised over its useful life		
Internally generated goodwill should never be recognised		
No internally generated intangible asset may be recognised		

Test 3

According to IAS 36 *Impairment of assets*, all non-current assets should be reviewed for impairment at least annually.

Is this statement True or False?

True	
False	

Test 4

Prepare brief notes to answer the following questions:

(a) What is an impairment loss, according to IAS 36 *Impairment of Assets*?

(b) What is an asset's recoverable amount?

(c) When should an impairment loss be recognised in other comprehensive income?

Test 5

Prepare brief notes to answer the following questions:

(a) Why is an adjustment made for closing inventories in the financial statements?

(b) What is meant by the cost of inventories, according to IAS 2 *Inventories*?

(c) How should inventories be valued in the financial statements?

(d) Why are inventories an asset?

Test 6

A company started to trade on 1 April and made the following purchases of inventory:

	Units	Price per unit	
	£	£	£
1 April	60	20	1,200
15 April	40	22	880
30 April	50	25	1,250
			3,330

On 30 April 125 units were sold. Total proceeds were £5,000.

The company uses the first in first out method (FIFO) to arrive at the cost of inventories.

What is the gross profit for April?

£2,170	
£2,225	
£2,295	
£2,670	

chapter 8:
LIABILITIES

CURRENT TAX

Companies in the UK pay corporation tax on their taxable profits.

You will not be asked to calculate corporation tax in the assessment. You do need to know how to account for and disclose corporation tax in the financial statements once the amount of tax has been calculated.

Accounting for corporation tax

At the end of each accounting period, tax is calculated on the profit for the year.

- The tax charge is included in profit or loss.
- The liability for tax is included in current liabilities in the statement of financial position.

Task 1

The tax charge of X Ltd is £150,000 for the year ended 31 December 20X2.

Show the journal entry that is needed to adjust the financial statements.

Journal

Account name	Debit £	Credit £

The tax expense included in the financial statements is only an estimate of the amount to be paid. The company does not usually know the actual amount of corporation tax until after the year-end, when this is agreed with Her Majesty's Revenue and Customs (HMRC).

The amount that is actually paid could be greater or smaller than the tax charge and the tax liability that have been included in the financial statements.

HOW IT WORKS

The following information relates to Pullman Ltd:

- The tax expense for the year ended 31 March 20X2 is estimated as £38,000.
- During the year ended 31 March 20X3 the company agrees the amount at £42,000 and this is paid to HMRC.
- The tax expense for the year ended 31 March 20X3 is estimated as £40,000.

The following adjustment is made to the accounts for the year ended 31 March 20X2:

DEBIT	Tax expense (profit or loss)	£38,000
CREDIT	Tax payable (statement of financial position)	£38,000

On 1 April 20X2, opening liabilities include a balance of £38,000 for tax payable. After the tax liability has been settled, the tax account is as follows:

Tax payable

	£		£
Bank	42,000	Balance b/f	38,000
		Balance c/f	4,000
	42,000		42,000
Balance b/f	4,000		

The debit balance of £4,000 is included in the trial balance when the accounts for the year ended 31 March 20X3 are prepared. It represents the difference between the estimate of £38,000 and the actual tax charge of £42,000.

After the year end adjustments have been made, the tax account is as follows:

Tax payable

	£		£
Balance b/f	4,000	Profit or loss	44,000
Balance c/f	40,000		
	44,000		44,000
		Balance b/f	40,000

The tax charge in the statement of comprehensive income is:

	£
Tax expense based on profits for the year	40,000
Adjustment in respect of prior period (underprovision)	4,000
	44,000

The amount included in the statement of financial position is the tax liability for the year ended 31 March 20X3: £40,000.

Task 2

Tolkein Ltd estimated the corporation tax charge for the year ended 30 June 20X4 as £45,000. The actual amount payable was £43,000. The estimated corporation tax charge for the year ended 30 June 20X5 is £50,000.

Indicate whether the following statements are True or False:

	True	False
The tax expense for the year ended 30 June 20X5 is £48,000	✓	
The tax liability at 30 June 20X5 is £48,000		

IAS 12 Income taxes

IAS 12 sets out the way in which current tax must be treated in the financial statements.

- Unpaid current tax (for both current and previous periods) should be recognised as a liability.

- Current tax should be measured at the amounts expected to be paid (or recovered) using the tax rates and laws that have been enacted by the year-end. This means that if the rate of tax changes between the year-end and the date on which the financial statements are approved, the rates used are the rates in force at the year-end (the reporting date).

- The tax expense relating to the profit or loss for the period is presented in profit or loss.

- Any tax relating to a gain or loss that has been recognised in other comprehensive income (for example, a gain when a property is revalued) should be separately disclosed in other comprehensive income.

HOW IT WORKS

At 31 March 20X3 the tax payable (corporation tax) account of Pullman Ltd is as follows:

Tax payable

	£		£
Balance b/f	4,000	Profit or loss	44,000
Balance c/f	40,000		
	44,000		44,000
		Balance b/f	40,000

The way in which this information is disclosed in the financial statements is shown below:

Statement of comprehensive income for the year ended 31 March 20X3 (extract)

	£
Profit before tax	X
Tax (W)	(44,000)
Profit for the year	X

Working

	£
Tax expense based on profits for the year	40,000
Adjustment in respect of prior period	4,000
	44,000

Statement of financial position at 31 March 20X3 (extract)

	£
Current liabilities:	
Tax payable	40,000

DEFERRED TAX

Why deferred tax is recognised in financial statements

Deferred tax is not an actual tax. It is a way of applying the accruals concept to accounting for corporation tax (current tax).

The profit before tax that is reported in the statement of comprehensive income is not the actual amount on which corporation tax is charged. There are two main reasons for this:

- PERMANENT DIFFERENCES: some items (such as entertainment expenditure) are not allowed as a deduction from income for tax purposes. They must be added back to reported profit when calculating the tax charge for the year.

- TEMPORARY DIFFERENCES: these are differences between the carrying amount of an asset or liability in the statement of financial position and its valuation for tax purposes (tax base).

Temporary differences can occur for a number of reasons. For example:

- Depreciation is not an allowable expense for tax purposes. Instead, a business claims capital allowances when assets are purchased. To calculate taxable profits, depreciation is added back to reported profit and capital allowances are deducted.

- Interest receivable is recognised as income in the financial statements, but is not taxable until the cash is received.

Because of temporary differences, some items are charged to tax or allowed for tax in a period that is different from the one in which they are recognised in the accounts.

HOW IT WORKS

A company placed £500,000 in a bank deposit account on 1 July 20X7 and kept it there until it was used to buy new plant on 30 June 20X8. Interest of 8% per annum was received on 30 June 20X8.

The company recognised interest receivable of £20,000 (£500,000 × 8% × 6/12) in its financial statements for each of the two years ended 31 December 20X7 and 31 December 20X8. It received cash of £40,000 (£500,000 × 8%) on 30 June 20X8.

Profit from operations (excluding interest) was £450,000 for each of the two years ended 31 December 20X8. There was no interest payable.

The rate of corporation tax is 30%. Interest income is not taxable until the cash is actually received.

Profit chargeable to tax is as follows for the two years:

	20X7 £'000	20X8 £'000	Total £'000
Profit before tax per financial statements (450 + 20)	470	470	940
Less: interest receivable	(20)	(20)	(40)
Add: interest received	–	40	40
Taxable profit	450	490	940
Tax @ 30%	135	147	282

Without these adjustments the company would have paid tax of £141,000 (470,000 × 30%) for each of the two years. The total tax paid during the whole period is exactly the same as it would have been if profit before tax had been the same as taxable profit, but the timing of the payment is different. The tax charge is lower in 20X7, but higher in 20X8.

The differences are:

	20X7	20X8	Total
	£'000	£'000	£'000
Profit before tax × 30%	141	141	282
Tax expense	(135)	(147)	(282)
Tax effect of temporary timing differences	6	(6)	–

The tax effect of the temporary timing differences is the deferred tax charge or credit that should be recognised in profit or loss each year.

Definition of deferred tax

IAS 12 *Income Taxes* defines DEFERRED TAX LIABILITIES as the amounts of income taxes payable in future periods in respect of taxable temporary differences.

TAXABLE TEMPORARY DIFFERENCES are temporary differences that will result in taxable amounts in determining taxable profit (or tax loss) of future periods.

Accounting treatment

IAS 12 states that a deferred tax liability must be recognised for all taxable temporary differences.

- Deferred tax liabilities are reported under non-current liabilities in the statement of financial position.

- Increases and decreases in the deferred tax liability are recognised in profit or loss for the year, unless they relate to a gain or loss that has been recognised in other comprehensive income.

- All deferred tax recognised in profit or loss is included as part of the tax on profit or loss for the year.

By recognising a liability for deferred tax, an entity recognises the estimated future tax consequences of transactions and events recognised in the financial statements of the current period.

HOW IT WORKS

You will not be asked to calculate deferred tax in the assessment, but you may be asked to account for it.

In the previous example, the tax charge for the year ended 31 December 20X7 was £135,000. Tax on the temporary difference was £6,000.

Therefore the company recognises a deferred tax liability of £6,000. The double entry to make the adjustment is:

| DEBIT | Deferred tax (profit or loss) | £6,000 | |
| CREDIT | Deferred tax liability (statement of financial position) | | £6,000 |

In the year ended 31 December 20X8 there is a credit to profit or loss of £6,000:

| DEBIT | Deferred tax liability (statement of financial position) | £6,000 | |
| CREDIT | Deferred tax (profit or loss) | | £6,000 |

The liability for deferred tax reduces to nil. Deferred tax is recognised as part of the tax expense in the statement of comprehensive income.

Task 3

At 31 December 20X4, Williams Ltd had the following balances in its trial balance:

	Dr	Cr
	£'000	£'000
Tax payable	5	
Deferred tax liability		110

The corporation tax charge for the year has been estimated at £150,000. The deferred tax liability is to be increased by £20,000.

(a) Calculate the tax expense to be recognised in profit or loss for the year ended 31 December 20X4

£	

(b) Show how the tax liability would be presented in the statement of financial position at 31 December 20X4

Statement of financial position for the year ended 31 December 20X4 (extract)

	£'000
Non-current liabilities:	
Current liabilities:	

LEASES

A LEASE is a contract between a lessor and a lessee for the hire of a specific asset. The lessor retains ownership of the asset, but the lessee has the right to use the asset for an agreed period of time in return for the payment of specified rentals.

Many entities use leases to finance the purchase or use of non-current assets. By leasing an asset rather than buying it, the entity spreads the cash outflow over several accounting periods.

Types of lease

IAS 17 *Leases* classifies leases into two types.

A FINANCE LEASE is a lease that **transfers substantially all the risks and rewards of ownership of an asset to the lessee**. Title (ownership) may or may not eventually be transferred. Although the lessor continues to own the asset, the substance of the contract is that the lessee has purchased the asset and has obtained a loan from the lessor to finance the purchase.

A lease is almost certainly a finance lease if all or some of the following apply:

- The lease transfers ownership of the asset to the lessee by the end of the lease term.

- The lessee has the option to purchase the asset and at the inception (start) of the lease it is reasonably certain that the lessee will exercise the option. This will be the case if the price of the option is expected to be significantly lower than the asset's fair value at the date the option becomes exercisable.

- The lease contract is for all or most of the asset's useful life, even if ownership is not transferred.

- At the inception (start) of the lease, the present value of the minimum lease payments amounts to at least substantially all of the fair value of the leased asset. The MINIMUM LEASE PAYMENTS are the total payments that the lessee is, or can be, required to make over the lease term.

- The leased assets are so specialised that only the lessee can use them without major modifications.

A lease could be a finance lease if either of the following apply:

- If the lease is cancelled, the lessee bears any losses incurred by the lessor as a result of the cancellation.

- After the initial lease term ends, the lessee has the option of continuing to lease the asset for a secondary period at a rent that is substantially lower than the market rent.

However, IAS 17 is clear that the key factor is the **transfer of the risks and rewards of ownership.**

An OPERATING LEASE is a lease other than a finance lease. An operating lease is similar to a rental agreement.

IAS 17 requires entities to account for the substance of a lease contract rather than its legal form. This means that finance leases and operating leases are treated differently in the financial statements.

Task 4

Witney Ltd leases an item of plant. Under the terms of the lease, Witney Ltd makes payments of £20,000 each year for five years. The present value of the minimum lease payments is £95,500. The plant has a useful life of five years and would cost £98,000 to purchase outright.

This lease is an operating lease.

Is this statement True or False?

True	
False	

Land and buildings

Land and buildings are often leased together under the same agreement.

- Land normally has a very long useful life. This means that when land is leased, the agreement often covers only a very small part of its useful life, so that the risks and rewards of ownership are not transferred to the lessee. Leases of land are normally operating leases.

- Leases of buildings may be either finance leases or operating leases.

- For accounting purposes, the land element and the buildings element must be separated. Each part is then classified as a finance lease or an operating lease independently of the other.

Accounting for finance leases

At the start of the lease

- The leased asset is recognised in the lessee's statement of financial position at its **fair value**, or, if this is lower, the **present value of the minimum lease payments**.

- The lessee also recognises a liability for the loan. This is the same amount as the value of the asset.

- **Fair value** is the amount for which an asset could be exchanged, or a liability settled, between knowledgeable, willing parties in an arm's length transaction. In practice, this is usually the same as the purchase price of the asset.

- To arrive at the present value of the minimum lease payments, the payments are discounted using the **interest rate implicit in the lease**, or, if this is not possible, the lessee's **incremental borrowing rate**.

- The INTEREST RATE IMPLICIT IN THE LEASE is the discount rate that, at the inception of the lease, causes the total present value of the minimum lease payments to be equal to the fair value of the leased asset.

- The idea here is that the lease is really a loan for the sum of money that the lessee would need to buy the asset outright (its fair value). The fair value of the asset is the capital amount of the loan and the lessor charges interest on this at a rate that takes account of the time value of money.

- The lessee's INCREMENTAL BORROWING RATE is the rate of interest that the lessee would have to pay on a similar lease or on a similar sum of money over a similar term.

Over the term of the lease

- The asset is depreciated over its **useful life**. The depreciation rate and method used must be the same as those used for similar assets that are owned by the entity.

- The useful life of a leased asset is the shorter of the normal useful life of a similar asset and the lease term. IAS 17 defines the useful life of a leased asset more formally as 'the estimated remaining period over which the economic benefits embodied in the asset are expected to be consumed by the entity'.

- The total payments under the lease are usually more than the value of the leased asset in the statement of financial position. The difference is the lease interest.

- The lease payments are split between capital and interest. As each instalment is paid, the capital portion reduces the outstanding liability, while the interest is charged to profit or loss.

HOW IT WORKS

Faringdon Ltd leases a machine under a finance lease.

- The lease runs for four years from 1 January 20X1.

- The company pays £40,000 on 31 December each year.

- The present value of the lease payments is £126,800.

- The rate of interest implicit in the lease is 10%.

- The machine would have cost £127,000 if the company had been able to purchase it outright.

- The useful life of the machine is four years.

At the start of the lease term

We are actually told that the lease is a finance lease. In addition, there are two indications that this is the case:

- The term of the lease is the same as the useful life of the machine: four years.

- The present value of the minimum lease payments (£126,800) is substantially all (99%) of the fair value of the lease (£127,000).

Therefore Faringdon Ltd recognises:

- An asset (the machine)
- A liability (the outstanding lease payments)

measured at the lower of the present value of the minimum lease payments and the fair value of the machine: £126,800.

The double entry is:

DEBIT	Property, plant and equipment at cost	£126,800	
CREDIT	Lease liability		£126,800

Over the term of the lease: the asset

The asset is depreciated over the lease term of four years, in exactly the same way as any other item of property, plant and equipment.

The double entry is:

DEBIT	Depreciation expense (£126,800 ÷ 4)	£31,700	
CREDIT	Property, plant and equipment: accumulated depreciation		£31,700

Over the term of the lease: the liability

The lease liability is similar to a loan. Interest is charged on the loan over the term of the lease and Faringdon Ltd repays the loan in equal instalments at the end of each year.

IAS 17 states that each lease instalment must be split between capital and interest. Interest must be allocated to each period so as to produce a constant periodic rate of interest on the remaining balance of the liability.

This is normally done by using the **actuarial method** (sometimes called the **effective interest rate method**).

Interest is charged at 10% on the outstanding liability at the beginning of each year and is recognised as an expense in profit or loss. The double entry for 20X1 is:

DEBIT	Finance cost (£126,800 × 10%) (profit or loss)	£12,680	
CREDIT	Lease liability (statement of financial position)		£12,680

The double entry for the repayment on 31 December is:

DEBIT	Lease liability	£40,000	
CREDIT	Cash		£40,000

Each year, the lease liability is increased by the interest on the outstanding amount and then reduced by the repayment. At the end of the first year, the outstanding liability is £99,480 (£126,800 + £12,680 − £40,000).

What happens over the whole term of the lease is shown below:

	Liability at 1 January	Interest at 10%	Repayment	Liability at 31 December
	£	£	£	£
20X1	126,800	12,680	(40,000)	99,480
20X2	99,480	9,948	(40,000)	69,428
20X3	69,428	6,942	(40,000)	36,370
20X4	36,370	3,630*	(40,000)	–

*   There is a rounding difference of £7 and this has been deducted from the interest charge for 20X4.

At the end of each year, the lease liability is shown in the statement of financial position. The total amount of £99,480 must be split between current liabilities and non-current liabilities. As the repayment is made at the end of the year, the current liability is the £40,000 instalment payable on 31 December 20X2 (ie, within 12 months) less the interest charge for the year on the liability at 1 January 20X2:

	£
Repayment on 31 December 20X2	40,000
Less: interest for 20X2 (£99,480 × 10%)	(9,948)
Current liabilities	30,052
Non-current liabilities (balancing figure)	69,428
	99,480

Alternatively, calculate the total liability at 31 December 20X2 and deduct it from the total liability at 31 December 20X1: £99,480 – £69,428 = £30,052.

It is very unlikely that you will be asked to do this calculation in the assessment, but you need to understand the way in which leases are presented in the financial statements.

Extracts from the financial statements

Statement of financial position at 31 December

	20X1 £	20X2 £	20X3 £	20X4 £
Property, plant and equipment				
Cost	126,800	126,800	126,800	126,800
Depreciation	(31,700)	(64,300)	(95,100)	(126,800)
Net carrying amount	95,100	64,300	31,700	–
Non-current liabilities				
Finance lease obligation	69,428	36,370	–	–
Current liabilities				
Finance lease obligation	30,052	33,058	36,370	–

The following amounts are included in the statement of comprehensive income for the year ended 31 December.

	20X1 £	20X2 £	20X3 £	20X4 £
Depreciation	31,700	31,700	31,700	31,700
Finance costs	12,680	9,948	6,942	3,630

Calculating the interest charge for the year: an alternative method

IAS 17 states that interest must be allocated to each period so as to produce a constant periodic rate of interest on the remaining balance of the liability. However, it does not actually require a lessee to use a specific method.

In this example we have used the **actuarial method,** which is generally accepted as being the most accurate.

IAS 17 explains that in practice a lessee can use an approximate calculation. The **sum-of-the digits method** is sometimes used as an alternative to the actuarial method. You could be asked to use either in the assessment.

We will recalculate the annual interest charges for the lease using the sum-of-the digits method. As before, on 1 January 20X1 Faringdon recognises an asset of £126,800 and depreciates it over its useful life of four years. It also recognises a liability of £126,800.

- The total interest payable over the term of the lease is calculated below:

	£
Total lease rentals (4 × 40,000)	160,000
Less: present value of minimum lease payments	(126,800)
Total interest	33,200

- There are four lease instalments. A digit is applied to each of the four instalments: the first instalment is 4, the second is 3, and so on.

- The digits are totalled: 4 + 3 + 2 + 1 = 10. (If there is a large number of instalments, use the formula $\dfrac{n(n+1)}{2}$ where n is the number of instalments.)

- The interest charge for each year is calculated as: total interest × $\dfrac{\text{Digit applicable to the instalment}}{\text{Sum of the digits}}$. The interest for the first year is £13,280 (33,200 × 4/10)

The double entry for 20X1 is:

DEBIT	Finance cost (profit or loss)	£13,280	
CREDIT	Lease liability (statement of financial position)		£13,280

As before, the double entry for the repayment on 31 December is:

DEBIT	Lease liability	£40,000	
CREDIT	Cash		£40,000

At the end of 20X1, the outstanding liability is £100,080 (£126,800 + £13,280 − £40,000).

What happens over the whole term of the lease is shown below:

	Liability at 1 January	Interest	Repayment	Liability at 31 December
	£	£	£	£
20X1	126,800	13,280	(40,000)	100,080
20X2	100,080	9,960	(40,000)	70,040
20X3	70,040	6,640	(40,000)	36,680
20X4	36,680	3,320	(40,000)	–
		33,200		

Extracts from the financial statements (using the sum-of-the-digits method)

Statement of financial position at 31 December

	20X1	20X2	20X3	20X4
Property, plant and equipment	£	£	£	£
Cost	126,800	126,800	126,800	126,800
Depreciation	(31,700)	(64,300)	(95,100)	(126,800)
Net carrying amount	95,100	64,300	31,700	–
Non-current liabilities				
Finance lease obligation	70,040	36,680	–	–
Current liabilities				
Finance lease obligation	30,040	33,360	36,680	–

The following amounts are included in the statement of comprehensive income for the year ended 31 December

	20X1	20X2	20X3	20X4
	£	£	£	£
Depreciation	31,700	31,700	31,700	31,700
Finance costs	13,280	9,960	6,640	3,320

Task 5

Wantage Ltd leases an item of plant under a finance lease. Under the terms of the lease, Wantage Ltd makes payments of £10,000 each year on 1 January for four years, **starting on 1 January 20X1** (the start of the lease). The present value of the minimum lease payments is £34,870 and the rate of interest implicit in the lease is 10%.

Calculate the total lease liability at 31 December 20X1. (Use the actuarial method.)

£

Accounting for operating leases

- The lease payments are charged to profit or loss on a straight line basis, unless another systematic basis is more representative of the time pattern of the user's benefit. (The asset is not recognised in the statement of financial position.)

- Information about the operating lease is disclosed in the notes to the financial statements.

HOW IT WORKS

Faringdon Ltd leases a machine under an operating lease.

- The lease runs for four years from 1 January 20X1.
- The company pays £20,000 on 31 December each year.
- The useful life of the machine is fifteen years.

Faringdon Ltd recognises an expense of £20,000 in profit or loss for each of the four years of the lease term.

Statement of comprehensive income (extract)

	20X1 £	20X2 £	20X3 £	20X4 £
Lease rental	20,000	20,000	20,000	20,000

PROVISIONS, CONTINGENT LIABILITIES AND CONTINGENT ASSETS

Provisions

The term 'provision' is often used in a very general way. For example, an entity makes 'provisions' for depreciation and doubtful debts. These are not really provisions at all, but the result of normal accounting estimates. The term has a much more precise meaning.

IAS 37 *Provisions, Contingent Liabilities and Contingent Assets* states that:

- A PROVISION is a liability of uncertain timing or amount

- A LIABILITY is a present obligation arising from past events, the settlement of which is expected to result in an outflow of resources embodying economic benefits

Uncertainty is what distinguishes a provision from another type of liability. For example, if an entity has a liability to pay a supplier, management usually knows how much it must pay and when. If a claim is made against an entity, management knows that it will possibly have to pay damages, but not the precise amount (because this normally depends on the outcome of a court case).

Financial statements must be reliable. This means that expenses and liabilities should not be understated. In addition, users of the financial statements need information about all potential liabilities of an entity, even if there is uncertainty.

On the other hand, if an entity provides for all potential liabilities even where the likelihood of payment is remote, the financial statements will be equally misleading. Before the issue of IAS 37 provisions were sometimes used for profit smoothing (a form of 'creative accounting'). An entity would set up a large general provision for future expenditure or future losses (sometimes known as 'the big bath') in a year where it had made high profits. The provision was then released to profit or loss in future years when profits were not as high, to make the results seem better than they really were. For this reason, IAS 37 sets out conditions which must be met before a provision can be recognised.

Recognising a provision

IAS 37 states that a provision should be recognised when:

- An entity has a present obligation as a result of a past event

- It is probable that an outflow of resources embodying economic benefits will be required to settle the obligation

- A reliable estimate can be made of the amount of the obligation

No provision is recognised if these conditions are not met.

If there is an **obligation** to transfer economic benefits an entity **cannot avoid making payment** in some form.

An obligation can be legal or constructive:

- A LEGAL OBLIGATION arises as the result of a contract, legislation or other operation of law.

- A CONSTRUCTIVE OBLIGATION occurs where:

    - an entity indicates that it will accept certain responsibilities (for example, by past practice, published policies or statements)

    - as a result, the entity has created a valid expectation on the part of those other parties that it will discharge those responsibilities.

For example, suppose that a shop has a policy of refunding the cost of goods purchased by dissatisfied customers. The shop makes customers aware of this policy. As a result, the shop has a constructive obligation to make refunds.

Other points to note:

- The obligation must be the result of a past event; in other words, the event giving rise to the obligation must have happened before the end of the reporting period.

- Probable means more likely than not.

- Only in extremely rare cases is it not possible to make a reliable estimate of the amount of an obligation.

Task 6

A company guarantees to repair or replace items that become defective within three years from the date of sale. The chance of an individual item needing to be repaired or replaced are small. However, past experience suggests that it is probable that there will be some claims under the guarantee.

The company should recognise a provision for the costs or repairing and replacing items under the guarantee.

Is this statement True or False?

True	
False	

Measuring a provision

IAS 37 states that:

- The amount recognised should be the best estimate of the expenditure required to settle the present obligation at the end of the reporting period (the year-end).

- Risks, uncertainties and future events should be taken into account.

- Where the effect of the time value of money is material, the amount of the provision should be the present value of the expenditures required to settle the obligation (the amount is discounted).

- A provision should be reviewed at the end of the reporting period and adjusted to reflect the current best estimate.

- A provision should only be used for expenditures for which it was originally recognised.

Specific situations

IAS 37 deals with specific situations in which excessive or unnecessary provisions were sometimes made in the past.

- A RESTRUCTURING is a programme that is planned and controlled by management and materially changes either:

  - The scope of a business undertaken by an entity; or
  - The manner in which that business is conducted.

- ■ Examples:
  - – Sale or termination of a line of business
  - – Closure of business locations in a country or region or a relocation of business activities from one country or region to another
  - – Changes in management structure
  - – Fundamental reorganisations that have a material effect on the nature and focus of an entity's operations
- ■ Provisions should not be recognised for restructuring unless the entity has a constructive obligation to restructure. This means that:
  - – It has a detailed formal plan for the restructuring
  - – It has raised a valid expectation in those affected that it will carry out the restructuring by starting to implement the plan or announcing its main features to those affected by it

  A management or board decision on its own is not sufficient.
- ■ A restructuring provision should include only the direct expenditures arising from the restructuring, those that are both:
  - – Necessarily entailed by the restructuring; and
  - – Not associated with the entity's ongoing activities.

  For example, it should not include:
  - – The cost of retraining or relocating staff who will continue to be employed
  - – Marketing
  - – Investment in new systems

  This is because these costs relate to the future activities of the business and are not liabilities of the entity at the year-end.
- ■ Provisions should not be recognised for **future operating losses**. These do not meet the definition of a liability.

Contingent liabilities

A provision can only be recognised if the liability is probable (more likely than not to occur). Users of the financial statements also need information about contingent liabilities.

A CONTINGENT LIABILITY is:

- A possible obligation that arises from past events and whose existence will be confirmed only by the occurrence of one or more uncertain future events not wholly within the entity's control

- A present obligation that arises from past events but is not recognised because:

    - It is not probable that a transfer of economic benefits will be required to settle the obligation

    - The amount of the obligation cannot be measured with sufficient reliability

There are two important things to notice:

- For there to be a liability, there must be an obligation. A liability is contingent if it is **uncertain** whether the entity has an obligation.

- A contingent liability is a liability that **does not meet the recognition criteria** (if there is an obligation it is not probable and/or the amount cannot be measured reliably).

IAS 37 states that contingent liabilities should not be recognised.

Instead, information about contingent liabilities is disclosed in the financial statements unless the possibility of a transfer of economic benefits is remote.

Contingent assets

A CONTINGENT ASSET is a possible asset that arises from past events and whose existence will be confirmed only by the occurrence of one or more uncertain future events not wholly within the entity's control.

For example, an entity makes a claim for damages. The outcome is uncertain, but if it is successful it will receive a significant amount of cash. The entity has a contingent asset.

IAS 37 states that:

- Contingent assets should not be recognised (they might never be realised and the financial statements would be misleading as a result).

- If the possibility of an inflow of economic benefits is probable information about the contingent asset should be disclosed.

- If the asset is virtually certain to be realised it should be recognised. It is not a contingent asset but an actual asset.

Provisions

For each class of provision, disclose:

- The carrying amount at the beginning and end of the period
- Additional provisions made in the period
- Amounts used during the period
- Unused amounts reversed during the period

Also disclose:

- A brief description of the nature of the obligation and expected timing of any resulting transfers of economic benefit

- An indication of the uncertainties about the amount or timing of those transfers of economic benefit

Contingent liabilities and assets

For each class of contingent liability and for probable contingent assets disclose:

- A brief description of its nature

- An estimate of its financial effect

- An indication of the uncertainties relating to the amount or timing of any outflow

Illustration

Notes to the financial statements

Provisions

A provision has been recognised for expected repairs to products sold in accordance with our guarantee to customers. This provision has been classified as a current liability as our guarantee is limited to goods returned within six months of purchase.

Changes in the provision during the year were:

	£'000
At the beginning of the year	4,000
Additional provision recognised during the year	5,250
Cost of product repairs and replacement during the year	(3,400)
At the end of the year	5,850

Contingent liabilities

During the year a customer initiated legal proceedings against the company for injuries caused by a faulty product. The customer is claiming damages of £75,000.

No provision has been recognised in these financial statements as the company's legal advisers do not consider it probable that the claim will succeed.

Summary

Provisions and contingent liabilities

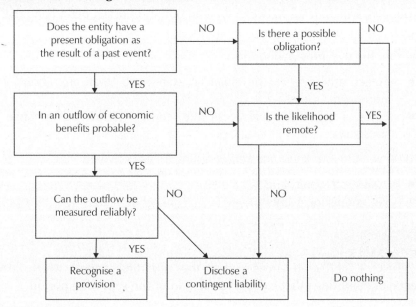

Contingent assets

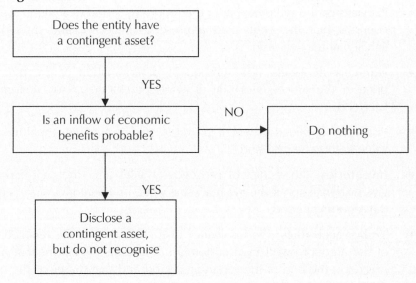

EVENTS AFTER THE REPORTING PERIOD

EVENTS AFTER THE REPORTING PERIOD are those events, both favourable and unfavourable, which occur between the end of the reporting period and the date on which the financial statements are authorised for issue.

Events after the reporting period may:

- Affect amounts in the financial statements that are about to be approved
- Have a significant effect on the entity's future performance and prospects.

IAS 10 *Events After the Reporting Period* distinguishes between:

- Adjusting events, and
- Non-adjusting events

Adjusting events

ADJUSTING EVENTS are events after the reporting period which provide **evidence of conditions that existed at the end of the reporting period**.

Examples of adjusting events:

- **Provisions**: the settlement after the reporting period of a court case that confirms that the entity had a present obligation (and therefore a liability) at the year-end.

- **Non-current assets**: the subsequent determination of the purchase price or the proceeds of sale of assets purchased or sold before the year-end.

- **Property**: a valuation which provides evidence of an impairment in value before the year-end.

- **Inventories**: the receipt of proceeds of sales after the year-end may give evidence about the net realisable value of inventories at the end of the reporting period.

- **Trade receivables**: the insolvency of a customer (or the renegotiation of the amount owed by a customer). This usually confirms that a loss existed at the end of the reporting period and that therefore the entity should write-off all or part of the amount receivable.

- **Claims**: amounts received or receivable in respect of insurance claims which are in the course of negotiation at the year-end.

- **Discoveries**: discovery of errors or frauds which show that the financial statements were incorrect.

Non-adjusting events

NON-ADJUSTING EVENTS are events after the reporting period which are indicative of **conditions which arose after the reporting period**.

Examples of non-adjusting events:

- Business combinations occurring after the reporting period

- Reconstructions and proposed reconstructions (such as discontinuing an operation)

- Issues of shares and loan stock

- Purchases or sales of property and investments

- Classifying an asset as held for sale, if the asset is material

- Losses of non-current assets or inventories as a result of catastrophe such as fire or flood

- Opening new trading activities or extending existing trading activities

- Closing a significant part of the trading activities if this was not anticipated at the year-end

- Changes in rates of foreign exchange, or rates of taxation

- Major litigation if this results from events after the reporting period

- Entering into significant commitments or contingent liabilities, for example, by issuing guarantees

The basic principle

Financial statements are prepared on the basis of **conditions existing at the end of the reporting period.**

- Where there are adjusting events after the reporting period the entity should adjust the amounts recognised in the financial statements.

- Where there are non-adjusting events after the reporting period, an entity should **not** adjust the amounts recognised in its financial statements.

- A material non-adjusting event after the reporting period should be disclosed where it could influence the economic decisions of users taken on the basis of the financial statements.

Disclosure

For each material non-adjusting event after the reporting period, the notes to the financial statements should disclose the following:

- The nature of the event; and

- An estimate of the financial effect, or a statement that it is not practicable to make such an estimate.

Separate disclosure of adjusting events is not normally required.

The date on which the financial statements were authorised for issue and who gave that authorisation should be disclosed in the financial statements.

Dividends

Equity (ordinary) dividends declared after the end of the reporting period should not be recognised as a liability. However, they should be disclosed in the notes to the financial statements.

Going concern

Some events after the reporting period could indicate that an entity may not be a going concern. For example, an entity could suffer significant losses shortly after the year-end (perhaps as a result of a serious accident or the loss of a major customer). This type of event would normally be non-adjusting, because it concerns conditions which did not exist at the end of the reporting period.

IAS 10 states that an entity should not prepare its financial statements on a going concern basis if this is not appropriate (for example, if management has no alternative but to cease trading). When an entity ceases to be a going concern, the effect is so pervasive that the amounts in the financial statements must reflect this.

Summary

If an event occurs after the year-end but before the financial statements are authorised for issue:

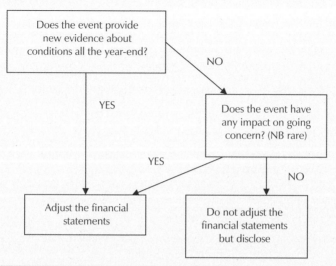

Task 7

Lessing Ltd has prepared financial statements for the year ended 31 December 20X4. The financial statements are due to be approved on 31 March 20X5.

1   On 20 January 20X5 Lessing Ltd sold land and buildings for £250,000. At 31 December 20X4 they had had a carrying amount of £100,000.

2   On 15 February 20X5 a major customer went into liquidation. The directors of Lessing Ltd were advised that they were unlikely to receive any amounts owing to them. At 15 February 20X5 the customer owed £20,000 of which £15,000 related to sales made before the year-end.

Which of the above events should be treated as a non-adjusting event after the reporting period?

1 only	✓
2 only	
Neither 1 nor 2	
Both 1 and 2	

CHAPTER OVERVIEW

- The corporation tax charge is included in the statement of comprehensive income (as part of profit or loss) and described as 'tax expense'

- The liability for corporation tax is included in current liabilities

- Deferred tax is a way of dealing with the effect of temporary differences on the corporation tax charge for the year. It applies the accruals concept

- Deferred tax should be recognised on all taxable temporary differences

- Deferred tax liabilities should be reported under non-current liabilities in the statement of financial position

- All deferred tax recognised in the statement of comprehensive income should be included within the heading 'tax expense'

- IAS 17 requires entities to account for the substance of a lease contract rather than its legal form

- A lease is either an operating lease or a finance lease. The classification of a lease determines the accounting treatment

- If the lease is a finance lease, the lease is treated as if the lessee has purchased an asset and financed the purchase by taking out a loan. The leased asset and the liability for the loan are recognised in the lessee's statement of financial position. The statement of comprehensive income includes depreciation and interest on the loan

- If the lease is an operating lease, the lease payments are charged to the lessee's profit or loss as rental and the leased asset is not recognised in the statement of financial position

- A provision should only be recognised when:
  - An entity has a present obligation as a result of a past event; and
  - It is probable that a transfer of economic benefits will be required to settle the obligation; and
  - A reliable estimate can be made of the amount of the obligation

- The amount recognised should be the best estimate of the expenditure required to settle the present obligation at the year-end

- Contingent liabilities should not be recognised. They should be disclosed in the financial statements unless the possibility of a transfer of economic benefits is remote

- Contingent assets should not be recognised. Probable contingent assets should be disclosed

- Financial statements should be prepared on the basis of conditions existing at the year-end

CHAPTER OVERVIEW CONTINUED

- An adjusting event after the year-end requires changes in the amounts to be included in the financial statements

- A material non-adjusting event after the year-end should be disclosed

Keywords

Permanent differences – differences between taxable profit and reported profit which arise because some items are not allowed as a deduction from income for tax purposes

Temporary differences – differences between taxable profit and reported profit which arise because some items are charged to tax or allowed for tax in a period that is different from the one in which they are recognised in the accounts

Deferred tax liabilities – the amounts of income taxes payable in future periods in respect of taxable temporary differences

Taxable temporary differences – temporary differences that will result in taxable amounts in determining taxable profit (or tax loss) of future periods

Lease – a contract for the hire of a specific asset. The lessor retains ownership of the asset, but the lessee has the right to use the asset for an agreed period of time in return for the payment of specified rentals

Finance lease – a lease that transfers substantially all the risks and rewards of ownership of an asset to the lessee

Operating lease – a lease other than a finance lease; similar to a rental agreement

Minimum lease payments – the total payments that the lessee is required to make over the lease term

Interest rate implicit in the lease – the discount rate that, at the inception of the lease, causes the total present value of the minimum lease payments to be equal to the fair value of the leased asset

Incremental borrowing rate – the rate of interest that the lessee would have to pay on a similar lease or on a similar sum of money over a similar term

Provision – a liability of uncertain timing or amount

Liability – a present obligation arising from past events, the settlement of which is expected to result in an outflow of resources embodying economic benefits

Legal obligation – an obligation which arises as the result of a contract, legislation or other operation of law

Constructive obligation – an obligation which occurs where: an entity indicates that it will accept certain responsibilities; and as a result, the entity has created a valid expectation that it will discharge those responsibilities

Restructuring – a programme that is planned and controlled by management and materially changes either: the scope of a business undertaken by an entity; or the manner in which that business is conducted

Contingent liability – a possible obligation that arises from past events and whose existence will be confirmed only by the occurrence of one or more uncertain future events not wholly within the entity's control; or a present obligation that arises from past events but is not recognised because: it is not probable that a transfer of economic benefits will be required to settle the obligation; or the amount of the obligation cannot be measured with sufficient reliability

Contingent asset – a possible asset that arises from past events and whose existence will be confirmed only by the occurrence of one or more uncertain future events not wholly within the entity's control

Events after the reporting period – those events, both favourable and unfavourable, which occur between the end of the reporting period and the date on which the financial statements are authorised for issue

Adjusting events – events after the reporting period which provide evidence of conditions existing at the end of the reporting period

Non-adjusting events – events after the reporting period which are indicative of conditions which arose after the end of the reporting period

TEST YOUR LEARNING

Test 1

For the year ended 30 June 20X3, Angle Ltd estimated that the charge to corporation tax was £85,500. The deferred tax provision was increased by £25,400. The estimated charge for corporation tax recognised in the financial statements for the year ended 30 June 20X2 was £11,000 higher than the actual amount paid to HMRC during 20X2/20X3.

What is the tax expense that should be recognised in profit or loss for the year ended 30 June 20X3?

£74,500	
£99,900	
£110,900	
£121,900	

Test 2

You have prepared draft financial statements for Craswall Ltd. The directors have noticed that the statement of financial position includes a deferred tax liability.

Prepare brief notes to answer the following questions:

(a) What is deferred tax?

(b) What are taxable temporary differences?

Test 3

A company's financial statements include the following note:

Profit from operations:

Profit from operations is stated after charging the following:

Depreciation:	owned assets	X
	leased assets	X

Assuming that the company has followed the correct accounting treatment set out in IAS 17 *Leases*, which type of lease agreement has it entered into?

A finance lease	
An operating lease	

Test 4

Clanfield Ltd leases a machine under a finance lease.

- The lease runs for four years from 1 January 20X1
- The company pays £20,000 on 31 December each year
- The present value of the minimum lease payments is £76,000.

Calculate the total lease liability at 31 December 20X1, using the sum-of-the-digits method.

£

Test 5

Proper Ltd operates a chain of restaurants. The directors of Proper have drawn your attention to two events that have occurred during the year ended 31 December 20X5:

- After a private function in one of the restaurants, several people became ill, possibly as a result of food poisoning. Legal proceedings were started seeking damages from the company. At 31 December, the case had not yet been settled, but the directors were advised that the company would probably not be found liable.

- As a result of this incident, the directors have decided to retrain most of the catering staff to make sure that they are aware of health and hygiene issues. The staff training means that the restaurants will have to close temporarily and the resulting loss of income is expected to be material. At 31 December 20X5 no staff training had taken place and the directors had not announced their decision to anybody likely to be affected.

Explain how each of the events should be treated in the financial statements for the year ended 31 December 20X5.

Test 6

The events listed below all took place between the end of a company's reporting period and the date on which the financial statements were authorised for issue.

Which ONE of these events is likely to be an adjusting event after the reporting period?

Damage to inventory as a result of a flood	
Discovery of a fraud committed by one of the accounts staff	
Issue of new share capital	
Sale of a freehold property	

chapter 9:
FURTHER ACCOUNTING STANDARDS

---

chapter coverage 📖

In this chapter we look at the requirements of four more accounting standards. The first two explain the treatment of particular items relating to profit or loss in the statement of comprehensive income. We then look briefly at two further standards that require an entity to provide additional information about its performance. The earnings per share figure is widely used by investors and their advisors. IAS 33 sets out the way in which it should be calculated. IFRS 8 requires public companies which carry out several different activities to provide information about the performance of each business 'segment'.

The topics covered are:

- ✍ Revenue
- ✍ Government grants
- ✍ Earnings per share
- ✍ Segment reporting

REVENUE

REVENUE is an entity's income from its main operating activities.

IAS 18 *Revenue* defines it more formally as:

- The gross inflow of economic benefits during the period arising in the course of the **ordinary activities** of the entity, when those inflows result in increases in equity, other than increases relating to contributions from equity shareholders (ie, increases in share capital).

Notice that this is very similar to the definition of income in the IASB's *Conceptual Framework*:

- **Income** is increases in economic benefits during the accounting period in the form of inflows or enhancement of assets or decreases of liabilities that result in increases in equity, other than those relating to contributions from owners.

This repeats the idea that if there is income, there will also be an increase in an asset or a decrease in a liability. The most obvious example of this is where an entity sells goods or services:

- Revenue is recognised in profit or loss (CREDIT entry)

- So the entity also recognises an asset: either cash or a trade receivable (DEBIT entry)

The other thing to notice is that not all income is revenue. Revenue only arises from an entity's **normal business activities**.

Task 1

A manufacturing company sells an item of property, plant and equipment at a profit. The income should be treated as revenue.

Is this statement True or False?

True	
False	

IAS 18 applies to:

- The sale of goods

- The rendering of services

- The use by others of entity assets yielding interest, royalties and dividends

The basic principle

Revenue is measured at the **fair value** of the consideration received or receivable.

For example, where an entity makes a sale the amount recognised is the amount invoiced. This is the amount of cash that the entity will eventually receive.

IAS 18 defines fair value in the same way as other Standards: **fair value** is the amount for which an asset could be exchanged, or a liability settled, between knowledgeable, willing parties in an arm's length transaction.

Sale of goods

Revenue from the sale of goods is recognised when all the following conditions have been satisfied:

- The entity has transferred to the buyer the significant risks and rewards of ownership of the goods

- The entity retains neither continuing managerial involvement to the degree usually associated with ownership nor effective control over the goods sold

- The amount of revenue can be measured reliably

- It is probable that the economic benefits associated with the transaction will flow to the entity

- The costs incurred or to be incurred in respect of the transaction can be measured reliably

Notice that IAS 18 uses the same recognition criteria as the *Conceptual Framework:* there must be a probable inflow of economic benefits; and these must be capable of being measured reliably.

Task 2

A customer orders some goods from Bampton Ltd which have to be specially manufactured for it. Because of the amount of work involved, the customer pays Bampton Ltd in full at the time the goods are ordered.

How should Bampton Ltd treat this payment in its financial statements?

It should recognise a liability	
It should recognise revenue	

Rendering of services

When the outcome of a transaction involving the rendering of services can be estimated reliably, revenue associated with the transaction is recognised by reference to the stage of completion of the transaction at the end of the reporting period.

The outcome of a transaction can be estimated reliably when:

- The amount of revenue can be measured reliably

- It is probable that the economic benefits associated with the transaction will flow to the entity

- The stage of completion of the transaction at the end of the reporting period can be measured reliably

- The costs incurred for the transaction and the costs to complete the transaction can be measured reliably

For example, suppose that a publicity company agrees to place a series of advertisements in magazines on behalf of a client over a period of six months to 31 March 20X3. It receives the total fee of £30,000 on 1 October 20X2 (the start of the six month period) but only recognises £15,000 (30,000 x 3/6) in profit or loss for the year ended 31 December 20X2.

Dividends

Revenue from dividends is recognised when:

- It meets the normal recognition criteria:

    - It is probable that the economic benefits associated with the transaction will flow to the entity; and

    - The amount of the revenue can be measured reliably; and

- The shareholder's right to receive payment is established.

GOVERNMENT GRANTS

Central and local government and other bodies make grants to entities (for example, to encourage them to operate in particular areas of the country or to employ particular groups of people). IAS 20 *Accounting for Government Grants and Disclosure of Government Assistance* explains how government grants should be treated.

Definitions

IAS 20 defines GOVERNMENT GRANTS as:

- Assistance by government in the form of transfers of resources to an entity in return for past or future compliance with certain conditions relating to the operating activities of the entity.

There are two types of government grant:

- GRANTS RELATED TO ASSETS are government grants whose primary condition is that an entity qualifying for them should purchase, construct or otherwise acquire long-term assets.

- GRANTS RELATED TO INCOME are government grants other than those related to assets (for example grants made to cover all or part of specific expenses).

Government grants exclude:

- Those forms of government assistance which cannot reasonably have a value placed upon them. (For example, a business may receive free assistance or advice).

- Transactions with government which cannot be distinguished from the normal trading transactions of the entity. (For example, government departments may buy goods or services from an entity in the normal course of business).

In return for receiving a grant an entity may have to comply with conditions. For example, where the grant is towards the cost of assets the entity may only be allowed to purchase a specific type of asset, or to use it in a particular factory or area. Entities may have to spend the grant money within a particular period.

Recognising grants: the general rule

IAS 20 states that government grants should not be recognised until there is reasonable assurance that:

- The entity will comply with the conditions attaching to them; and
- The grants will be received.

Government grants should be recognised in profit or loss on a systematic basis over the periods in which the entity recognises the related costs for which the grants are intended to compensate.

In other words, an entity should apply the accruals concept.

Grants related to assets

There are two possible methods of accounting for a grant related to assets:

- Recognise the grant as deferred income (a liability) and then recognise the income in profit or loss on a systematic basis over the useful life of the asset.

- Deduct the grant from the carrying amount of the asset (normally its cost or purchase price). The income is recognised in profit or loss in the form of a reduced depreciation expense.

HOW IT WORKS

Cinnamon Ltd purchases an asset for £90,000 and receives a government grant of £30,000 towards its cost. The asset has a useful life of three years and a residual value of nil.

The effect on each method on the financial statements is shown below.

Recognise deferred income and then recognise in profit or loss over the useful life of the asset.

Year	1	2	3
	£'000	£'000	£'000
Statement of financial position			
Property, plant and equipment:			
Cost	90	90	90
Accumulated depreciation	(30)	(60)	(90)
Net carrying amount	60	30	–
Non-current liabilities			
Deferred income	10	–	–
Current liabilities			
Deferred income	10	10	–
	20	10	–
Statement of comprehensive income (profit or loss)			
Depreciation charge	30	30	30
Government grant	(10)	(10)	(10)
	20	20	20

Deduct the grant from the cost of the asset and depreciate the net amount

Year	1	2	3
	£'000	£'000	£'000
Statement of financial position:			
Property, plant and equipment			
Cost (net of grant) (90 – 30)	60	60	60
Accumulated depreciation	(20)	(40)	(60)
Net carrying amount	40	20	–

Statement of comprehensive income (profit or loss)			
	£'000	£'000	£'000
Depreciation charge	20	20	20

The two methods compared

- Both methods recognise the grant in profit or loss over the useful life of the asset (ie, over the periods in which the entity recognises the cost of the asset as depreciation). Therefore IAS 20 allows both methods.

- The net effect on profit or loss is the same under both methods.

- Deducting the grant from the cost of the asset is simpler to apply.

- When a grant is recognised as deferred income, the asset is recorded at its actual cost. Because it avoids offsetting the grant against the cost of the asset, many people believe this method presents the statement of financial position more fairly.

Grants related to income

Grants related to income are recognised as a credit (as income) in the statement of comprehensive income. They can be presented:

- As a separate line item; or
- Under a general heading such as 'other income'; or
- They can be deducted from the related expense.

Task 3

Thyme Ltd has a year-end of 31 December. On 31 October 20X2 it received a government grant of £25,000. The grant covers part of the cost of training three new members of staff who were previously unemployed. The new members of staff joined the company on 1 October 20X2 and their training will last until 28 February 20X3.

How much income from grants should Thyme Ltd recognise in profit or loss for the year ended 31 December 20X2?

£Nil	
£6,250	
£15,000	
£25,000	

EARNINGS PER SHARE

Earnings per share is an important measure of financial performance. Investors and analysts use it to assess and compare the performance of different companies. It is also used to calculate other important ratios for assessing a company's performance.

IAS 33 *Earnings Per Share* states that:

- All companies that publicly trade their shares must calculate and disclose earnings per share. (In practice, this means that most public companies must disclose earnings per share.)

- The Standard also applies to any other company that chooses to disclose earnings per share.

The basic calculation

Earnings per share is calculated by dividing the profit or loss for the period attributable to ordinary equity holders (ie, ordinary shareholders) by the weighted average number of ordinary shares outstanding during the period.

At its simplest, the calculation is:

$$\frac{\text{Profit after tax}}{\text{Number of issued ordinary shares}}$$

Profit or loss for the period

The earnings per share ratio measures the amount of the profit for the year that has been earned for each ordinary share held.

It is based on the profit for the year that 'belongs' to ordinary (or equity) shareholders.

- An **ordinary share** is an equity instrument that is subordinate to all other classes of equity instruments. Ordinary shareholders only share in the profit for the period after preference shareholders have received their dividends.

- Therefore the profit or loss for the period attributable to ordinary equity holders is the profit or loss **after** deducting preference dividends.

  However, if preference shares are treated as non-current liabilities, preference dividends are included in finance costs. They will already have been deducted in arriving at profit or loss for the year.

- If there are no preference shares, the profit or loss figure used in the calculation is **profit after tax**. This must include **all** items of income and expense, even those that are unusually large or not expected to recur.

Number of ordinary shares

The number of ordinary shares used in the earnings per share calculation is the **weighted average** number of ordinary shares outstanding during the period.

Where there has been a change in the number of shares in issue during the year (for example, because there has been a share issue) the calculation uses an average number. The average is based on the proportion of the year for which each share was in issue. In practice, this is normally calculated to the nearest month.

HOW IT WORKS

At 1 January 20X1 Ranby plc had 500,000 ordinary shares of 50p each. On 30 June 20X1 it issued 100,000 new ordinary shares of 50p each. There were no preference shares in issue.

An extract from the statement of comprehensive income for the year ended 31 December 20X1 is shown below:

	£'000
Profit before tax	100
Tax	(40)
Profit for the year	60

Dividends of £20,000 were paid during the year, so retained profit for the year was £40,000.

Step 1   Calculate net profit attributable to ordinary equity holders

Net profit attributable to ordinary equity holders is profit after tax, which is £60,000.

Step 2   Calculate the weighted average number of ordinary shares outstanding during the year

There has been a share issue exactly half way through the year. The weighted average number of shares is calculated accordingly:

	'000
1 January – 30 June (500,000 × 6/12)	250
1 July – 31 December (600,000 × 6/12)	300
	550

Step 3   Calculate earnings per share

Earnings per share is expressed in pence.

$$\frac{\text{Profit after tax}}{\text{Weighted average number of shares}}$$

$$= \frac{60,000}{550,000} = 10.9p$$

Task 4

At 1 July 20X1 Limoges plc had 800,000 £1 ordinary shares in issue. On 31 March 20X2 a further 200,000 £1 ordinary shares were issued. Profit after tax for the year ended 30 June 20X1 was £760,000.

Calculate earnings per share for the year ended 30 June 20X2.

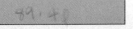

Presentation and disclosure

Earnings per share must be presented in the statement of comprehensive income for the period.

Illustration

	£'000
Profit before tax	X
Tax	(X)
Profit for the period from continuing operations	X
Earnings per share	X

- Where a company has discontinued operations during the period, earnings per share must be calculated and disclosed in the statement of comprehensive income:

  – for the company as a whole; **and**
  – for continuing operations.

- Earnings (or loss) per share for discontinued operations can be shown either in the statement of comprehensive income or in the notes.

Using earnings per share

Earnings per share provides a useful starting point for looking at a company's performance and comparing it with the performance of similar companies. However, some users of financial statements focus on earnings per share and do not go any further.

This can cause problems:

- If users only focus on one figure they may miss other important information in the statement of comprehensive income and elsewhere in the financial statements. This other information would give users a far better idea of how a company had performed **and was likely to perform in the future** than the earnings per share figure alone.

- If the performance of a company (and its directors) is judged almost entirely on earnings per share, the directors will be under pressure to make earnings per share as high as possible. This means that they may employ 'creative accounting' to boost the figure for profit after tax.

SEGMENT REPORTING

Some companies carry out several different activities or operate in several different geographical locations. Users of the financial statements need information that enables them to judge how profitable each of these operations is and how each of them contributes to the company's total sales revenue and profit.

Suppose that a company has three divisions, each operating in a different country. The following information is available:

	Revenue	Profit for the period
	£'000	£'000
UK	10,000	200
USA	25,000	(200)
Mexico	2,000	500
	37,000	500

The total amounts for revenue and net profit would tell the reader very little on their own. The figures for each geographical market give the reader much more information: the USA operation is the biggest but makes a loss, while the operation in Mexico is the smallest but is highly profitable. Comparative figures for the previous year would provide still more information: the reader would be able to see whether, for example, the company has been withdrawing its business from the USA and expanding its operations in Mexico.

Segmental information:

- Helps users to understand an entity's past performance and therefore to assess its future prospects

- Makes users aware of the impact that changes in significant components of a business have on the business as a whole

Therefore IFRS 8 *Operating Segments* states that an entity should disclose information to enable users of its financial statements to evaluate the nature and financial effects of the business activities in which it engages and the economic environments in which it operates.

Operating segments

IFRS 8 applies to public companies (those whose equity or debt securities are publicly traded) and to companies in the process of becoming public companies. IFRS 8 also applies to other companies that choose to disclose segment information.

IFRS 8 states that an entity should disclose information about each of its operating segments.

An OPERATING SEGMENT is a component of an entity:

- That engages in business activities from which it earns revenues and incurs expenses;

- Whose operating results are regularly reviewed by the entity's chief operating decision-maker to make decisions about resources to be allocated to the segment and to assess its performance; and

- For which discrete financial information is available.

Management receives financial and other information at regular intervals to enable it to see how the company has performed and to make decisions about the future running of the business. Most companies analyse this information between different parts of the business. Usually this analysis is based on different products and services or on different geographical markets. Each of these different parts of the business is an operating segment.

Some parts of an entity are not operating segments or part of an operating segment. For example, a company's head office is not an operating segment because its main purpose is to carry out administration for the business; it does not normally earn revenue from third parties.

Reportable segments

An entity's operating segments reflect the way in which it is managed internally. This means that for many entities it will be obvious what the operating segments are.

However, some entities may be organised in such a way that there are a large number of relatively small divisions. If this is the case, management needs to determine which of these must be reported separately and which can be aggregated (combined) for the purpose of the financial statements.

Combining segments

IFRS 8 states that two or more operating segments may be aggregated into a single operating segment if the segments have similar economic characteristics, and the segments are similar in each of the following respects:

- The nature of the products and services

- The nature of the production processes

- The type or class of customer for their products and services

- The methods used to distribute their products or provide their services

- If applicable, the nature of the regulatory environment (this would apply if an entity carried out any operations such as banking or insurance, which have to comply with special regulations in addition to the Companies Act 2006)

The '10% test'

Information about an operating segment must be reported separately if it meets **any** of the following thresholds:

- Its reported revenue, (sales to external customers plus sales to other segments), is 10% or more of the combined revenue, internal and external, of all operating segments.

- Its reported profit or loss is 10% or more of the combined reported profit of all operating segments that did not report a loss (or the combined reported loss of all operating segments that reported a loss if this is greater).

- Its assets are 10% or more of the combined assets of all operating segments.

Operating segments that **do not meet any of the quantitative thresholds** may be reported separately if management believes that the information would be useful to users of the financial statements.

The '75% test'

The total **external** revenue reported by operating segments must be at least 75% of the entity's total external revenue.

If the total revenue of the operating segments that meet the '10% test' is less than 75% of total external revenue, additional operating segments must be identified as reportable until the 75% threshold is reached.

HOW IT WORKS

Alston plc has organised its business activities into five operating segments. It has no other activities. There are no inter-segment sales.

Operating segment	Total revenue	Profit (loss)	Assets
	£m	£m	£m
A	85	15	115
B	475	135	165
C	75	10	20
D	80	(10)	35
E	185	30	45
Total	900	180	380

Step 1   **Apply the '10% test'**

The thresholds are:

- Revenue: £90m (900 × 10%)
- Profit: £19m (190 ×10%)
- Assets: £38m (380 × 10%)

Remember that segment D has made a loss of £10m, so the threshold is based on the combined profit of all segments **except** D (15 + 135 + 10 + 30 = 190).

The reportable segments are:

- A: because its assets are more than £38m
- B: because it exceeds all three thresholds
- E: because it exceeds all three thresholds

Step 2   **Apply the '75% test'**

Revenue of reportable segments:

	£m
A	85
B	475
E	185
	745

This is 83% of total revenue (745/900), so no more segments need to be reported. The reportable operating segments are A, B and E.

Why the usefulness of segment information is limited

There are a number of problems:

- Management defines operating segments. There is still some scope for 'hiding' loss-making divisions.

- Because the identification of operating segments depends on judgement and the way in which the entity is organised, segment information is not normally comparable with that of other companies.

- It can be difficult to allocate common costs to segments and to deal with inter-segment transactions.

CHAPTER OVERVIEW

- Revenue is the income from an entity's main operating activities

- Revenue is measured at the fair value of the consideration received or receivable

- Revenue from the sale of goods is recognised when:

  - The entity has transferred the significant risks and rewards of ownership of the goods

  - The entity no longer has effective control over the goods sold

  - The amount of revenue and the related costs of the transaction can be measured reliably

  - It is probable that the economic benefits associated with the transaction will flow to the entity

- When the outcome of a transaction involving the rendering of services can be estimated reliably, revenue associated with the transaction is recognised by reference to the stage of completion of the transaction at the year-end

- Government grants can be grants related to assets or grants related to income

- Grants should not be recognised until there is reasonable assurance that: the entity will comply with the conditions attached to them; and that they will be received.

- Government grants should be recognised in profit or loss over the periods in which the entity recognises the related costs

- To account for a grant related to assets: recognise the grant as deferred income and recognise the income in profit or loss over the useful life of the asset; **or** deduct the grant from the cost of the asset and then depreciate the net amount

- All companies that publicly trade their shares must calculate and disclose earnings per share in the statement of comprehensive income

- Earnings per share $= \dfrac{\text{Profit after tax}}{\text{Number of issued ordinary shares}}$

- IFRS 8 applies to public companies (those whose equity or debt securities are publicly traded) and to companies in the process of becoming public companies. IFRS 8 also applies to other companies that choose to disclose segment information

- An entity should disclose information about each of its operating segments

Keywords

Revenue – the gross inflow of economic benefits during the period arising in the course of the ordinary activities of the entity, when those inflows result in increases in equity, other than increases relating to contributions from equity shareholders

Government grants – assistance by government in the form of transfers of resources to an entity in return for past or future compliance with certain conditions relating to the operating activities of the entity

Grants related to assets – government grants whose primary condition is that an entity qualifying for them should purchase, construct or otherwise acquire long-term assets

Grants related to income – government grants other than those related to assets

Operating segment – a component of an entity that engages in business activities from which it earns revenue and incurs expenses and whose operating results are regularly reviewed by the entity's chief operating decision-maker in order to make decisions about resources to be allocated to the segment and to assess its performance

TEST YOUR LEARNING

Test 1

Prepare brief notes to answer the following questions:

(a)   What is revenue, according to IAS 18 *Revenue?*

(b)   When should an entity recognise revenue from the sale of goods?

Test 2

When an entity receives a government grant that contributes to the cost of purchasing an asset the amount that it recognises in the statement of financial position is always the cost of the asset less the amount of the grant.

Is this statement True or False?

True	
False	

Test 3

Indicate which of the following statements are True or False.

	True	False
All companies must calculate and present earnings per share.		
Earnings per share is disclosed in the statement of comprehensive income.		
The calculation is always based on profit after tax.		
The calculation is based on the number of shares in issue at the end of the year.		

Test 4

At 1 July 20X4 Bailey plc had 4,000,000 ordinary shares of £1 each. On 1 April 20X5 it issued a further 1,000,000 ordinary shares of £1 each. There were no preference shares in issue. Profit for the year was £1,750,000. During the year the company paid a dividend of £150,000.

What was earnings per share for the year ended 30 June 20X5?

35.0 pence	
37.6 pence	
41.2 pence	
43.7 pence	

Test 5

Diffuse plc is organised in several geographical divisions. Each of these divisions maintains its own accounting records which it then uses to prepare monthly reports for the Managing Director, who is the chief operating decision-maker. Revenue earned by each of the divisions for the year ended 31 December 20X5 is shown below. There are no inter-division sales.

Revenue:

	£'000
Northern	145,000
Eastern	42,500
Midlands	39,500
Southern	108,000
Western	37,000
Highland	28,000
	400,000

On the basis of this information, only Northern, Eastern and Southern are reportable segments according to IFRS 8 *Operating Segments*.

Is this statement True or False?

True	
False	

chapter 10:
GROUP ACCOUNTS: THE CONSOLIDATED STATEMENT OF FINANCIAL POSITION

---

chapter coverage 📖

The next two chapters explain how to prepare simple accounts for a group of companies.

A group consists of a parent company and one or more subsidiary companies controlled by the parent. As well as its own financial statements, the parent prepares financial statements for the group as a single entity. These are known as consolidated financial statements.

This chapter concentrates on the consolidated statement of financial position.

The topics covered are:

✍ Groups

✍ The consolidated statement of financial position

✍ Intra-group adjustments

GROUPS

A GROUP of companies consists of a **parent (holding) company** and all its **subsidiaries**. The parent controls the subsidiaries.

The individual companies within the group are separate legal entities. Each group company prepares its own financial statements.

In the financial statements of the parent:

- Investments in subsidiaries are included in the statement of financial position at cost (or fair value), under non-current assets

- Dividends receivable from subsidiaries are included in the statement of comprehensive income

Consolidated financial statements

The individual financial statements of a parent do not reflect the commercial reality of the situation.

- Because the parent can control the subsidiary, it has the benefits and risks attaching to the subsidiary's assets and liabilities, even though it may not directly own them.

- The parent is directly affected by the subsidiary's results, because it can appropriate the subsidiary's profits as dividends.

In practice, the parent and the subsidiary operate as a single economic entity: the group.

The Companies Act and IAS 27 *Consolidated and Separate Financial Statements* both require a parent to prepare consolidated financial statements for its group.

CONSOLIDATION is the process of adjusting and combining financial information from the individual financial statements of a parent and its subsidiary to prepare CONSOLIDATED FINANCIAL STATEMENTS that present financial information for the group as a single economic entity.

IAS 27 *Consolidated and Separate Financial Statements* and IFRS 3 *Business Combinations* apply to all situations in which a parent and one or more subsidiaries come together to form a group.

Business combinations

A BUSINESS COMBINATION is a transaction or other event in which an acquirer obtains control of one or more businesses.

IFRS 3 defines a BUSINESS as an integrated set of activities and assets that is capable of being conducted and managed for the purpose of providing a return in the form of dividends, lower costs or other economic benefits directly to investors or other owners.

If an entity simply acquires the separate assets and liabilities of another entity this is not a business combination. The entity should account for the transaction or other event as an asset acquisition.

There are several ways in which a business combination can occur, but the most common way is that one company acquires equity shares in another company.

- Equity shares can be purchased for cash or for other assets, or by issuing equity shares to the owners of the acquired entity in exchange for shares in the parent company. In this situation, the owners of the acquired entity become shareholders of the parent (the acquirer) instead of shareholders of the subsidiary (the acquiree).

- There may be more than one type of consideration (for example, an entity might pay cash **and** issue shares).

- IFRS 3 explains that an entity can also obtain control of another entity by incurring liabilities or through a contract.

- A subsidiary is normally a company, but it could be a partnership or another type of unincorporated body.

Control

A PARENT is an entity that has one or more subsidiaries.

A SUBSIDIARY is an entity that is controlled by another entity (the parent).

IFRS 3 also uses the terms **acquiree** and **acquirer**.

The ACQUIREE is the business or businesses that the acquirer obtains control of in a business combination.

The ACQUIRER is the entity that obtains control of the acquiree.

CONTROL is the power to govern the financial and operating policies of an entity so as to obtain benefits from its activities.

Control is presumed to exist where the parent owns more than half the **voting power** of an entity, unless it can be clearly demonstrated that such ownership does not constitute control.

Control also exists when the parent owns half or less of the voting power of an entity when there is:

- Power over more than half of the voting rights by virtue of an agreement with other investors

- Power to govern the financial and operating policies of the entity under a statute or an agreement

- Power to appoint or remove the majority of the members of the board of directors

- Power to cast the majority of votes at meetings of the board of directors

Notice that the crucial factor is not the number of shares that an investor holds, but the amount of voting power that they represent. In most companies, one equity share carries one vote, so in practice, if a company holds more than 50% of the equity (ordinary) shares in another company it is normally able to control that other company. You should assume that this is the case unless you are told otherwise.

However, it is important to remember that a company may be able to control another company even though it owns less than 50% of its issued equity share capital.

Task 1

Moat Ltd owns 6,000 'A' £1 ordinary shares in Grange Ltd. The share capital of Grange Ltd consists of:

Ordinary voting 'A' shares	10,000
Ordinary non-voting 'B' shares	20,000

Grange Ltd is a subsidiary of Moat Ltd.

Is this statement True or False?

True	
False	

THE CONSOLIDATED STATEMENT OF FINANCIAL POSITION

The basic idea

To prepare a consolidated statement of financial position:

- Add together the individual assets and liabilities of the parent and the subsidiary

- Make adjustments to cancel out intra-group items

HOW IT WORKS

On 1 January 20X0 P Ltd acquired 100% of the issued ordinary share capital of S Ltd. S Ltd was incorporated on that date. At 31 December 20X0, the individual company statements of financial position were as follows:

	P Ltd	S Ltd
	£'000	£'000
Property, plant and equipment	25,000	4,000
Investment in S Ltd	5,000	–
Current assets	30,000	16,000
	60,000	20,000
Share capital	20,000	5,000
Retained earnings	30,000	5,000
	50,000	10,000
Current liabilities	10,000	10,000
	60,000	20,000

Step 1 **Cancel P Ltd's investment in S Ltd against the share capital of S Ltd.**

Consolidation has the effect of replacing the cost of the investment with the net assets that it represents.

P Ltd bought the whole of the share capital of S Ltd for £5,000,000, its nominal value. The two items cancel exactly.

Step 2 **Add the individual assets and liabilities of P Ltd and S Ltd together.**

The share capital of the subsidiary never appears in the consolidated statement of financial position.

Consolidated statement of financial position as at 31 December 20X0

	£'000
Property, plant and equipment (25,000 + 4,000)	29,000
Current assets (30,000 + 16,000)	46,000
	75,000
Share capital (P Ltd only)	20,000
Retained earnings (30,000 + 5,000)	35,000
	55,000
Current liabilities (10,000 + 10,000)	20,000
	75,000

Dealing with goodwill

In practice, where a parent acquires a subsidiary the cost of the investment is almost always more than the total fair value of the subsidiary's individual assets and liabilities. The difference represents goodwill.

IFRS 3 defines GOODWILL more formally as: an asset representing the future economic benefits arising from other assets acquired in a business combination that are not individually identified and separately recognised.

IFRS 3 states that goodwill acquired in a business combination must be recognised as an asset.

- Unlike many other intangible assets, goodwill is not amortised.

- Instead it is carried in the statement of financial position at its cost less any accumulated impairment losses.

- It must be tested for impairment annually, or more frequently if there are any indications that it might be impaired.

- IAS 36 *Impairment of Assets* explains how to carry out an impairment review (see Chapter 7).

HOW IT WORKS

On 1 January 20X0 P Ltd acquired 100% of the issued ordinary share capital of S Ltd. S Ltd was incorporated on that date. At 31 December 20X0, the individual company statements of financial position were as follows:

	P Ltd	S Ltd
	£'000	£'000
Property, plant and equipment	25,000	4,000
Investment in S Ltd	10,000	–
Current assets	30,000	16,000
	65,000	20,000
Share capital	20,000	5,000
Retained earnings	35,000	5,000
	55,000	10,000
Current liabilities	10,000	10,000
	65,000	20,000

Calculate goodwill:

	£'000
Cost of investment in S Ltd (price paid)	10,000
Less: net assets acquired	(5,000)
	5,000

The individual assets and liabilities are added together to produce the consolidated statement of financial position.

Consolidated statement of financial position as at 31 December 20X0

	£'000
Intangible assets: goodwill	5,000
Property, plant and equipment (25,000 + 4,000)	29,000
Current assets (30,000 + 16,000)	46,000
	80,000
Share capital (P Ltd only)	20,000
Retained earnings (35,000 + 5,000)	40,000
	60,000
Current liabilities (10,000 + 10,000)	20,000
	80,000

Impairment of goodwill

In the example above, P Ltd would have reviewed the goodwill for impairment at 31 December 20X0 (one year after acquisition). We assumed that the goodwill was not impaired.

If goodwill is impaired, intangible assets and the retained earnings reserve are both reduced by the amount of the impairment loss.

HOW IT WORKS

Suppose that in the example above, goodwill had been tested for impairment and found to have suffered an impairment loss of 20% of its original cost.

Calculate goodwill:

	£'000
Cost of investment in S Ltd (price paid)	10,000
Less: net assets acquired	(5,000)
	5,000
Less: impairment (20% × 5,000)	(1,000)
	4,000

Consolidated retained earnings are also reduced by £1,000,000.

Consolidated statement of financial position as at 31 December 20X0

	£'000
Intangible assets: goodwill (5,000 – 1,000)	4,000
Property, plant and equipment (25,000 + 4,000)	29,000
Current assets (30,000 + 16,000)	46,000
	79,000
Share capital (P Ltd only)	20,000
Retained earnings (35,000 + 5,000 – 1,000)	39,000
	59,000
Current liabilities (10,000 + 10,000)	20,000
	79,000

Pre-acquisition profits and post-acquisition profits

A parent may acquire a subsidiary that has already been trading for some time. This means that the parent's interest includes retained profits, as well as share capital.

Consolidated financial statements only include profits made by the group. Profits made by the subsidiary before the acquisition were not made by the group; instead they are part of the net assets acquired so belong in the goodwill calculation.

Pre-acquisition profits must be excluded from the consolidated retained earnings reserve.

HOW IT WORKS

On 1 January 20X4 A Ltd acquired 100% of the issued ordinary share capital of B Ltd. On that date, the retained earnings reserve of B Ltd was £10,000,000. At 31 December 20X4, the statements of financial position of A Ltd and B Ltd were as follows:

	A Ltd £'000	B Ltd £'000
Property, plant and equipment	50,000	10,000
Investment in B Ltd	25,000	–
Current assets	40,000	25,000
	115,000	35,000
Share capital	25,000	10,000
Retained earnings	75,000	15,000
	100,000	25,000
Current liabilities	15,000	10,000
	115,000	35,000

Step 1 Calculate goodwill

The net assets acquired consist of B Ltd's share capital plus its retained profits at the date of acquisition.

	£'000	£'000
Cost of investment (price paid)		25,000
Less: net assets acquired		
Share capital	10,000	
Retained earnings	10,000	
		(20,000)
Goodwill		5,000

Step 2 Calculate the consolidated retained earnings reserve

This consists of the retained earnings of A Ltd, plus the post-acquisition profits of B Ltd.

	£'000	£'000
A Ltd		75,000
B Ltd: at 31 December 20X4	15,000	
Less: at acquisition	(10,000)	
		5,000
Group retained earnings		80,000

Step 3 **Prepare the consolidated statement of financial position**

Consolidated statement of financial position as at 31 December 20X4

	£'000
Intangible assets: goodwill	5,000
Property, plant and equipment	60,000
Current assets	65,000
	130,000
Share capital	25,000
Retained earnings (as above)	80,000
	105,000
Current liabilities	25,000
	130,000

Task 2

The following information relates to Church Ltd and Steeple Ltd:

	Church Ltd £'000	Steeple Ltd £'000
Share capital (£1 ordinary shares)	480	400
Retained earnings at 1 January 20X5	1,080	600
Profit for the year ended 31 December 20X5	96	50

On 1 January 20X5 Church Ltd purchased 100% of the ordinary share capital of Steeple Ltd for £1,000,000.

Calculate consolidated retained earnings at 31 December 20X5.

£

Non-controlling interests

The consolidated statement of financial position includes 100% of the subsidiary's individual assets and liabilities. This reflects the fact that the parent controls the subsidiary and therefore controls its assets and liabilities.

Suppose that the parent owns 80% of the subsidiary's equity share capital. This means that it controls 100% of the subsidiary's assets and liabilities, but it only owns 80% of them.

Equity (share capital and reserves) is analysed to show:

- The group's share
- The share owned by other shareholders

The part of the equity share capital and reserves not owned by the parent is the **non-controlling interest**.

IFRS 3 contains a more formal definition:

- NON-CONTROLLING INTEREST is the equity in a subsidiary not attributable, directly or indirectly, to a parent.

The non-controlling interest in the net assets of the subsidiary is shown on a separate line within equity:

	£
Equity attributable to owners of the parent:	
Share capital	X
Retained earnings	X̲
	X
Non-controlling interest	X̲
Total equity	X̲

The sub-total below retained earnings shows the equity that 'belongs' to the parent.

Calculating goodwill where there is a non-controlling interest

In simple terms, goodwill is the difference between the cost of the parent's investment in a subsidiary and the fair value of the net assets acquired.

Where there is a non-controlling interest, IFRS 3 states that goodwill is calculated as:

	£
Consideration transferred (ie, cost of investment)	X
Plus: non-controlling interest	X
Less: fair value of net assets acquired	(X)
Goodwill	X̲

IFRS 3 allows the non-controlling interest to be measured as either:

- The proportionate share of the fair value of the subsidiary's net assets, or
- Fair value

The proportionate share of net assets means that the non-controlling interest is measured at its share of the subsidiary's net assets at acquisition. So, if the non-controlling interest owned 20% of a subsidiary, then it would be measured at 20% of the net assets at the date of acquisition.

Unusually, an entity does not have to choose one method and then apply it to every business combination. For example, if A plc acquired 80% of the shares in B Ltd and then 75% of the shares in C Ltd it could measure the non-controlling interest in B Ltd at the proportionate share of B Ltd's net assets and the non-controlling interest in C Ltd at fair value.

The first method (proportionate share of subsidiary's net assets) is the method that is normally used and this is the method that you will be expected to use in the assessment.

In the examples in this book, you should always assume that non-controlling interests are measured at the proportionate share of the subsidiary's net assets.

HOW IT WORKS

On 1 January 20X4 A Ltd acquired 8,000,000 ordinary shares in B Ltd. On that date, the retained earnings reserve of B Ltd was £10,000,000. At 31 December 20X4, the statements of financial position of A Ltd and B Ltd were as follows:

	A Ltd £'000	B Ltd £'000
Property, plant and equipment	50,000	10,000
Investment in B Ltd	25,000	–
Current assets	40,000	25,000
	115,000	35,000
Share capital (£1 ordinary shares)	25,000	10,000
Retained earnings	75,000	15,000
	100,000	25,000
Current liabilities	15,000	10,000
	115,000	35,000

Step 1   Establish the group structure

A Ltd owns 80% (8,000/10,000) of the equity share capital of B Ltd.

Step 2   Calculate goodwill

Because there is a non-controlling interest, goodwill is calculated as the cost of the investment **plus the non-controlling interest**, less the net assets acquired.

The non-controlling interest (NCI) is measured as the non-controlling interest's share of B Ltd's net assets at the date of acquisition.

	£'000	£'000
Consideration transferred (price paid)		25,000
Plus: non-controlling interest:		
Fair value of net assets acquired:		
Share capital	10,000	
Retained earnings	10,000	
NCI share (20%)	20,000	4,000
Less: fair value of net assets acquired		(20,000)
		9,000

Where this method of measuring non-controlling interest is used, goodwill can also be calculated as the cost of the investment (consideration transferred) less the group share of the net assets acquired:

	£'000
Cost of investment (price paid)	25,000
Less: fair value of net assets acquired	
Share capital attributable to parent (80% × 10,000)	(8,000)
Retained earnings attributable to parent (80% × 10,000)	(8,000)
	9,000

This is the way that you will be expected to calculate goodwill in the Assessment.

Step 3   Calculate the consolidated retained earnings reserve

The consolidated retained earnings reserve only includes the **group share** of post-acquisition profits.

	£'000	£'000
A Ltd		75,000
B Ltd: at 31 December 20X4	15,000	
Less: at acquisition	(10,000)	
Group share (80%)	5,000	4,000
		79,000

Step 4   Calculate the non-controlling interest

This is the non-controlling interest's share of the net assets of B Ltd at the reporting date.

	£'000
Share capital attributable to NCI (20% × 10,000)	2,000
Retained earnings attributable to NCI (20% × 15,000)	3,000
	5,000

Step 5   Prepare the consolidated statement of financial position

Consolidated statement of financial position as at 31 December 20X4

	£'000
Intangible assets: goodwill (Step 2)	9,000
Property, plant and equipment	60,000
Current assets	65,000
	134,000
Share capital	25,000
Retained earnings (Step 3)	79,000
	104,000
Non-controlling interest (Step 4)	5,000
	109,000
Current liabilities	25,000
	134,000

In the assessment, you will be given a pro-forma statement to complete. You will also be given pro-forma workings for goodwill, consolidated retained earnings, non-controlling interests and possibly other figures. These will be in a similar format to the workings above. You do not have to use these workings, but any data entered into them will be taken into account if the final figures in the consolidated statement of financial position are incorrect.

Some pro-forma workings will ask you to select the correct items from a 'pick-list' ('drop-down' list). The terminology used in the workings may vary slightly from task to task. For example, the working for goodwill includes a line for the cost of the investment. In examples, tasks and questions in this Text we normally use the terms 'Cost of investment' or 'Price paid', but you may also see 'Consideration transferred' (the term used in IFRS 3) or 'Consideration'.

Task 3

Thatch Ltd acquired 600,000 £1 ordinary shares in Straw Ltd for £4,000,000 on 1 January 20X2. At that date, the capital and reserves of Straw Ltd were:

	£'000
Share capital (£1 ordinary shares)	1,000
Retained earnings	5,000
	6,000

Calculate the amount of goodwill arising on the acquisition.

£

Reflecting fair values

The subsidiary's statement of financial position normally shows its assets and liabilities at their original cost to the subsidiary. This is not necessarily the same as their cost to the parent and the group.

Suppose that P Ltd acquires 100% of the shares in S Ltd. The statement of financial position of S Ltd includes a freehold property which it purchased for £100,000 some years ago. The market value of the property (its fair value) is now £150,000.

The statement of financial position of S Ltd records the property at (say) £90,000 (original cost less accumulated depreciation). However, the price that P Ltd has paid for its investment in S Ltd reflects the fact that the fair value of the property is now £150,000. It would be incorrect to include the property in the consolidated statement of financial position at £90,000.

IFRS 3 states that the identifiable assets and liabilities of a subsidiary that are acquired by a parent should be recognised in the consolidated financial statements at their **fair values** at the date of the acquisition.

- FAIR VALUE is the amount for which an asset could be exchanged, or a liability settled between knowledgeable, willing parties in an arm's length transaction.

There are two reasons why fair value adjustments are required:

- The consolidated statement of financial position includes all the assets and liabilities controlled by the group (the parent's own assets and liabilities plus the assets and liabilities of the subsidiary). The group has purchased these assets and liabilities and so the consolidated statement of financial position should reflect their cost to the group.

- The goodwill calculation is based on the fair values of the identifiable assets and liabilities acquired. If the subsidiary's assets and liabilities are not adjusted to fair value, goodwill will be over-stated.

Note that fair value adjustments **only** affect the consolidated financial statements. The subsidiary continues to record assets at their book values (carrying amounts) in its own financial statements.

The consideration transferred (cost of the investment) must also be recognised at its fair value. For example, if all or part of the consideration is in the form of shares in the parent, these are included in the goodwill calculation at their market value.

HOW IT WORKS

On 1 January 20X6, P Ltd acquired 100% of the ordinary shares in S Ltd. At that date the retained earnings of S Ltd were £140,000,000. On 31 December 20X6, the summarised statements of financial position of the two companies were as follows:

	P Ltd	S Ltd
	£'000	£'000
Net assets	540,000	252,000
Investment in S Ltd	280,000	
	820,000	252,000
Share capital	400,000	50,000
Retained earnings	420,000	202,000
	820,000	252,000

At 1 January 20X6 the fair values of the assets and liabilities of S Ltd were equal to their book values with one exception. Some land that had a carrying amount (book value) of £90,000,000 had a fair value of £120,000,000.

Step 1   Calculate goodwill

The net assets acquired must be increased by £30,000,000 (the difference between the book value/carrying amount and the fair value of the land).

	£'000	£'000
Price paid		280,000
Less: Fair value of net assets acquired:		
Share capital	50,000	
Retained earnings at acquisition	140,000	
Fair value adjustment (120,000 – 90,000)	30,000	
		(220,000)
		60,000

Step 2   Calculate group net assets (excluding goodwill)

These include S Ltd's land and therefore the total must take account of the fair value adjustment of £30,000,000.

	£'000	£'000
P Ltd		540,000
S Ltd:		
Carrying amount	252,000	
Fair value adjustment	30,000	
		282,000
		822,000

Step 3 **Calculate consolidated retained earnings**

The fair value adjustment of £30,000,000 is included in pre-acquisition reserves (as a revaluation surplus).

	£'000	£'000
P Ltd		420,000
S Ltd:		
At 31 December 20X6	202,000	
At acquisition	(140,000)	
		62,000
		482,000

Consolidated statement of financial position as at 31 December 20X6

	£'000
Goodwill	60,000
Other net assets	822,000
	882,000
Share capital	400,000
Retained earnings	482,000
	882,000

Recognising the subsidiary's identifiable assets and liabilities

At the acquisition date, a parent (an acquirer) should recognise:

- All the subsidiary's identifiable assets that it has acquired
- All the liabilities that it has assumed
- Any non-controlling interest

in the consolidated financial statements, provided that they meet the definitions of assets and liabilities in the *Conceptual Framework for Financial Reporting*:

- An asset is recognised if it is probable that any associated future economic benefits will flow to the acquirer; and its fair value can be measured reliably.

- A liability is recognised if it is probable that an outflow of resources embodying economic benefits will be required to settle the obligation; and its fair value can be measured reliably.

If an asset is IDENTIFIABLE, it is either:

- Separable (capable of being separated or divided from the rest of the business and sold or otherwise disposed of); or

- It arises from contractual or other legal rights, whether or not these rights are themselves separable or transferable.

At first sight, this appears to be different from the normal rules for recognising an item in the financial statements. There is no requirement for an item to be capable of being measured reliably at a monetary amount.

This means that there are two exceptions to the normal rules for recognising assets and liabilities:

- Intangible assets acquired are normally recognised even if they are not included in the subsidiary's statement of financial position because they were internally generated. (IAS 38 prohibits the recognition of most internally generated assets).

- IFRS 3 states that contingent liabilities of the subsidiary are recognised if they exist at the date of the acquisition. (IAS 37 normally prohibits their recognition).

The reason why these items are recognised in the consolidated financial statements is that the parent has purchased its investment in the subsidiary and the purchase price takes the existence of items such as internally generated intangibles and contingent liabilities into account. Therefore they **can** be reliably measured at the price that the acquirer is willing to pay for them (or to assume them, in the case of contingent liabilities).

Notice that an entity only recognises assets and liabilities that exist **at the acquisition date**. Once a subsidiary has been acquired, the acquirer often restructures its operations, for example, by closing a loss-making division. An acquirer cannot recognise a liability for the costs of restructuring, because these are not liabilities at the acquisition date. Instead, they must be recognised as expenses in the period in which the restructuring occurs.

IFRS 3 states that the identifiable assets acquired and liabilities assumed must be part of what the acquirer and the acquiree exchanged as part of the business combination. Any assets and liabilities transferred in separate transactions (for example, goods sold by one entity to the other) should not be included in the goodwill calculation.

Bargain purchases

Sometimes the fair value of the identifiable net assets acquired is greater than the cost of the investment. IFRS 3 describes this as a **bargain purchase**.

For example, an entity might acquire a subsidiary cheaply in a forced sale (where the seller acts under compulsion).

Bargain purchases are relatively **rare**.

In a bargain purchase, the difference between the fair value of the net assets acquired and the consideration transferred is often called a GAIN ON A BARGAIN PURCHASE (or NEGATIVE GOODWILL).

IFRS 3 states that this should be recognised as a **gain** in profit or loss on the acquisition date.

Task 4

The following information relates to Valencia Ltd and Vella Ltd

	Valencia Ltd £'000	Vella Ltd £'000
Share capital (£1 ordinary shares)	500	200
Retained earnings at 1 January 20X6	1,250	500
Profit for the year ended 31 December 20X6	110	60

On 1 January 20X6 Valencia Ltd purchased 90% of the ordinary share capital of Vella Ltd for £600,000.

Calculate consolidated retained earnings at 31 December 20X6.

£

INTRA-GROUP ADJUSTMENTS

Group companies normally enter into transactions with each other. These may include:

- Sales by one group company to another
- Loans by one group company to another
- Receipts and payments of dividends.

Consolidated financial statements reflect the financial performance and position of the group as if it were a single economic entity. Therefore:

- The effect of any intra-group transactions must be eliminated from the consolidated financial statements (because the group cannot trade with itself)

- Any balances due to or from another group company must be eliminated from the statement of financial position (because the group cannot owe money to itself or be owed money from itself)

Intra-group balances

If one group company sells goods to another there may be trade receivables and trade payables that relate to group companies at the year-end.

These are cancelled against each other on consolidation.

Task 5

X Ltd owns 80% of the equity share capital of Y Ltd. At the year-end X Ltd has trade receivables of £20,000 and Y Ltd has trade receivables of £15,000. The trade receivables of Y Ltd include an amount of £1,500 which is due from X Ltd.

Calculate the amount for trade receivables included in the consolidated statement of financial position.

£ [   ]

 Intra-group sales

Suppose that P Ltd sells goods costing £10,000 to its subsidiary S Ltd for £20,000.

- The revenue of P Ltd and the cost of sales of S Ltd both increase by £20,000.

- P Ltd makes a profit of £10,000 on the sale.

At the year-end S Ltd still has half the goods in inventory.

- Although P Ltd has made a profit of £10,000 as a result of the sale, **the group** has only made a profit of £5,000 (10,000 ÷ 2) which is the profit on the sale of goods to parties outside of the group.

- The goods which S Ltd still has in inventory are valued at their cost to S Ltd of £10,000 which includes the profit made by P Ltd on the transaction. The cost of the inventory **to the group** is the price that P Ltd originally paid for the goods: £5,000 (10,000 ÷ 2).

- From the perspective of the **group**, both inventories and profits are over-stated.

The profit on the sale of the goods to S Ltd which still remain in inventory at the year-end cannot be recognised as it is not yet realised. This is because we view the group as a **single economic entity.** The group cannot sell goods to itself. Profit can only be recognised once the goods have left the group.

Therefore the following adjustment must be made in the consolidated statement of financial position:

DEBIT   Consolidated retained earnings   £5,000

CREDIT   Inventories   £5,000

HOW IT WORKS

Perch Ltd acquired 80% of the equity share capital of Sild Ltd many years ago. At the date of acquisition the retained earnings reserve of Sild Ltd was £200,000. The statements of financial position of the two companies at 31 December 20X7 are shown below:

	Perch Ltd £'000	Sild Ltd £'000
Assets		
Non-current assets		
Property, plant and equipment	1,000	600
Investment in S Ltd	400	–
	1,400	600
Current assets:		
Inventories	200	150
Trade and other receivables	200	100
Cash	60	40
	460	290
Total assets	1,860	890
Equity and liabilities		
Equity		
Share capital	500	100
Retained earnings	1,160	640
Total equity	1,660	740
Current liabilities:		
Trade payables	200	150
Total equity and liabilities	1,860	890

The following information is relevant:

- During the year, Perch Ltd sold goods costing £20,000 to Sild Ltd for £25,000. At 31 December 20X7 all of these goods were still included in the inventories of Sild Ltd.

Step 1   **Calculate goodwill**

	£'000	£'000
Price paid		400
Less: Fair value of net assets acquired		
Share capital attributable to Perch Ltd		
(80% × 100)	80	
Retained earnings attributable to Perch Ltd		
(80% × 200)	160	
		(240)
		160

Step 2   **Calculate the provision for unrealised profit**

Unrealised profit on goods sold to		
Sild Ltd (25,000 – 20,000)	£5,000	
Adjustment required:		
DEBIT Consolidated retained	£5,000	
Earnings		
CREDIT Inventories		£5,000

Step 3   **Calculate the consolidated retained earnings**

	£'000	£'000
Perch Ltd		1,160
Less: provision for unrealised profit		(5)
Sild Ltd	640	
Less: pre-acquisition	(200)	
	440	
Group share (80%)		352
		1,507

Step 4   **Calculate the non-controlling interest**

	£'000
Share capital attributable to NCI (20% × 100)	20
Retained earnings attributable to NCI (20% × 640)	128
	148

Step 5   **Prepare the consolidated statement of financial position**

	£'000	£'000
Assets		
Non-current assets		
Intangible: Goodwill (Step 1)		160
Property, plant and equipment		1,600
		1,760
Current assets		
Inventories (200 + 150 – 5)	345	
Trade and other receivables	300	
Cash	100	
		745
Total assets		2,505
Equity and liabilities		
Equity attributable to owners of		
the parent		
Share capital		500
Retained earnings (Step 3)		1,507
		2,007
Non-controlling interest (Step 4)		148
Total equity		2,155
Current liabilities:		
Trade payables		350
Total equity and liabilities		2,505

BPP
LEARNING MEDIA

Task 6

Kilvert Ltd owns 60% of the issued share capital of Woodford Ltd. At the year-end, their statements of financial position showed inventories of £100,000 and £50,000 respectively. Kilvert Ltd sells goods to Woodford Ltd at a mark-up of 25% on cost. At the year-end, goods which had been purchased from Kilvert Ltd for £30,000 remained in the inventories of Woodford Ltd.

Calculate the amount of inventories that should be recognised in the consolidated statement of financial position of the group at the year-end.

£ [   ]

Sales from the subsidiary to the parent

Suppose that in the example above, Sild Ltd sells the goods to Perch Ltd.

- The unrealised profit arises in the accounts of Sild Ltd, instead of the accounts of Perch Ltd.

- The adjustment for unrealised profit affects both the group and the non-controlling interest.

HOW IT WORKS

During the year, Sild Ltd sold goods costing £20,000 to Perch Ltd for £25,000. At 31 December 20X7 all these goods were still included in the inventories of Perch Ltd.

As before:

- Unrealised profit on goods sold to Perch Ltd   £5,000

Adjustment required:

DEBIT	Consolidated retained earnings	£4,000
	(£5,000 × 80%)	
DEBIT	Non-controlling interest	£1,000
	(£5,000 × 20%)	
CREDIT	Inventories	£5,000

In the consolidated statement of financial position, the figure for inventories is the same as before, when the parent made the unrealised profit. The figures for consolidated retained earnings and non-controlling interest are different as the unrealised profit is allocated between the group and the non-controlling interest.

Consolidated retained earnings

	£'000	£'000
Perch Ltd		1,160
Sild Ltd (640 less unrealised profit 5)	635	
Less: pre-acquisition	(200)	
	435	
Group share (80%)		348
		1,508

Non-controlling interest

	£'000
Share capital attributable to NCI (20% × 100)	20
Retained earnings attributable to NCI (20% × 640 - 5)	127
	147

CHAPTER OVERVIEW

- A group of companies consists of a parent (holding) company and one or more subsidiaries under the control of the parent

- A parent must prepare consolidated financial statements for its group

- An entity is a subsidiary of another (the parent) if that other entity can control it

- Control exists where:

  - The parent owns more than half the voting power of an entity; or where it has:

  - Power over more than half of the voting rights by virtue of an agreement with other investors;

  - Power to govern the financial and operating policies of the entity under a statute or an agreement;

  - Power to appoint or remove the majority of the members of the board of directors; or

  - Power to cast the majority of votes at meetings of the board of directors.

- To prepare a consolidated statement of financial position:

  (1) Calculate the proportion of the subsidiary's shares owned by the parent

  (2) Calculate goodwill: consideration transferred (cost of investment) plus non-controlling interest less net assets acquired

  (3) Calculate consolidated retained earnings reserve: parent plus group share of post acquisition reserves of subsidiary

  (4) Calculate non-controlling interest: non-controlling interest's share of net assets of subsidiary at year-end

  (5) Complete the consolidated statement of financial position by adding the parent's assets and liabilities and the subsidiary's assets and liabilities together, line by line

- Goodwill is recognised as an asset and carried at cost. It must be reviewed for impairment at least annually

- Non-controlling interest at acquisition is normally measured at the proportionate share of the fair value of the subsidiary's net assets

- The identifiable assets and liabilities of a subsidiary are included in the consolidated financial statements at their fair values at the date of the acquisition

CHAPTER OVERVIEW CONTINUED

- Adjustment to eliminate unrealised profit on intra-group sales:
  Sale from parent to subsidiary

  DEBIT   Consolidated retained earnings

  CREDIT   Inventories

  Sale from subsidiary to parent

  DEBIT   Consolidated retained earnings (group share)

  DEBIT   Non-controlling interest (non-controlling interest's share)

  CREDIT   Inventories

Keywords

Group – a **parent (holding) company** and all its **subsidiaries**

Consolidation – the process of adjusting and combining financial information from the individual financial statements of a parent and its subsidiary to prepare consolidated financial statements

Consolidated financial statements – the financial statements of a group presented as those of a single economic entity

Business combination – a transaction or other event in which an acquirer obtains control of one or more businesses

Business – an integrated set of activities and assets that is capable of being conducted and managed for the purpose of providing a return in the form of dividends, lower costs or other economic benefits directly to investors or other owners

Parent – an entity that has one or more subsidiaries

Subsidiary – an entity that is controlled by another entity (the parent)

Acquiree – the business that the acquirer obtains control of in a business combination

Acquirer – the entity that obtains control of the acquiree

Control – the power to govern the financial and operating policies of an entity or business so as to obtain benefits from its activities

Goodwill – an asset representing the future economic benefits arising from other assets acquired in a business combination that are not individually identified and separately recognised

Non-controlling interest – the equity in a subsidiary not attributable to the parent

Fair value – the amount for which an asset could be exchanged, or a liability settled between knowledgeable, willing parties in an arm's length transaction

Identifiable – either separable; or arising from contractual or other legal rights

Gain on a bargain purchase (negative goodwill) – the excess of the fair value of the net assets acquired over the consideration transferred

TEST YOUR LEARNING

Test 1

A plc owns the following investments in other companies:

- B Ltd: 15% of the ordinary shares and 80% of the preference shares
- C Ltd: 80% of the ordinary shares
- D Ltd: 45% of the ordinary shares
- E Ltd: 25% of the ordinary shares and 60% of the loan stock

A plc has the right to appoint three of the four directors of D Ltd.

Which of the four companies are subsidiaries of A plc?

C Ltd only	
B Ltd and C Ltd	
C Ltd and D Ltd	
All four companies	

Test 2

The directors of Sella Ltd are considering acquiring a significant investment of equity shares in another company.

Prepare brief notes for the directors of Sella Ltd to answer the following questions:

(a) What is a subsidiary, according to IAS 27 *Consolidated and Separate Financial Statements*?

(b) Under what circumstances does one company control another?

Test 3

The summarised consolidated statements of financial position of Left plc and Right Ltd as at 31 December 20X9 were as follows:

	Left plc	*Right Ltd*
	£'000	£'000
Investment in Right Ltd	9,000	–
Other assets	45,000	15,000
	54,000	15,000
Share capital	10,000	5,000
Retained earnings	28,000	3,000
	38,000	8,000
Liabilities	16,000	7,000
	54,000	15,000

On 1 January 20X9 Left plc acquired 95% of the share capital of Right Ltd for £9,000,000 in cash. At that date the retained earnings of Right Ltd were £2,000,000. There is no impairment of goodwill.

(a)　How much goodwill arose on the combination?

£1,000,000	
£1,400,000	
£2,000,000	
£2,350,000	

(b)　What amount should be recognised as consolidated retained earnings at 31 December 20X9?

£28,950,000	
£29,000,000	
£30,850,000	
£31,000,000	

(c)　What amount should be recognised as non-controlling interest at 31 December 20X9?

£250,000	
£300,000	
£350,000	
£400,000	

Test 4

Explain why the assets and liabilities of an acquired subsidiary should be adjusted to fair value before they are included in the consolidated statement of financial position.

Test 5

Grand plc sells goods which cost £15,000 to its 100% subsidiary, Small Ltd, for £20,000. None of these goods remain in the inventories of Small Ltd at the year-end.

No adjustment for unrealised profit is required in the consolidated financial statement of financial position.

Is this statement true or false?

True	
False	

Test 6

The following statements of financial position relate to Salt plc and its subsidiary, Pepper Ltd, at 31 March 20X7:

	Salt plc £'000	Pepper Ltd £'000
Assets		
Non-current assets:		
Property, plant and equipment	8,000	6,000
Investment in Pepper Ltd	4,000	–
	12,000	6,000
Current assets:		
Inventories	2,400	1,440
Trade and other receivables	2,640	2,400
Cash and cash equivalents	480	360
	5,520	4,200
Total assets	17,520	10,200
Equity and liabilities		
Equity		
Share capital (£1 ordinary shares)	5,000	1,000
Retained earnings	7,960	6,200
Total equity	12,960	7,200
Non-current liabilities	1,200	1,080
Current liabilities:		
Trade payables	2,500	1,700
Tax payable	860	220
	3,360	1,920
Total liabilities	4,560	3,000
Total equity and liabilities	17,520	10,200

Additional data:

(1) Salt plc purchased 800,000 ordinary shares in Pepper Ltd on 1 April 20X5 when the retained earnings reserve of Pepper Ltd was £2,500,000.

(2) At 31 March 20X7, the trade payables of Salt plc included £960,000 which was owed to Pepper Ltd.

Required

Prepare the consolidated statement of financial position of Salt plc and its subsidiary as at 31 March 20X7.

Consolidated statement of financial position as at 31 March 20X7

	£'000
Assets	
Non-current assets:	
Intangible assets: Goodwill	
Property, plant and equipment	
Current assets:	
Inventories	
Trade and other receivables	
Cash and cash equivalents	
Total assets	
Equity and liabilities	
Equity attributable to owners of the parent	
Share capital	
Retained earnings	
Non-controlling interest	
Total equity	
Non-current liabilities	
Current liabilities:	
Trade payables	
Tax payable	
Total liabilities	
Total equity and liabilities	

Workings

(Complete the left hand column by writing in the correct narrative from the list provided.)

Goodwill		£'000
	▼	
	▼	
	▼	

Picklist:

Price paid
Retained earnings attributable to Salt plc
Share capital attributable to Salt plc

Retained earnings		£'000
	▼	
	▼	

Picklist:

Pepper Ltd attributable to Salt plc
Salt plc

Non-controlling interest		£'000
	▼	
	▼	

Picklist:

Current assets attributable to NCI
Non-current assets attributable to NCI
Price paid
Retained earnings attributable to NCI
Share capital attributable to NCI

chapter 11:
GROUP ACCOUNTS: FURTHER ASPECTS

---

chapter coverage 📖

This chapter explains how to prepare a consolidated statement of comprehensive income and looks at a number of further aspects of group accounts.

The topics covered are:

✍ The consolidated statement of comprehensive income

✍ Groups: further points

✍ Associates

THE CONSOLIDATED STATEMENT OF COMPREHENSIVE INCOME

The basic idea

As for the consolidated statement of financial position, there are basically two steps:

- Add together the statements of the parent and the subsidiary
- Make adjustments to cancel out intra-group items

HOW IT WORKS

P Ltd has owned 80% of the share capital of S Ltd for many years. The individual company statements of comprehensive income for the year ended 31 December 20X0 are shown below:

	P Ltd £'000	S Ltd £'000
Continuing operations		
Revenue	100,000	50,000
Cost of sales	(50,000)	(25,000)
Gross profit	50,000	25,000
Other income (dividend from S Ltd)	4,000	–
Operating expenses	(30,000)	(10,000)
Profit before tax	24,000	15,000
Tax	(7,000)	(4,000)
Profit for the year	17,000	11,000

During the year, S Ltd paid a dividend of £5,000,000.

Step 1   Add together the statements of the parent and the subsidiary, line by line, from revenue to profit for the year

- This reflects the fact that the parent **controls** 100% of the results of the subsidiary, even though it only owns 80% of the equity shares.

- The investment income is P Ltd's share of S Ltd's dividend (80% × £5,000,000). This is not included in the consolidated statement of comprehensive income. Intra-group dividends are eliminated on consolidation.

	£'000
Revenue	150,000
Cost of sales	(75,000)
Gross profit	75,000
Operating expenses	(40,000)
Profit before tax	35,000
Tax	(11,000)
Profit for the year	24,000

Step 2 Deal with the non-controlling interest

- Calculate the non-controlling interest's share of profit for the year in the accounts of the subsidiary: £2,200,000 (20% × 11,000,000).

- Therefore the profit for the year attributable to the group is the total profit for the year less the non-controlling interest: £21,800,000 (24,000,000 – 2,200,000).

- Profit for the year is analysed between profits owned by the non-controlling interest and profits owned by the group. The analysis is shown at the foot of the consolidated statement of comprehensive income.

Attributable to:	£'000
Equity holders of the parent (bal fig)	21,800
Non-controlling interest (20% × 11,000)	2,200
	24,000

Consolidated statement of comprehensive income for the year ended 31 December 20X0

	£'000
Continuing operations	
Revenue	150,000
Cost of sales	(75,000)
Gross profit	75,000
Operating expenses	(40,000)
Profit before tax	35,000
Tax	(11,000)
Profit for the year from continuing operations	24,000
Attributable to:	
	£'000
Equity holders of the parent	21,800
Non-controlling interest (20% × 11,000)	2,200
	24,000

Goodwill

Any impairment loss is normally included in administrative expenses.

Intra-group interest

Interest payable by one group company to another is cancelled against interest receivable in the statement of comprehensive income of the other company.

Task 1

Thatch plc owns 75% of the issued share capital of Slate Ltd.

Extracts from statements of comprehensive income for the year ended 30 June 20X9:

	Thatch plc	Slate Ltd
	£'000	£'000
Profit from operations	685	90
Dividends received from Slate Ltd	15	–
Profit before tax	700	90
Tax	(150)	(30)
Profit for the year	550	60

Prepare the consolidated statement of comprehensive income for Thatch plc and its subsidiary, for the year ended 30 June 20X9.

Consolidated statement of comprehensive income for the year ended 30 June 20X9 (extract):

	£'000
Profit before tax	
Tax	
Profit for the year from continuing operations	
Attributable to:	
Equity holders of the parent	
Non-controlling interests	

Intra-group sales

Suppose that P Ltd sells goods costing £10,000 to its subsidiary S Ltd for £20,000.

- The revenue of P Ltd and the cost of sales of S Ltd both increase by £20,000.

- P Ltd makes a profit of £10,000 on the sale.

At the year-end S Ltd still has half the goods in inventory.

From the perspective **of the group**:

- Revenue and cost of sales are both overstated by £10,000
- Profit is overstated by £5,000 (£10,000 ÷ 2)

Where one company sells goods to another two adjustments must be made to the consolidated statement of comprehensive income:

- Intra-group sales and purchases are cancelled against each other; and
- The unrealised profit is removed.

HOW IT WORKS

Arden Ltd has owned 75% of the share capital of Baker Ltd for many years. The individual company statements of comprehensive income for the year ended 31 December 20X1 are shown below:

	Arden Ltd £'000	Baker Ltd £'000
Continuing operations		
Revenue	6,000	3,000
Cost of sales	(4,000)	(2,000)
Gross profit	2,000	1,000
Operating expenses	(1,000)	(500)
Profit before tax	1,000	500
Tax	(300)	(100)
Profit for the year	700	400

- During the year, Arden Ltd made sales totalling £1,000,000 to Baker Ltd. Arden Ltd made a gross profit of 30% on these sales. All the goods were still in the inventory of Baker Ltd at 31 December 20X1.

Intra-group sales

To cancel the sale from Arden Ltd to Baker Ltd:

DEBIT	Revenue	£1,000,000	
CREDIT	Cost of sales		£1,000,000

Or: **deduct** the sale from consolidated revenue **and** from consolidated cost of sales.

To eliminate the unrealised profit of £300,000 (£1,000,000 × 30%):

DEBIT	Cost of sales (statement of comprehensive income)	£300,000	
CREDIT	Closing inventories (statement of financial position)		£300,000

Closing inventories are **deducted** from cost of sales. Therefore the reduction in closing inventories **increases** cost of sales.

Method of working

Add the statements of comprehensive income of Arden Ltd and Baker Ltd together line by line, making adjustments to cancel:

- Intra-group sales
- Intra-group interest and dividends (if any)

It is helpful to build up the figures for revenue and cost of sales using workings:

Revenue

	£'000
Arden Ltd	6,000
Baker Ltd	3,000
Adjustment: intra-group sale	(1,000)
	(8,000)

Cost of sales

	£'000	£'000
Arden Ltd		4,000
Baker Ltd		2,000
Adjustment: intra-group sale	(1,000)	
Provision for unrealised profit	300	
		(700)
		(5,300)

Consolidated statements of comprehensive income for the year ended 31 December 20X1

	£'000
Continuing operations	
Revenue (W)	8,000
Cost of sales (W)	(5,300)
Gross profit	2,700
Operating expenses (1,000 + 500)	(1,500)
Profit before tax	1,200
Tax (300 + 100)	(400)
Profit for the year from continuing operations	800
Attributable to:	
Equity holders of the parent	700
Non-controlling interest (25% × 400)	100
	800

Intra-group sales from the subsidiary to the parent

Where the subsidiary sells goods to the parent, the profit on sale arises in the subsidiary's accounts. The non-controlling interest must be adjusted for its share of the unrealised profit.

DEBIT   Cost of sales (statement of comprehensive income)

CREDIT   Closing inventories (statement of financial position)
             with the full amount of unrealised profit

The adjustment (above) to the consolidated statement of comprehensive income is the same as we have seen already when the parent made the sale. The difference is that the non-controlling interest's share of income must now be reduced to take account of their share of the unrealised profit:

DEBIT   Non-controlling interest in statement of financial position

CREDIT   Non-controlling interest in statement of comprehensive income
             with the non-controlling interest's share of unrealised profit

HOW IT WORKS

During the year, Baker Ltd made sales totalling £1,000,000 to Arden Ltd. Baker Ltd made a gross profit of 30% on these sales. All the goods were still in the inventory of Arden Ltd at 31 December 20X1.

To cancel the sale from Baker Ltd to Arden Ltd:

DEBIT	Revenue	£1,000,000	
CREDIT	Cost of sales		£1,000,000

To eliminate the unrealised profit of £300,000:

DEBIT	Cost of sales	£300,000	
CREDIT	Closing inventories		£300,000
DEBIT	Non-controlling interest – statement of financial position (25% × 300,000)	£75,000	
CREDIT	Non-controlling interest – statement of comprehensive income		£75,000

Workings

Revenue

	£'000
Arden Ltd	6,000
Baker Ltd	3,000
Adjustment: intra-group sale	(1,000)
	(8,000)

Cost of sales

	£'000	£'000
Arden Ltd		4,000
Baker Ltd		2,000
Adjustment: intra-group sale	(1,000)	
Provision for unrealised profit	300	
		(700)
		(5,300)

Non-controlling interest in statement of comprehensive income:

	£'000
Share of subsidiary's profit after tax (25% × 400)	100
Less: share of unrealised profit (25% × 300)	(75)
	25

Consolidated statement of comprehensive income for the year ended 31 December 20X1

	£'000
Continuing operations	
Revenue (6,000 + 3,000 – 1,000)	8,000
Cost of sales (4,000 + 2,000 – 1,000 + 300)	(5,300)
Gross profit	2,700
Operating expenses (1,000 + 500)	(1,500)
Profit before tax	1,200
Tax (300 + 100)	(400)
Profit for the year from continuing operations	800
Attributable to:	
Equity holders of the parent	775
Non-controlling interest (25% × (400 – 300))	25
	800

Task 2

Timber Ltd is a 100% owned subsidiary of Wood Ltd. During the year, Timber Ltd sold goods that originally cost £30,000 to Wood Ltd for £40,000. At the year-end, half those goods remained in inventory.

What adjustment should be made to the cost of sales figure in the consolidated statement of comprehensive income to reflect this transaction?

Reduce by £25,000	
Reduce by £30,000	
Reduce by £35,000	
Reduce by £40,000	

GROUPS: FURTHER POINTS

Scope of consolidated accounts

IAS 27 states that the consolidated financial statements must include **all** subsidiaries of the parent. Subsidiaries cannot be excluded simply because their activities are very different from those of the parent.

Accounting policies

Consolidated financial statements must be prepared using uniform accounting policies for similar transactions and other events in similar circumstances.

If a subsidiary uses different accounting policies from the parent its financial statements are adjusted before consolidation.

The acquisition method

When two companies combine to form a group, one company (the parent) acquires (takes over) the other (the subsidiary). The shareholders of the parent become the ultimate shareholders of the subsidiary and the parent exercises control over the subsidiary. Almost all business combinations are ACQUISITIONS.

IFRS 3 states that an entity should account for each business combination by using the acquisition method. (In theory there are other methods of accounting for a business combination, but the acquisition method is the only method allowed.)

Applying the acquisition method requires four steps:

- Identifying the acquirer;
- Determining the acquisition date;
- Recognising and measuring the identifiable assets acquired, the liabilities assumed and any non-controlling interest in the acquiree; and
- Recognising and measuring goodwill or a gain from a bargain purchase (negative goodwill).

We have already looked at the last two steps in the previous chapter.

Identifying an acquirer

One of the combining entities must be identified as the acquirer. This is the entity that **obtains control** of the acquiree. IAS 27 *Consolidated and Separate Financial Statements* explains when control is presumed.

It is usually clear which of the two entities is the acquirer. The acquirer is almost always the entity that transfers cash or issues its equity shares to acquire equity shares in the other entity.

Determining the acquisition date

The acquirer should identify the acquisition date, which is the date on which it **obtains control** of the acquiree.

This is usually the date on which the acquirer legally transfers the consideration (eg cash or equity shares), acquires the assets and assumes the liabilities of the acquiree (the closing date).

However, it is possible for the acquirer to obtain control earlier or later than this, for example, by written agreement.

Separate financial statements

SEPARATE FINANCIAL STATEMENTS are the parent's individual financial statements. They show the parent as a separate entity.

IAS 27 applies to separate financial statements where an entity has investments in subsidiaries or in associates. (Associates are covered in the section below.)

- Separate financial statements recognise the parent's investment in the subsidiary as a non-current asset in the statement of financial position.

- The investment is measured either at **cost** or in accordance with IAS 39 (normally at **fair value**). (IAS 39 is not assessable.)

ASSOCIATES

A company can have three types of investment in another company:

- A simple investment: the investor has little or no influence

- A subsidiary: the investor has control

- An associate: the investor does not have control, but can exercise significant influence

Definition

- An ASSOCIATE is an entity over which the investor has **significant influence** and that is not a subsidiary.

- SIGNIFICANT INFLUENCE is the power to participate in the financial and operating policy decisions of the investee but is not control or joint control over those policies.

If an investor holds 20% or more of the voting power of the investee it is presumed that the investor has significant influence unless it can be clearly demonstrated that this is not the case.

If an investor holds less than 20% of the voting power, it is presumed that the investor does not have significant influence, unless it can be clearly demonstrated otherwise.

In most cases, a holding of between 20% and 50% of the equity share capital of a company gives significant influence (but not control).

However:

- It is possible for an investor to exercise significant influence with a shareholding of less than 20%. For example, it might have the right to appoint and remove directors.

- It is possible for an investor to have a shareholding of more than 20% without being able to exercise significant influence. For example, the remainder of the shares might be held by another company.

IAS 28 *Investments in Associates* explains that an investor usually has significant influence if:

- It is represented on the board of directors

- It takes part in policy-making processes, including decisions about dividends and other distributions

- There are material transactions between the investor and the investee

- There is interchange of management personnel

- It provides essential technical information to the investee

The accounting treatment of associates

Associates are not consolidated, as this would imply that the investor has control over their assets and liabilities. However, they are too significant to be treated as simple investments.

IAS 28 states that the EQUITY METHOD should be used.

- At acquisition, the investment is recognised at cost.

- In subsequent periods the value of the investment is adjusted for changes in the investor's share of the net assets of the associate (which are post-acquisition profits and losses).

- The investor's share of the associates' profit or loss is included in the statement of comprehensive income.

The financial statements must be prepared using uniform accounting policies for both investor and associate. If an associate uses different accounting policies from the investor its financial statements are adjusted before consolidation.

In the consolidated statement of financial position

The investment in the associate is recognised as a non-current asset investment and disclosed as a separate line item (as required by IAS 1).

The carrying amount of the investment is:

- Cost; plus

- The investor's (group's) share of the associate's post-acquisition profits and losses.

Alternatively, the carrying amount of the investment can be calculated as:

- The group share of the net assets of the associate; plus
- Any goodwill arising on the acquisition.

Goodwill is the cost of the investment less the parent's (group's) share of the net assets acquired.

In the consolidated statement of comprehensive income

The group share of the associate's profit after tax is included as a separate line item above profit before tax.

HOW IT WORKS

Python Ltd, which has one wholly owned subsidiary, acquired 40% of the issued ordinary share capital of Adder Ltd on 1 January 20X1, when the retained earnings reserve of Adder Ltd stood at £1,000,000. The financial statements of Python Ltd and its subsidiary and Adder Ltd for the year ended 31 December 20X1 are shown below:

Statements of comprehensive income for the year ended 31 December 20X1

	Python group £'000	Adder Ltd £'000
Continuing operations		
Revenue	10,000	2,000
Cost of sales	(7,000)	(1,000)
Gross profit	3,000	1,000
Operating expenses	(2,000)	(500)
Profit before tax	1,000	500
Tax	(300)	(100)
Profit for the year	700	400

Statement of financial position as at 31 December 20X1

	Python group £'000	Adder Ltd £'000
Assets		
Non-current assets		
Property, plant and equipment	10,000	2,000
Investment in Adder Ltd	1,500	–
	11,500	2,000
Current assets:		
Inventories	1,500	400
Trade and other receivables	1,600	500
Cash and cash equivalents	200	100
	3,300	1,000
Total assets	14,800	3,000
Equity and liabilities		
Equity		
Share capital	5,000	1,000
Retained earnings	7,300	1,400
	12,300	2,400
Current liabilities:		
Trade and other payables	2,000	500
Tax liabilities	500	100
	2,500	600
Total equity and liabilities	14,800	3,000

Step 1   Calculate the investment in the associate

	£'000
Cost of investment	1,500
Add: share of associate's profit since acquisition	
(40% × 400)	160
	1,660

Alternative calculation (proof)

	£'000
Group share of net assets at year end (40% × 2,400)	960
Add: goodwill (see below)	700
	1,660

Goodwill:	£'000	£'000
Cost of investment		1,500
Less: net assets acquired:		
Share capital	1,000	
Retained earnings	1,000	
	2,000	
Group share (40%)		(800)
		700

Step 2   **Calculate consolidated retained earnings reserve**

	£'000
Python group	7,300
Add: share of associate's profit since acquisition	
(40% × 400)	160
	7,460

Step 3   **Prepare the consolidated financial statements**

Consolidated statement of comprehensive income for the year ended 31 December 20X1

	£'000
Continuing operations	
Revenue	10,000
Cost of sales	(7,000)
Gross profit	3,000
Operating expenses	(2,000)
Share of profit of associates (40% × 400)	160
Profit before tax	1,160
Tax	(300)
Profit for the year from continuing operations	860

Consolidated statement of financial position as at 31 December 20X1

	£'000	£'000
Assets		
Non-current assets:		
Property, plant and equipment		10,000
Investment in associate (Step 1)		1,660
		11,660
Current assets:		
Inventories	1,500	
Trade and other receivables	1,600	
Cash and cash equivalents	200	
		3,300
Total assets		14,960
Equity and liabilities		
Equity attributable to owners of the parent		
Share capital		5,000
Retained earnings (Step 2)		7,460
		12,460
Current liabilities:		
Trade and other payables	2,000	
Tax liabilities	500	
		2,500
Total equity and liabilities		14,960

Task 3

Plaster Ltd purchased a 30% interest in Paint Ltd for £500,000 on 1 April 20X6 when the total net assets of the company amounted to £1,000,000. Since acquisition Paint Ltd has made profits amounting to £250,000 and at 31 March 20X8, the total net assets of the company amounted to £1,250,000.

Calculate the amount of the investment in Paint Ltd that should be recognised in the group statement of financial position of Plaster Ltd at 31 March 20X8.

£

CHAPTER OVERVIEW

- To prepare a consolidated statement of comprehensive income:

  - Add together the statements of the parent and the subsidiary, line by line

  - Split the profit for the year between the parent and the non-controlling interest

- Where one company sells goods to another two adjustments must be made to the consolidated statement of comprehensive income:

  (1) To eliminate the sale:

    DEBIT   Revenue

    CREDIT   Cost of sales

  (2) To eliminate unrealised profit:

    Increase cost of sales by amount of unrealised profit

    If the sale is from subsidiary to parent, deduct NCI's share of unrealised profit from profit or loss attributable to NCI

- Consolidated financial statements must include all subsidiaries of the parent

- Uniform accounting policies must be used

- All business combinations must be accounted for by applying the acquisition method

- In separate financial statements, the parent's investment in the subsidiary is measured either at cost or at fair value

- Associates are included in the consolidated financial statements using the equity method

- The consolidated statement of financial position includes the group share of the associate's net assets

- The consolidated statement of comprehensive income includes the group share of the associate's profit after tax

Keywords

Acquisition – a business combination in which one company (the parent) acquires and controls the other (the subsidiary)

Separate financial statements – the parent's individual financial statements, showing the parent as a separate entity

Associate – an entity over which the investor has **significant influence** and that is not a subsidiary

Significant influence – the power to participate in the financial and operating policy decisions of the investee

Equity method – a method of accounting whereby the investment is initially recognised at cost and adjusted thereafter for the post-acquisition change in the investor's share of net assets of the investee. The profit or loss of the investor includes the investor's share of the profit or loss of the investee

TEST YOUR LEARNING

Test 1

Explain why adjustments are made in consolidated financial statements when one group company sells goods to another.

Test 2

Stansfield Ltd is a 75% subsidiary of Purton Ltd. An extract from its statement of comprehensive income is shown below:

	£'000
Profit before tax	7,500
Tax	(2,000)
Profit for the year	5,500

During the year, Purton Ltd sold goods to Stansfield Ltd. As a result, inventories in the consolidated statement of financial position have been reduced to reflect unrealised profit of £12,000.

The profit for the year attributable to non-controlling interests is £1,375,000.

Is this statement True or False?

True	
False	

Test 3

Denston Ltd has owned 60% of the share capital of Hawkedon Ltd and 30% of the share capital of Clare Ltd for many years. Revenue for the year ended 30 September 20X9 for each of the three companies was as follows:

	£
Denston Ltd	950,000
Hawkedon Ltd	500,000
Clare Ltd	300,000

What figure for revenue will be reported in the consolidated statement of comprehensive income for the year ended 30 September 20X9?

£1,250,000	
£1,340,000	
£1,450,000	
£1,540,000	

Test 4

Aldeburgh plc has owned 100% of the share capital of Southwold Ltd for many years. Cost of sales for the year ended 31 December 20X9 for each of the two companies was as follows:

	£
Aldeburgh plc	800,000
Southwold Ltd	600,000

During the year Aldeburgh plc sold goods that had originally cost £100,000 to Southwold Ltd for £125,000. All of these goods remained in the inventories of Southwold Ltd at 31 December 20X9.

What figure for cost of sales will be reported in the consolidated statement of comprehensive income for the year ended 30 September 20X9?

£1,250,000	
£1,275,000	
£1,300,000	
£1,400,000	

Test 5

Prepare brief notes to answer the following questions:

(a)   What is an associate, according to IAS 28 *Investments in Associates*?
(b)   What is significant influence?
(c)   What are the signs that an investor is likely to have significant influence?

Test 6

The statements of comprehensive income of Thames plc and Stour Ltd for the year ended 31 December 20X3 are shown below.

	Thames plc £'000	Stour Ltd £'000
Continuing operations		
Revenue	2,280	1,200
Cost of sales	(1,320)	(660)
Gross profit	960	540
Other income (dividend from Stour Ltd)	85	–
Operating expenses	(360)	(180)
Profit before tax	685	360
Tax	(240)	(120)
Profit for the year	445	240

BPP LEARNING MEDIA

Further information:

(1) The issued share capital of Stour Ltd consists of 100,000 ordinary shares of £1 each.

(2) Thames plc acquired 85,000 of the ordinary shares of Stour Ltd on 1 January 20X0.

(3) During the year, Stour Ltd made sales totalling £600,000 to Thames plc. All these goods had been sold by 31 December 20X3.

(4) There is no impairment of goodwill.

(5) During the year Stour Ltd paid a dividend of £100,000.

Required

Prepare the consolidated statement of comprehensive income of Thames plc and its subsidiary for the year ended 31 December 20X3.

Consolidated statement of comprehensive income for the year ended 31 December 20X3

	£'000
Continuing operations	
Revenue	
Cost of sales	
Gross profit	
Other income	
Operating expenses	
Profit before tax	
Tax	
Profit for the year	
Attributable to:	
Equity holders of the parent	
Non-controlling interest	

Workings

Revenue	£'000
Thames plc	
Stour Ltd	
Total intercompany adjustment	

Cost of sales	£'000
Thames plc	
Stour Ltd	
Total intercompany adjustment	

chapter 12:
INTERPRETING FINANCIAL STATEMENTS

chapter coverage 📖

The objective of financial statements is to enable users to make economic decisions. This chapter concentrates on the start of the decision-making process: analysing and interpreting the information in financial statements.

The topics covered are:

- ✍ Users of financial statements and their needs
- ✍ Ratio analysis
- ✍ Profitability
- ✍ Liquidity
- ✍ Use of resources
- ✍ Financial position
- ✍ Interpreting ratios
- ✍ Writing the answer
- ✍ Limitations of ratio analysis

USERS OF FINANCIAL STATEMENTS AND THEIR NEEDS

The main objective of financial statements is to **help users make economic decisions.**

Users

Several different groups of people may be interested in the information provided by financial statements.

- Investors and potential investors
- Employees
- Lenders and potential lenders.
- Suppliers
- Customers
- Governments and their agencies (for example, tax authorities)
- The public

Different types of limited company

Different types of company may have slightly different objectives.

- **Public companies and large private companies**: to provide a return to investors by maximising profit.

- **Owner-managed businesses (small private companies, partnerships and sole traders)**: to make sufficient profit to support the owners and their dependants.

They may also be financed differently.

- **Public companies and large private companies**: ordinary shares (equity); preference shares; debentures and other types of loan (debt), including bank loans.

- **Owner-managed businesses**: ordinary shares; owners' capital; loans (normally from the bank).

The main providers of finance are normally the most important users of an entity's financial statements. Public companies and large private companies are managed by directors on behalf of their equity investors (shareholders). Management is responsible for using the company's assets efficiently to generate profit and otherwise benefit the shareholders. Many small businesses are financed by bank loans and other debt and therefore management may be 'accountable' to lenders.

Task 1

The IASB *Conceptual Framework for Financial Reporting* states that the objective of general purpose financial reporting is to provide financial information about the reporting entity that is useful to potential investors, lenders and other creditors in making decisions about providing resources to the entity.

Is this statement True or False?

True	✓
False	

False   existing (handwritten)

What decisions do users of financial statements need to make?

Investors and potential investors need information that helps them to decide whether to buy, hold or sell their investment or (for a potential investor) whether to invest in the company at all.

- They need to assess the return that they are likely to obtain on their investment: how large a dividend can they hope to receive relative to the amount they have invested?

- These users are most interested in the profitability of the entity and in its efficiency (the way in which it has used its resources to generate profit).

- They also need information which helps them to assess the ability of the entity to pay dividends (normally profits but possibly also cash flow and liquidity).

- They may also be interested in assessing the riskiness of an investment: for example, is there any chance that the company will start to make losses or get into financial difficulties?

Lenders and potential lenders need to decide whether to lend (or continue to lend) money to the business and on what terms.

- They need to be satisfied that the business can pay interest on the loan.

- They also need to be satisfied that the loan will be repaid when it is due.

- These users are most interested in an entity's cash flows and in its ability to meet its debts as they fall due, both in the short term and in the longer term (its liquidity and solvency).

Investors and lenders are the users that you are most likely to have to think about in the assessment. However, you may be asked to consider the needs of other users.

- **Employees** need information that helps them to assess their employer's ability to provide wages, salaries and other benefits and employment opportunities. Therefore they need information about their employer's stability and profitability (particularly in relation to the part of the organisation in which they work).

- **Suppliers** need information that helps them to decide whether to sell to the entity and to assess the likelihood that amounts owing to them will be paid when due (liquidity, cash flows and profits).

- **Customers** need information about the entity's continued existence, particularly if they are dependent on the entity's products (for example, because they may need specialised replacement parts).

- **Governments and their agencies** need information that helps them to allocate resources, assess taxation and regulate the activities of businesses and other organisations. For example, Her Majesty's Revenue and Customs (HMRC) needs to be satisfied that the business has paid the right amount of tax, based on its profit for the period. It is interested in the profit figure and in the make-up of revenue and expenses.

- **The public** is interested in information that is useful in assessing the trends and recent developments in an entity's prosperity and the range of its activities. This is because businesses and other organisations all affect the community in some way, for example, by providing employment or by using local suppliers.

In the assessment, you will almost certainly be asked to prepare a report or to draft a letter or an e-mail which interprets information in the financial statements. Ask yourself:

- Who is the interpretation intended for?
- What are they most interested in?
- What decision do they need to make?

RATIO ANALYSIS

RATIO ANALYSIS is a technique used to interpret financial information. It involves calculating ratios by comparing one figure in the financial statements with another.

For example, revenue is £100,000 and gross profit is £25,000. The gross profit margin is 25%.

However, this tells us very little on its own. Is a gross profit margin of 25% good or bad? The ratios must be compared with other information:

- The previous year's financial statements (is the gross profit margin better or worse than last year?)

- Budgeted financial statements (is gross profit more or less than forecast?)

- The financial statements of another company (is the gross profit margin better or worse than that of a competitor?)

- Average figures for the industry (how profitable is the company in relation to the industry as a whole?)

Types of ratios

Ratios can be used to assess:

- Profitability
- Liquidity
- Efficient use of resources
- Financial position.

The statements of comprehensive income and statements of financial position below will be used to illustrate the ratio calculations.

Statements of comprehensive income for the year ended 31 December 20X8

	Smith Ltd £'000	Jones Ltd £'000
Continuing operations		
Revenue	2,200	3,000
Cost of sales	(770)	(2,100)
Gross profit	1,430	900
Operating expenses	(1,320)	(600)
Profit from operations	110	300
Finance cost	(10)	(15)
Profit before tax	100	285
Tax	(35)	(85)
Profit for the year from continuing operations	65	200

Statements of financial position as at 31 December 20X8

	Smith Ltd £'000	Jones Ltd £'000
Assets		
Non-current assets		
Property, plant and equipment	440	660
Current assets:		
Inventories	170	110
Receivables	220	100
Cash	–	20
	390	230
Total assets	830	890
Equity and liabilities		
Equity:		
Share capital	100	100
Retained earnings	230	440
	330	540
Non-current liabilities: bank loans	140	170
Current liabilities:		
Trade payables	220	90
Tax liabilities	30	90
Bank overdraft	110	–
	360	180
Total liabilities	500	350
Total equity and liabilities	830	890

PROFITABILITY

Return on capital employed

RETURN ON CAPITAL EMPLOYED (ROCE) is regarded as the key measure of a business' profitability. It measures the profit (the return) that a business generates from the resources available to it (its capital employed). CAPITAL EMPLOYED is total equity plus non-current liabilities or can also be calculated as total assets less current liabilities.

$$\textbf{ROCE} = \frac{\text{Profit from operations}}{\text{Total equity} + \text{Non-current liabilities}} \times 100\%$$

	Smith Ltd	Jones Ltd
ROCE	$\dfrac{110}{330+140} \times 100\% = 23.4\%$	$\dfrac{300}{540+170} \times 100\% = 42.2\%$

Notice that both interest and long-term liabilities are included in the calculation. ROCE measures the total return made by the company on both loans (debt capital) and share capital, not simply the return to shareholders.

Interpreting ROCE

A high ROCE is a good sign. It means that the company is generating a good return on the capital that shareholders and lenders have invested in it.

As we will see later in this chapter, ROCE reflects:

- the company's profitability; and
- the company's use of assets (capital employed)

If the ROCE of a company has fallen compared with the previous year the cause could be a lower operating profit or an increase in capital employed (net assets) or a combination of the two. If ROCE has improved the opposite applies: either profits have increased or capital employed has decreased.

Other calculations

A variation of ROCE measures the return to shareholders only:

$$\textbf{Return on equity} = \frac{\text{Profit after tax}}{\text{Total equity}} \times 100\%$$

This ratio is sometimes known as return on shareholders' equity (capital) or return on owners' equity.

	Smith Ltd	Jones Ltd
ROE	$\frac{65}{330} \times 100\% = 19.7\%$	$\frac{200}{540} \times 100\% = 37.0\%$

In this ratio interest and tax are deducted from profit, as we are only concerned with the profit for the shareholders.

Another variation of ROCE measures the return on total assets, rather than assets less current liabilities.

$$\textbf{Return on total assets} = \frac{\text{Profit from operations}}{\text{Total assets}} \times 100\%$$

	Smith Ltd	Jones Ltd
Return on total assets	$\frac{110}{830} \times 100\% = 13.2\%$	$\frac{300}{890} \times 100\% = 33.7\%$

Operating profit percentage

OPERATING PROFIT PERCENTAGE (sometimes called **net profit margin**) measures the overall profitability of a business, or the operating profit generated as a percentage of sales.

$$\textbf{Operating profit percentage} = \frac{\text{Profit from operations}}{\text{Revenue}} \times 100\%$$

	Smith Ltd	Jones Ltd
Operating profit percentage	$\dfrac{110}{2,200} \times 100\% = 5\%$	$\dfrac{300}{3,000} \times 100\% = 10\%$

Interpreting operating profit percentage

If a company's operating profit percentage has improved compared with the previous year, this may be because:

- Sales revenue has decreased, but operating profit has remained constant or increased (i.e. costs have not fallen, or not fallen as sharply as sales)

- Costs have fallen (increasing operating profit), but sales revenue has remained constant or decreased

- Operating profit has risen by a higher percentage than sales revenue. So if operating profit increases by 20%, but sales revenue increases by only 10%, then the overall operating profit percentage will increase.

It is logical then, that if a company's operating profit percentage has deteriorated, this is because:

- Sales revenue has increased, but operating profit has remained constant or decreased

- Costs have risen (decreasing operating profit), but sales revenue has remained constant or increased

- Operating profit has risen by a lower percentage than sales revenue

All of the above reasons are linked to the fact that operating profit percentage is measuring what proportion of each £1 of sales revenue is converted into operating profit. For example, earlier we saw that on average Smith Ltd turned 5% (5p) of each £1 of sales revenue into an operating profit. Smith Ltd's sales revenue of £2,200 therefore resulted in £110 (£2,200 x £0.05) of operating profit. So to improve the operating profit percentage, it is not a matter of selling more or less, but instead a matter of generating more profit for each £1 sold.

So we now know operating profit percentage depends on the sales revenue and operating cost values. Therefore we shall look at possible reasons for changes in each of these.

A change in sales revenue may be the result of:

- A change in the volume of sales (perhaps because of promotions, price cutting, or special offers)

- A change in sales prices

- A change in the sales mix (for example, so that a greater proportion of high-value items are being sold than previously);

- New or improved products;

- A competitor entering or leaving the market.

A change in operating costs may be the result of:

- A change in cost of sales (for example, an increase in the cost of raw materials);

- A change in other operating costs, such as administrative expenses;

- Poor cost control or improved cost control;

- Large, unusual items (such as legal fees, or a profit on disposal of non-current assets) that might not recur in future periods.

Gross profit percentage

GROSS PROFIT PERCENTAGE (or **gross profit margin**) measures gross profit as a percentage of sales.

$$\textbf{Gross profit percentage} = \frac{\text{Gross profit}}{\text{Revenue}} \times 100\%$$

	Smith Ltd	Jones Ltd
Gross profit percentage	$\frac{1,430}{2,200} \times 100\% = 65\%$	$\frac{900}{3,000} \times 100\% = 30\%$

Interpreting gross profit percentage

Many of the comments about interpreting the operating profit percentage also apply to the gross profit percentage. A change in the gross profit percentage compared with the previous year means that either the amount of sales revenue has changed or that cost of sales has changed. An increasing gross profit percentage means additional gross profit is being generated per £1 of sales revenue (e.g. 20p of each £1 of sales revenue is now converted to a gross profit compared to 10p for each £1 of sales revenue).

It can be useful to compare the gross profit percentage with the operating profit percentage (if both ratios are available).

For example, suppose that a company's operating profit percentage has fallen, but its gross profit percentage has shown a slight improvement. This means that the fall in operating profit percentage could have been caused by an increase in

operating expenses (expenses not included in cost of sales): either because of poor cost control, large 'one off' items or a significant increase in particular expenses. (For example, a rise in the price of petrol would increase selling and distribution costs.)

If sales had fallen or cost of sales had increased then the gross profit figure used in the gross profit percentage calculation would also have fallen.

Expenses ratios

The EXPENSE/REVENUE PERCENTAGE (sometimes called **expenses ratio** or **expenses/sales**) measures operating expenses as a percentage of sales. For this purpose, operating expenses are expenses other than those included in cost of sales (often presented as distribution costs and administrative expenses). It follows that if a business has a high expenses ratio it normally has a low operating profit percentage.

$$\textbf{Expense/revenue percentage} = \frac{\text{Operating expenses}}{\text{Revenue}} \times 100\%$$

	Smith Ltd	Jones Ltd
Expense/revenue percentage	$\frac{1,320}{2,200} \times 100\% = 60\%$	$\frac{600}{3,000} \times 100\% = 20\%$

The expense/revenue percentage can be calculated using a specific expense, for example, administrative expenses or depreciation:

$$\textbf{Expense/revenue percentage} = \frac{\text{Specific expense}}{\text{Revenue}} \times 100\%$$

Asset turnover

ASSET TURNOVER measures the efficiency with which a business uses its resources to generate sales. It measures the revenue generated by each £1 of assets.

It can be calculated based on total assets less current liabilities (which is the same as capital employed):

$$\textbf{Asset turnover} = \frac{\text{Revenue}}{\text{Total assets} - \text{Current liabilities}}$$

	Smith Ltd	Jones Ltd
Asset turnover	$\frac{2,200}{330 + 140} = 4.7 \text{ times}$	$\frac{3,000}{540 + 170} = 4.2 \text{ times}$

This is the most common version. It can also be calculated based on total assets:

Asset turnover $= \dfrac{\text{Revenue}}{\text{Total assets}}$

	Smith Ltd	Jones Ltd
Asset turnover	$\dfrac{2,200}{830} = 2.7 \text{ times}$	$\dfrac{3,000}{890} = 3.4 \text{ times}$

Asset turnover measures an entity's use of resources, rather than its profitability as such. However, it has been introduced here because it has an important relationship with the main profitability ratios.

Interpreting asset turnover

A change in asset turnover is the result of a change in sales revenue or a change in assets or net assets (depending on the formula used).

The possible reasons for a change in sales revenue have been considered above.

Possible causes of a change in assets or net assets include:

- Purchases of non-current assets;
- Disposals of non-current assets;
- Revaluation of non-current assets.

If non-current assets increase significantly during the year (for example, because of a revaluation) while sales remain at the same level, asset turnover will fall. The company will appear to be using its assets less efficiently, but this may not necessarily be the case.

The relationship between the ratios

A business' return on capital employed (ROCE) has two components:

- Its profitability (measured by operating profit percentage)
- Its use of assets (measured by asset turnover).

The relationship between the three ratios is:

$$\frac{\text{Profit from operations}}{\text{Revenue}} \times \frac{\text{Revenue}}{\text{Total assets} - \text{Current liabilities}} =$$

$$\frac{\text{Profit from operations}}{\text{Total equity} + \text{Non-current liabilities}}$$

$$\text{or:} \quad \frac{\text{Profit from operations}}{\text{Revenue}} \times \frac{\text{Revenue}}{\text{Capital employed}} =$$

$$\frac{\text{Profit from operations}}{\text{Capital employed}}$$

The nature of the business often affects the components of ROCE. For example, a manufacturing business and a business that provides services could both have the same ROCE, made up in different ways:

	Operating profit percentage	×	Asset turnover	=	ROCE
■ Manufacturer	10%	×	2.5	=	25%
■ Service provider	5%	×	5	=	25%

The service provider appears to make more efficient use of assets than the manufacturer because a manufacturer needs to invest in plant and equipment in order to generate revenue. Service industries normally have few non-current assets relative to their revenue; they rely on the expertise of their staff to generate profit.

Task 2

The summarised statement of financial position of Brookstream Ltd is shown below:

		£'000
Assets		
Non-current assets		1,400
Current assets		400
Total assets		1,800
Equity:		
Share capital		200
Share premium		100
Retained earnings		600
		900
Non-current liabilities	600	
Current liabilities	300	
Total liabilities		900
Total equity and liabilities		1,800

Sales revenue for the year was £2 million and profit from operations was £300,000.

Calculate the following ratios:

(a) Return on capital employed (ROCE)

(b) Operating profit percentage

(c)   Asset turnover (based on capital employed or net assets)

Earnings per share

The earnings per share ratio is an important measure of profitability. It measures the profit earned for each ordinary (equity) share and the basic calculation is as follows:

$$\textbf{Earnings per share} = \frac{\text{Profit after tax}}{\text{Number of issued ordinary shares}}$$

Earnings per share was covered in Chapter 9.

LIQUIDITY

A business' LIQUIDITY is its ability to meet its debts as they fall due.

Current ratio

This is an overall measure of a business' liquidity. It shows the extent to which current liabilities are covered by either cash or assets that can be converted into cash within a reasonably short time.

$$\textbf{Current ratio} = \frac{\text{Current assets}}{\text{Current liabilities}}$$

	Smith Ltd	Jones Ltd
Current ratio	$\frac{390}{360} = 1.1:1$	$\frac{230}{180} = 1.3:1$

Quick (acid test) ratio

This ratio measures the immediate solvency of a business by showing the extent to which its current liabilities are covered by cash and amounts receivable. Inventories are excluded from the calculation because they are less liquid than receivables. Inventories must be sold and converted into receivables before they can eventually be converted into cash.

$$\textbf{Quick ratio} = \frac{\text{Current assets} - \text{inventories}}{\text{Current liabilities}}$$

	Smith Ltd	*Jones Ltd*
Quick ratio	$\dfrac{220}{360} = 0.6:1$	$\dfrac{120}{180} = 0.7:1$

Interpreting the liquidity ratios

Generally, the higher the ratio of current assets to current liabilities, the better.

- If the current ratio and/or the quick ratio have improved, this will be because:

    - One or more of the components of current assets has increased (while current liabilities have remained stable or decreased)

    - One or more of the components of current liabilities has decreased (while current assets have remained stable or increased)

    - Current assets have increased by a higher percentage than current liabilities have.

- If the ratios have worsened, the opposite will be true and there may have been a decrease in current assets or an increase in current liabilities, or both.

Current assets include cash at bank and current liabilities include bank overdrafts. If a company moves from having a positive cash balance to having an overdraft, the ratios will deteriorate and vice versa. A low current or quick ratio may also mean that there are other significant liabilities. For example, the amount of trade payables may have increased (perhaps because the company has insufficient cash to pay them promptly).

It is possible for a company to have what appears to be an acceptable current ratio and still be short of cash. For example, it may have high inventories, high trade receivables, low trade payables and a bank overdraft. Working capital management is discussed in more detail in the next section.

Very high current and quick ratios may also be a sign that a company has problems.

- It may have built up large amounts of trade receivables which are not being converted into cash.

- If the current ratio is very high or it is much higher than the quick ratio, the company may be tying too much cash up in inventories (the quick ratio excludes inventories).

- Or it may simply have surplus cash that is not being used to generate future sales, for example, by purchasing new or more efficient plant and machinery, or by researching and developing new products.

Task 3

The following information has been extracted from the statement of financial position of Gloryline Ltd:

	£'000
Inventories	4,750
Receivables	11,350
Cash	2,900
Trade payables	7,400
Other current liabilities	2,100

Calculate the current ratio and the quick ratio.

Current ratio

Quick ratio

USE OF RESOURCES

This group of ratios measures the ability of a business to control its working capital and to use it efficiently. WORKING CAPITAL is an entity's resources that are available for use in its day-to-day trading operations. For most businesses working capital is current assets less current liabilities.

These ratios are also used to analyse liquidity, because they provide information about the individual components of working capital: inventories, receivables and payables.

If a business has a relatively high level of inventories and receivables it has cash tied up which cannot be used immediately. This means that:

- The business may not be able to meet its debts promptly

- It may miss opportunities for growth (for example, it may be more difficult to purchase new plant and equipment which might generate more revenue)

- Lack of cash may mean that the business has a bank overdraft or has to take out a loan. Profit is then reduced by interest charges

If a business has a relatively low level of trade payables, it may be paying its debts more quickly than is strictly necessary.

A business can improve its cash flow (and possibly avoid a bank overdraft) by:

- Keeping inventory levels as low as possible

- Collecting cash from customers promptly (by offering prompt payment discounts or by good credit control)

- Delaying payments to suppliers

However:

- A business must carry enough inventories to meet customer demand
- Customers must be allowed a reasonable amount of credit
- Suppliers must be paid within a reasonable amount of time

In practice, a business has to balance the need for cash against the need to maintain good relationships with customers and suppliers (in order to continue to generate sales and profits).

Inventory turnover

This shows how rapidly a business's inventory is sold on average during the year; or alternatively, the extent to which inventory levels are justified relative to sales.

$$\textbf{Inventory turnover} = \frac{\text{Cost of sales}}{\text{Inventories}}$$

	Smith Ltd	Jones Ltd
Inventory turnover	$\dfrac{770}{170} = 4.5\text{ times}$	$\dfrac{2,100}{110} = 19.1\text{ times}$

An alternative calculation is inventory holding period (sometimes called inventory days), or the average number of days for which a business holds an item of inventory.

$$\textbf{Inventory holding period} = \frac{\text{Inventories}}{\text{Cost of sales}} \times 365 \text{ days}$$

	Smith Ltd	Jones Ltd
Inventory holding period	$\dfrac{170}{770} \times 365 = 81 \text{ days}$	$\dfrac{110}{2,100} \times 365 = 19 \text{ days}$

Possible reasons for low inventory turnover or a long inventory holding period include:

- Poor inventory management (too much inventory has been ordered or allowed to build up)

- Inventories include significant amounts of obsolete or damaged items

344

- There has been a sudden fall in demand for the company's products
- The company has deliberately purchased higher amounts of inventory than before because it is planning to expand or to fill a particular very large order.

Trade receivables collection period

This is the average period taken to collect receivables. It is sometimes called receivables days.

$$\textbf{Trade receivables collection period} = \frac{\text{Trade receivables}}{\text{Revenue}} \times 365 \text{ days}$$

	Smith Ltd	Jones Ltd
Trade receivables collection period	$\frac{220}{2,200} \times 365 = 36$ days	$\frac{100}{3,000} \times 365 = 12$ days

Possible reasons for an increase in the trade receivables collection period include:

- Poor credit control (customers are not being 'chased' for payment or are being allowed too much credit)
- Sales have been increasing throughout the period or were unusually high just before the period end (so that trade receivables are high in relation to total sales for the period)
- Certain major customers have been allowed extended credit (for example, because they generate a large proportion of the company's revenue).

Trade payables payment period

This is the average period taken to pay suppliers. It is sometimes called payables days.

$$\textbf{Trade payables payment period} = \frac{\text{Trade payables}}{\text{Cost of sales}} \times 365 \text{ days}$$

	Smith Ltd	Jones Ltd
Payables days	$\frac{220}{770} \times 365 = 104$ days	$\frac{90}{2,100} \times 365 = 16$ days

Technically, payables days should be based upon purchases rather than cost of sales, but the purchases figure is not normally available from a set of financial statements. Therefore cost of sales is used as an approximation.

Possible reasons for an increase in the trade payables payment period include:

- Poor management (the company is not paying suppliers promptly)

- The company is expanding or planning to expand (so that trade payables are high in relation to total cost of sales for the period)

- The company is delaying payments to suppliers because it does not have enough cash to pay them.

Working capital cycle

There are normally several stages in an entity's day-to-day trading operations, for example:

- The entity buys inventories on credit (it then has inventories and it also has trade payables)

- Cash goes out of the business when the entity pays the supplier

- The entity holds the inventories

- The inventories are sold on credit (the entity now has trade receivables); and finally

- Cash comes back into the business when the customer pays the amount owing

The **working capital cycle** is the period of time from the point at which cash goes out of a business to pay for inventories and the point at which cash comes back into the business when those inventories are sold and the customer pays for the goods. It is sometimes called the **cash cycle** or the **operating cycle**.

Working capital cycle = Inventory days + Receivable days – Payable days

	Smith Ltd	Jones Ltd
Working capital cycle	81 + 36 – 104 = 13 days	19 + 12 – 16 = 15 days

Task 4

Draft statement of comprehensive income for the year ended 30 June 20X5 (extract):

	£'000	£'000
Sales		6,900
Opening inventories	900	
Purchases	4,500	
Closing inventories	(1,200)	
Cost of sales		(4,200)
Gross profit		2,700

Calculate inventory turnover (using cost of sales).

FINANCIAL POSITION

Gearing

Gearing ratios measure the extent to which a company is financed by debt rather than by shareholders' equity. Debt usually means non-current liabilities: loan stock (or debentures) and other long-term loans.

There are several ways of calculating the gearing ratio, but the formula that you will be expected to use in your assessment is:

$$\text{Gearing} = \frac{\text{Non-current liabilities}}{\text{Total equity} + \text{Non-current liabilities}} \times 100\%$$

This ratio measures non-current liabilities (debt) as a percentage of total financing (total capital employed).

	Smith Ltd	*Jones Ltd*
Gearing	$\dfrac{140}{330+140} \times 100\% = 30\%$	$\dfrac{170}{540+170} \times 100\% = 24\%$

If the gearing ratio increases, this normally means that the company has taken out additional long-term loans (for example, bank loans or loan stock).

The gearing ratio will also increase if the company enters into a finance lease (see Chapter 8). The company's obligation to make future lease payments is a non-current liability.

If a company repays its borrowings, the gearing ratio will improve (decrease).

Major purchases or revaluations of property, plant or equipment will also improve the gearing ratio. Non-current assets are part of shareholders' equity (capital employed).

Gearing and risk

A company with a high proportion of debt to equity is said to be HIGHLY GEARED. If a company is highly geared:

- Interest charges mean that less profit is available to pay dividends to equity shareholders. As a result, the company may be less attractive to investors and potential investors.

- It may be difficult to raise additional finance, because banks and other potential lenders are normally reluctant to lend to a company that is already heavily in debt.

- If the company makes losses, there is a greater likelihood that it will face severe problems as a result. If the company cannot make the interest payments, lenders can demand repayment of the entire loan. This may lead to the company going into liquidation.

HOW IT WORKS

A highly geared company is perceived as a risky investment. Consider the three companies below:

	A plc £'000	B plc £'000	C plc £'000
10% loan stock	Nil	1,000	2,000
Equity share capital	1,000	1,000	1,000
Reserves	1,000	1,000	1,000
	2,000	2,000	2,000
Gearing	0%	33%	50%

	A plc £'000	B plc £'000	C plc £'000
Profit from operations	1,000	1,000	1,000
Interest payable	–	(100)	(200)
Profit before tax	1,000	900	800
Tax at 30%	(300)	(270)	(240)
Profit available for shareholders	700	630	560

Suppose that profit from operations falls by 50%. This is the effect on equity shareholders:

	A plc £'000	B plc £'000	C plc £'000
Profit from operations	500	500	500
Interest payable	–	(100)	(200)
Profit before tax	500	400	300
Tax at 30%	(150)	(120)	(90)
Profit available for shareholders	350	280	210
Decrease in profits available to shareholders	50%	55%	62.5%

Suppose that profit from operations increases by 50%.

	A plc £'000	B plc £'000	C plc £'000
Profit from operations	1,500	1,500	1,500
Interest payable	–	(100)	(200)
Profit before tax	1,500	1,400	1,300
Tax at 30%	(450)	(420)	(390)
Profit available for shareholders	1,050	980	910
Increase in profits available to shareholders	50%	55%	62.5%

Risk is uncertainty as to the amount of benefits. If a company is highly geared, profits available for shareholders (and therefore dividends) may fluctuate considerably as the result of a relatively small change in the level of profit from operations.

Interest cover

This shows the extent to which interest payments are 'covered' by profit from operations; or whether a business is generating enough profit to meet its interest costs comfortably.

$$\textbf{Interest cover} = \frac{\text{Profit from operations}}{\text{Finance costs}}$$

	Smith Ltd	Jones Ltd
Interest cover	$\frac{110}{10} = 11$ times	$\frac{300}{15} = 20$ times

There are three possible causes of a change in interest cover compared with the previous period:

- An increase or decrease in profit from operations;

- An increase or decrease in the amount of the company's long-term loans;

- A change in interest rates.

Generally, a company with high gearing also has low interest cover (and vice-versa).

INTERPRETING RATIOS

Ratio calculations are the first step in interpreting financial statements. The calculations themselves do not provide firm answers. Rather, they focus attention on significant aspects of an entity's performance and position.

There is no such thing as an 'ideal' ratio. Whether a particular ratio is a sign of strength or weakness may depend on a number of factors, including:

- Whether the ratio is improving or deteriorating

- Any other information that is available (including possible reasons for a result)

- The nature of the business

For example, it is often said that the quick ratio should be greater than 1:1. A company has a quick ratio of 0.5:1. Does this mean that the company has severe liquidity problems?

Not necessarily: either of the following could apply:

- The company is a retailer. All sales are for cash; there are no trade receivables. The average quick ratio in the industry is 0.4:1.

- The quick ratio for the previous year was 0.2:1. Other information suggests that the company has had severe liquidity problems, but it is recovering.

In the assessment, you will be asked to comment on specific ratios. As well as making observations ('gross profit percentage has increased during the year') it is important that you attempt to **interpret** the ratios, for example, by suggesting reasons **why** gross profit percentage might have increased, based on any other relevant information you are given.

This means that as well as knowing how to calculate each ratio you need to understand:

- what each ratio means
- whether increases/decreases are good or bad

HOW IT WORKS

The following information relates to two companies. The ratios have been calculated for the year ended 31 December 20X8. The two companies operate in the same line of business.

	Smith Ltd	Jones Ltd
ROCE	23.4%	42.2%
Gross profit percentage	65%	30%
Operating profit percentage	5%	10%
Expenses/revenue percentage	60%	20%
Asset turnover (based on net assets)	4.7 times	4.2 times
Current ratio	1.1:1	1.3:1
Quick ratio	0.6:1	0.7:1
Inventory turnover	4.5 times	19.1 times
Trade receivables collection period	36 days	12 days
Trade payables payment period	104 days	16 days
Gearing	30%	24%
Interest cover	11 times	20 times

Profitability

- Smith Ltd has the higher gross profit percentage, 65% compared with Jones Ltd's 30%.

- However, overall Jones Ltd is performing much better than Smith Ltd, with ROCE of 42.2% compared with 23.4%.

- Asset turnover for the two companies is roughly comparable, so the difference in ROCE is largely a reflection of operating profit percentage. Smith Ltd has an operating profit percentage of 5%, only half that of Jones Ltd.

- The difference in gross profit percentage may indicate that the two companies have different strategies. Smith Ltd may be concentrating on low volume, high margin sales, while Jones Ltd may be selling its products very cheaply in order to generate more revenue.

- Smith Ltd incurs much higher operating expenses (relative to its sales revenue) than Jones Ltd, as shown by the expenses/revenue percentage, which is three times that of Jones Ltd. This may be because it is less efficient at controlling administrative costs. Alternatively, it may have incurred high 'one-off' costs, such as legal fees, during the year.

Liquidity and use of resources (working capital management)

- The current ratios are 1.1:1 and 1.3:1 respectively. Both companies are likely to be able to meet their current liabilities in the near future.

- However, Smith Ltd has an acid test ratio of 0.6:1 and Jones Ltd's position is only slightly better. This suggests potential liquidity problems for both companies, or a type of business which tends to have a low quick ratio (see above).

- Jones Ltd appears to be much better at managing its working capital than Smith Ltd.

  - Smith Ltd's inventory turnover is 4.5 times compared with 19 times for Jones Ltd. Given the healthy gross profit ratio, this difference seems to suggest poor management by Smith, rather than a decline in the company's business.

  - Smith Ltd takes over three months on average to pay its suppliers. In contrast, Jones Ltd's average supplier payment period is less than one month. Jones Ltd evidently has sufficient cash to pay its suppliers promptly. It is possible that Smith does not.

  - Smith Ltd takes just over one month on average to collect receivables. Most companies allow roughly 30 days' credit, but this compares badly with the performance of Jones Ltd (which has an average collection period of just under two weeks). This suggests either poor management by Smith or (more probably) that the management of Jones is extremely efficient. Alternatively, the two companies may have different types of customer. Smith's customers may be mainly large companies; Jones Ltd may deal mainly with individuals from whom it can demand payment almost immediately.

- All the above information seems to indicate that Smith Ltd may be suffering liquidity problems.

Gearing

- Although Smith Ltd is more highly geared than Jones Ltd, neither company's gearing ratio seems to be unduly high.

- Neither company appears to be having difficulty in generating enough profit to cover interest charges on their loans (interest cover is 11 times and 20 times respectively). Smith's lower interest cover reflects this company's much lower operating profit percentage, as well as its higher gearing.

Conclusion

On the basis of the information provided, Jones Ltd appears to be more profitable (in relative terms) and to be in a stronger financial position than Smith Ltd. Jones Ltd has a low acid test ratio, but there are no other signs of trading problems.

In contrast, Smith Ltd's financial position gives cause for concern. There are several signs that it may be experiencing liquidity problems. In addition, there are indications that working capital could be better managed.

Task 5

A business normally allows customers 30 days' credit. However, the information in the latest financial statements suggests that the average collection period is actually 45 days.

A major customer went into liquidation during the year and the debt was written-off. This could be a reason for the difference.

Is this statement True or False?

True	
False	

Suggest ONE other possible reason to explain the difference.

Further information

In the assessment, ratio analysis is normally based on a statement of financial position and a statement of comprehensive income. This information is very limited. For this reason, the conclusions drawn can often only be very tentative. Ratio analysis often poses questions, rather than providing definitive answers.

In the example above, on the basis of the analysis, Jones Ltd appears to be the safer choice. However, the following further information would be useful for both companies:

- Comparative figures for at least the previous year (and preceding periods if possible)

- Notes to the financial statements

- The directors' report, auditor's report and any other non-financial information that is available. (There is unlikely to be any further information because both companies are private companies. The published annual report of a public company includes a Chairman's Statement and normally includes an Operating and Financial Review, both of which may help to explain the view given by the financial statements)

- Budgeted figures for the current year (with actual figures for the period to date if these are available)

- Average figures for the industry

In addition, the following specific information might be helpful:

- Analysis of cost of sales and operating expenses for both companies. This may help to explain the differences in gross profit percentage and operating profit percentage and, in particular, the reason why Smith Ltd's operating expenses are so high.

- Statements of cash flow. These may help to explain the differences in liquidity and working capital management.

- Repayment dates and terms for the long-term loans. If the loans have to be repaid in the near future, Smith Ltd will probably then have severe liquidity problems and even Jones Ltd may have difficulty in finding the necessary cash.

- Details of movements in property, plant and equipment during the year. These might help to explain the reason for Smith Ltd's low ROCE. ROCE has been calculated on the closing capital employed. If Smith Ltd has purchased assets just before the year-end, the new assets will be included in capital employed, even though they will have generated very little if any profit during the year. As a result, ROCE will appear artificially low.

WRITING THE ANSWER

In the assessment, there are normally two interpretation tasks. The first is computational: you will be asked to select the correct formulae for specific ratios from 'pick lists' ('drop down lists') and to calculate those ratios for a company from a statement of comprehensive income and a statement of financial position.

The second task will probably require you to interpret a set of ratios and to draw a conclusion. You may be asked to set out your comments in the form of a report, a letter, or an e-mail.

Formats

- A **report** should begin with a heading showing the:
    - Addressee
    - Author
    - Date
    - Subject

- Example report:

REPORT	
To:	The Chief Accountant
From:	An accounting technician
Subject:	Analysis of the financial statements of Smith Ltd and Jones Ltd
Date:	23 June 20X2

- An **e-mail** should begin in a similar way. It should give e-mail addresses for the person sending it and the person receiving it.

- Example e-mail:

To:	chief.accountant@xyz.com
From:	accounting.technician@abc.co.uk
Subject:	Analysis of the financial statements of Smith Ltd and Jones Ltd
Date:	23 June 20X2

- A **letter** should either:
    - begin with 'Dear Sir/Madam' and end 'Yours faithfully'; or
    - begin with 'Dear (Name)' and end 'Yours sincerely'

- Example letter:

Sender's address
Name
Address
Date
Dear Ms X,
Analysis of the financial statements of Smith Ltd and Jones Ltd

- Note: the level of detail above should be enough; there is no need to invent addresses.

- Start with a **brief** introductory comment. This can normally be based on the wording of the task. For example:

    As requested, I have analysed the performance and financial position of Smith Ltd and Jones Ltd as shown by their financial statements for the year ended 31 December 20X1.

Comments

- In the main body of the answer, group your comments under headings or bullets. The wording of the task normally suggests suitable headings. For example, you could use the ratios that you have been asked to comment on.

- You will almost always be asked to compare a set of calculated ratios with:

    - Ratios of the previous accounting period for the same company; or
    - Ratios of another company; or
    - Industry average ratios.

- **Evaluate** the ratios. Are they better or worse than the ones with which they are being compared?

- **Explain why** each ratio is better or worse. For example, if the current ratio has decreased, there are less current assets compared to current liabilities. Why might this have happened? One possible reason is that the company could have moved from having a positive cash balance to having an overdraft.

Conclusion

- Assessment tasks almost always ask for a conclusion or for recommendations, for example:

    - Which of the two companies is the more profitable?
    - Should X invest in this company?
    - Should X lend money to this company?

- **Draw a firm conclusion, based on your observations about the information you have been given**. Candidates often lose marks because they try to avoid drawing a firm conclusion, for example, by saying there is not enough information available.

- Where you can, you should attempt to relate your conclusion back to any background information you are given in the question. Ask yourself:

- Who are the comments addressed to?
- What are they interested in?
- What decision do they need to make?

- For example, if you are writing to a potential investor who is interested in the profitability or performance of a company, you should base your conclusion at least partly on whether the company's revenue and/or profits have improved or deteriorated or (depending on the information you are given) are better or worse than the alternative company/the industry average.

- You may be asked to suggest ways in which particular ratios could be improved. This is usually easy if you understand what a ratio measures and the reasons why it may have deteriorated. For example, low inventory turnover shows that the business is carrying too much inventory relative to its level of sales. Inventory is not being sold quickly enough. So management should reduce inventories by ordering fewer items and/or by scrapping or writing down slow moving or obsolete items.

LIMITATIONS OF RATIO ANALYSIS

Ratio analysis is a useful technique, but as we have seen, it does not provide all the answers. Nor does it replace simple observation. For example, if revenue has increased, or the company has made an operating loss this should be immediately obvious, without calculations. Ratios should always be interpreted in the context of the financial statements as a whole and of any other information that is available.

Ratio analysis also has some serious limitations.

General limitations

- Financial statements are based on historical information. They may be several months out-of-date by the time that they are published. Very recent or forecast information is more useful for decision-making.

- Most ratios are calculated on closing figures taken from the statement of financial position. This means that ROCE, asset turnover and the working capital ratios may not compare like-with-like (because the figures taken from the statement of comprehensive income are for the whole period).

- Businesses can use 'window dressing' to improve the appearance of the statement of financial position. For example, they can order goods to be delivered just after the year-end so that inventories and payables are lower than usual or they can collect debts just before the year-end so that cash is higher than usual and receivables are lower than usual.

- Some businesses are seasonal. This means that the choice of reporting date (year-end) can be crucial, as the financial position varies according to the time of year.

- Financial statements only include information which can be measured in money terms. For example, they do not normally contain information about:

  - An entity's effect on the natural environment
  - Its effect on the community
  - The human resources available to it (its management and employees)
  - Some internally generated intangible assets, such as brand names

  These factors can have an important effect on an entity's performance. For example, consumers may choose to buy goods from entities that have been seen to adopt 'green' policies.

- Ratios are normally based on historic cost accounts. This means that they ignore the effect of inflation and trends can be distorted. If inflation is high, an entity may appear to be more profitable than is actually the case in real terms.

Comparisons between different businesses

Ratios for an individual business are often compared with ratios for a similar business, or with industry averages. These comparisons can be misleading.

- Businesses may use different accounting policies. For example, some businesses revalue non-current assets, while others carry them at historic cost. This can have a significant effect on key ratios.

- Businesses within the same industry can operate in completely different markets. They may also adopt different strategies. For example, some food stores may specialise in quality (relatively few sales at high margins), while other stores may concentrate on high volume, low-margin sales.

- Size differences may affect the way in which a business operates. A large company can often achieve economies of scale that are not available to a smaller business. For example, it may make use of trade discounts for bulk buying. Large companies are likely to have a different approach to managing working capital. They may be able to take advantage of extended credit terms and they may only hold fast-moving inventory lines. They may also adopt a more aggressive policy towards customers than would be the case in a small family business.

- Ratios may not always be calculated according to the same formula. For example, there are several possible variations on the calculation of gearing.

Task 6

Harkeats Ltd revalues some of its properties upwards. This affects its key ratios.

Indicate whether the following statements are True or False for the period immediately after the revaluation:

	True	False
Asset turnover is higher		
Gearing is higher		
Operating profit percentage is lower		
Return on capital employed is lower		

CHAPTER OVERVIEW

- Different types of limited company have different objectives

- The most important users of an entity's financial statements are usually the persons to whom management has stewardship responsibilities and/or the main providers of finance

- Ratio analysis is used to interpret financial information. Ratios are normally compared with other information (eg the previous years' financial statements, industry averages)

- Return on capital employed (ROCE) measures the profit that a business generates from the resources available to it

- Operating profit percentage measures the overall profitability of a business

- Gross profit percentage measures gross profit as a percentage of sales

- The expenses/revenue percentage measures operating expenses (or a specific expense) as a percentage of sales

- Asset turnover measures the efficiency with which a business uses its resources to generate sales

- The current ratio shows the extent to which a business' current liabilities are covered by current assets

- The quick ratio (acid test ratio) measures the immediate solvency of a business by showing the extent to which its current liabilities are covered by cash and receivables

- Inventory turnover shows how rapidly a business' inventory is sold on average during the year

- The trade receivables collection period is the average period taken to collect receivables

- The trade payables payment period is the average period taken to pay suppliers

- The working capital cycle is the period of time from the point at which cash goes out of a business to pay for inventories and the point at which cash comes back into the business as sales revenue

- The gearing ratio measures the extent to which a company is financed by debt rather than by owners' equity

- Interest cover shows the extent to which interest payments are 'covered' by profit from operations

- There is no such thing as an 'ideal' ratio. Whether a particular ratio is a sign of strength or weakness may depend on a number of factors

CHAPTER OVERVIEW CONTINUED

- Ratios should always be interpreted in the context of the accounts as a whole and of any other information that is available

- Ratio analysis has some serious limitations. Comparisons with ratios for a similar business or with industry averages can be misleading

Keywords

Ratio analysis – a technique used to interpret financial information. It involves calculating ratios by comparing one figure in the financial statements with another

$$\textbf{Return on capital employed (ROCE)} = \frac{\text{Profit from operations}}{\text{Total equity} + \text{Non-current liabilities}} \times 100\%$$

Capital employed = capital and reserves (equity) + non-current liabilities

$$\textbf{Return on equity} = \frac{\text{Profit after tax}}{\text{Total equity}} \times 100\%$$

$$\textbf{Return on total assets} = \frac{\text{Profit from operations}}{\text{Total assets}} \times 100\%$$

$$\textbf{Operating profit percentage} = \frac{\text{Profit from operations}}{\text{Revenue}} \times 100\%$$

$$\textbf{Gross profit percentage} = \frac{\text{Gross profit}}{\text{Revenue}} \times 100\%$$

$$\textbf{Expense/revenue percentage} = \frac{\text{Operating expenses}}{\text{Revenue}} \times 100\%$$

$$\text{Or } \frac{\text{Specified expense}}{\text{Revenue}} \times 100\%$$

$$\textbf{Asset turnover} = \frac{\text{Revenue}}{\text{Total assets} - \text{Current liabilities}}$$

$$\textbf{Asset turnover} \text{ (total assets)} = \frac{\text{Revenue}}{\text{Total assets}}$$

$$\textbf{Earnings per share} = \frac{\text{Profit after tax}}{\text{Number of issued ordinary shares}}$$

Liquidity – the ability of an entity to meet its debts as they fall due

$$\textbf{Current ratio} = \frac{\text{Current assets}}{\text{Current liabilities}}$$

$$\text{Quick ratio} = \frac{\text{Current assets} - \text{Inventories}}{\text{Current liabilities}}$$

Working capital – resources that are available for use in day-to-day trading operations (normally current assets less current liabilities)

$$\text{Inventory turnover} = \frac{\text{Cost of sales}}{\text{Inventories}}$$

$$\text{Inventory holding period} = \frac{\text{Inventories}}{\text{Cost of sales}} \times 365 \text{ days}$$

$$\text{Trade receivables collection period} = \frac{\text{Trade receivables}}{\text{Revenue}} \times 365 \text{ days}$$

$$\text{Trade payables payment period} = \frac{\text{Trade payables}}{\text{Cost of sales}} \times 365 \text{ days}$$

Working capital cycle = Inventory days + Receivable days – Payable days

$$\text{Gearing} = \frac{\text{Non-current liabilities}}{\text{Total equity} + \text{Non-current liabilities}} \times 100\%$$

Highly geared – having a high proportion of debt compared with equity

$$\text{Interest cover} = \frac{\text{Profit from operations}}{\text{Finance costs}}$$

TEST YOUR LEARNING

Test 1

Gross profit is £20,000 and operating expenses are £12,000. The gross profit percentage is 25%.

What is the operating profit percentage?

8%	
10%	
15%	
40%	

Test 2

If return on capital employed is 20% and the operating profit percentage is 10%, asset turnover is 0.5 times.

Is this statement True or False?

True	
False	

Test 3

State the formulas that are used to calculate each of the following ratios:

(a) Return on capital employed

(b) Acid test ratio

(c) Inventory holding period (days)

(d)   Interest cover

Test 4

The summarised statement of financial position of Bellbrock Ltd is shown below:

	£'000	£'000
Non-current assets		57,000
Current assets		22,800
		79,800
Equity:		
Ordinary shares		10,000
Revaluation reserve		4,600
Retained earnings		11,400
		26,000
Non-current liabilities	39,000	
Current liabilities	14,800	
		53,800
		79,800

What is the gearing ratio?

40%	
60%	
80%	
150%	

Test 5

The formula for calculating the operating profit percentage is:

$$\frac{\text{Profit from operations}}{\text{Total assets}} \times 100$$

Is this statement True or False?

True	
False	

Test 6

You have been asked to calculate ratios for Jackson Ltd in respect of its financial statements for the year ended 30 April 20X2.

Summarised statement of comprehensive income for the year ended 30 April 20X2 (extract)

	£'000
Revenue	4,100
Cost of sales	(2,625)
Gross profit	1,475

Additional information:

At 30 April 20X2, inventories were £480,000, trade receivables were £956,000 and trade payables were £267,000.

(a) State the formulae that are used to calculate each of the following ratios.

(Complete the middle column by writing in the correct formula from the list provided.)

(b) Calculate the ratios.

	Formula	Calculation
Gross profit percentage	▼	

Picklist for formulae:

Gross profit/Total equity × 100

Gross profit/Total assets – current liabilities × 100

Gross profit/Revenue × 100

Gross profit/Total assets × 100

	Formula	Calculation
Inventory turnover	▼	

Picklist for formulae:

Cost of sales/Inventories

Inventories/Cost of sales

Inventories/Revenue

Revenue/Inventories

	Formula	Calculation
Trade receivables collection period	▼	

Picklist for formulae:

Cost of sales/Trade receivables × 365

Revenue/Trade receivables × 365

Trade receivables/Cost of sales × 365

Trade receivables/Revenue × 365

	Formula	Calculation
Trade payables payment period	▼	

Picklist for formulae:

Trade payables/Revenue × 365

Trade payables/Cost of sales × 365

Revenue/Trade payables × 365

Cost of sales/Trade payables × 365

Test 7

The operating profit percentage can be improved by reducing administrative expenses.

Is this statement True or False?

True	
False	

Test 8

Michael Beacham has been asked to lend money to Goodall Ltd for a period of three years. He employed a financial adviser to advise him whether to make a loan to the company. The financial adviser has obtained the financial statements of the company for the past two years, calculated some ratios and found the industry averages. However, she was unable to complete her report. Michael has asked you to analyse the ratios and to advise him on whether he should make a loan to Goodall Ltd. The ratios are set out below.

	20X3	20X2	Industry average
Gearing ratio	67%	58%	41%
Interest cover	1.2	2.3	4.6
Quick ratio/acid test ratio	0.5	0.8	1.1
Return on equity	9%	13%	19%

Write a report for Michael Beacham that includes the following:

(a) Comments on Goodall's financial position and the performance of the company as shown by the ratios.

(b) A conclusion on whether Michael should lend money to Goodall Ltd. Base your conclusion only on the ratios calculated and the analysis performed.

ANSWERS TO CHAPTER TASKS

CHAPTER 1 **Limited companies**

Task 1

Amelia
Income statement for the year ended 30 June 20X1

	£	£
Sales		350,000
Opening inventories	12,700	
Purchases	221,200	
	233,900	
Less: closing inventories	(14,900)	
Cost of sales		(219,000)
Gross profit		131,000
Wages and salaries	55,000	
Rent and rates (9,600 – 900)	8,700	
Heat and light (4,500 + 700)	5,200	
Depreciation – equipment (91,000 × 10%)	9,100	
– motor vehicles (39,000 × 20%)	7,800	
Sundry expenses	7,300	
Total expenses		(93,100)
Net profit for the year		37,900

Amelia

Statement of financial position as at 30 June 20X1

	£	£
Non-current assets		
Equipment (91,000 – 20,500 – 9,100)		61,400
Motor vehicles (39,000 – 8,000 – 7,800)		23,200
		84,600
Current assets		
Inventories	14,900	
Trade receivables	48,000	
Prepayments	900	
Cash at bank (4,800 + 500)	5,300	
	69,100	
Current liabilities		
Trade payables	33,000	
Accruals	700	
	33,700	
Net current assets		35,400
		120,000
Capital		
Balance at 1 July 20X0		97,700
Add profit for the year		37,900
		135,600
Less: drawings		(15,600)
Balance at 30 June 20X1		120,000

Task 2

£125,000	✓
£500,000	
£750,000	

Task 3

Total interest payable for the year.

| £24,000 | (12% × 200,000) |

Journal

Account name	Debit	Credit
	£	£
Interest payable	10,000	
Accruals		10,000

This is five months' interest (12% × 200,000 × 5/12)

CHAPTER 2 **The frameworks**

Task 1

1	To make economic decisions
2	To assess the stewardship of management

Task 2

Neither of them	
(a) only	
(b) only	
Both of them	✓

Error (a) is certainly not material in the context of total sales revenue. However, cost of sales is correct, so net profit has also been overstated by £1,000 (this is 5% of total net profit).

Error (b) represents 6% of the company's net assets. Again, the error has affected net profit. Because the £30,000 has been treated as an expense instead of being capitalised, net profit has been reduced by more than half.

Task 3

(a) Non-current assets

1	Land and buildings
2	Plant and machinery
3	Motor vehicles

(b) Current assets

1	Inventories
2	Receivables
3	Bank account

Other possible examples of non-current assets: fixtures and fittings; development costs; long-term investments.

Other possible examples of current assets: prepayments; petty cash; short-term investments.

Task 4

True	
False	✓

An item that meets the definition of an element should be recognised if:

- It is probable that any future economic benefit associated with the item will flow to or from the entity

- The item has a cost or value that can be measured with reliability

The key word here is 'probable'. The advertising campaign is intended to generate sales income, but it is very difficult to predict whether it actually will do this in practice. No asset should be recognised; the £100,000 should be treated as an expense in the period in which it is incurred.

CHAPTER 3 The statement of financial position

Task 1

Examples:

1	Purchases are adjusted for opening and closing inventories to arrive at the cost of sales (to match the cost of sales to the sales made during the period)
2	Non-current assets are depreciated (to match the cost of an asset to the accounting periods expected to benefit from its use)

Task 2

	True	False
Intangible assets are current assets		✓
Long-term provisions are a current liability		✓
Share premium is part of equity	✓	
Tax payable is a current liability	✓	

Task 3

Sawyer Ltd: Statement of financial position as at 31 July 20X2

	£'000
Assets	
Non-current assets:	
Property, plant and equipment (W)	16,480
Current assets:	
Inventories	4,898
Trade and other receivables	6,870
	11,768
Total assets	28,248

	£'000
Equity and liabilities	
Equity:	
Share capital	5,800
Share premium	3,120
Revaluation reserve	840
Retained earnings	7,460
Total equity	17,220
Non-current liabilities	
Loan stock	6,000
Current liabilities	
Trade and other payables	1,930
Tax payable	2,333
Bank overdraft	765
	5,028
Total liabilities	11,028
Total equity and liabilities	28,248

Workings

Property, plant and equipment	£'000
Land and buildings at cost	12,350
Plant and machinery at cost	9,980
Buildings accumulated depreciation	(1,370)
Plant and machinery accumulated depreciation	(4,480)
	16,480

Task 4

Journal

Account name	Debit £	Credit £
Bank	125,000	
Share capital		125,000

Being the issue of 250,000 50p ordinary shares at par.

Task 5

	£
Share capital (25p ordinary shares)	135,000
Share premium	27,000
Retained earnings	170,000
	332,000

Working

	Number of shares	Share capital £	Share premium £
Original	400,000	100,000	30,000
Rights issue (1 for 5)	80,000	20,000	12,000
	480,000	120,000	42,000
Bonus issue (1 for 8)	60,000	15,000	(15,000)
	540,000	135,000	27,000

CHAPTER 4 The statements of financial performance

Task 1

	True	False
The gain is part of the company's performance	✓	
The gain should be recognised in profit or loss		✓

The building is part of the resources of the company, which have increased in value. In theory, it could now be sold for more than its original cost, resulting in extra income and a cash inflow.

The gain is not yet realised (the cash has not yet been received). It is not certain that the gain ever will be realised. The company may not sell the building, or the market may collapse so that the building falls in value in the future.

Task 2

Statement of comprehensive income for the year ended ...

	£'000
Continuing operations	
Revenue	3,534
Cost of sales (W)	(2,587)
Gross profit	947
Distribution costs (W)	(157)
Administrative expenses (W)	(416)
Profit from operations	374
Finance costs	(24)
Profit before tax	350
Tax	(105)
Profit for the period from continuing operations	245

Workings

Cost of sales	£'000
Opening inventories	228
Purchases	2,623
Closing inventories	(264)
	2,587
Distribution costs	£'000
Wages and salaries: Sales staff	131
Advertising and marketing costs	16
Depreciation: delivery vans	10
	157

Administrative expenses	£'000
Directors' salaries	32
Wages and salaries: Office staff	197
Office expenses	128
Light and heat	16
Depreciation: freehold buildings	2
Depreciation: fixtures and fittings	36
Audit fees	5
	416

Task 3

True	
False	✓

The profit for the year from discontinued operations is £15,000 (profit on disposal of £95,000 less post-tax loss for the year of £80,000).

Task 4

Statement of comprehensive income for the year ended 31 December 20X3 (extract)

	£'000
Profit for the year	609
Other comprehensive income for the year	
Gain on property revaluation	125
Total comprehensive income for the year	734

Statement of changes in equity for the year ended 31 December 20X3 (extract)

	Total equity
	£'000
Balance at 1 January 20X3	2,020
Changes in equity for 20X3	
Total comprehensive income	734
Dividends	(100)
Issue of share capital (200,000 × 1.50)	300
Balance at 31 December 20X3	2,954

Task 5

True	
False	✓

This is a change in accounting estimate. (Compare this with the next example, which **is** a change in accounting policy: this is a change from no depreciation to depreciation, rather than simply a change in the way that depreciation is calculated.)

Task 6

True	
False	✓

This is not a prior period error, because the doubtful debt allowance was an accounting estimate based on the information available at the time (see the definition). Routine adjustments and corrections to previous accounting estimates should not normally be treated as prior period errors.

The shortfall would only be a prior period error if there had been misuse of information that was available before the financial statements were authorised for issue. This would be the case, if, for example, the directors knew that one of their major customers was about to go into liquidation and they ignored this when making the allowance.

CHAPTER 5 **The statement of cash flows**

Task 1

Cash received from the sale of property, plant and equipment	
Dividends paid	
Interest received	
Repayment of loans	✓

Cash received from the sale of property, plant and equipment is reported under 'cash flows from investing activities'

Equity dividends paid are normally reported under 'cash flows from financing activities', but may also be included under 'cash flows from operating activities'.

Interest received is reported under 'cash flows from investing activities'.

Task 2

£14,900	
£15,100	
£24,500	
£24,900	✓

	£
Profit from operations	20,000
Depreciation	5,000
Decrease in inventories (£5,100 – £5,800)	700
Increase in receivables (£7,500 – £7,000)	(500)
Decrease in payables (£5,700 – £6,000)	(300)
Cash generated from operations	24,900

Task 3

Statement of cash flows for the year ended...

	£'000	£'000
Net cash from operating activities		39,000
Investing activities:		
Purchase of property, plant and equipment	(65,000)	
Proceeds on disposal of property, plant and equipment	10,000	
Dividends received	4,000	
Net cash used in investing activities		(51,000)
Financing activities:		
Proceeds of share issue	50,000	
Repayment of long-term loan	(20,000)	
Dividends paid	(8,000)	
Net cash from financing activities		22,000
Net increase (decrease) in cash and cash equivalents for the year		10,000
Cash and cash equivalents at the beginning of the year		7,000
Cash and cash equivalents at the end of the year		17,000

Task 4

£100,000	
£1,000,000	
£1,100,000	✓
£1,400,000	

Cash flows from financing activities:

	£'000
Proceeds from issue of share capital (2,200 – 1,600)	600
Additional loan stock (1,500 – 1,000)	500
Net cash from financing activities	1,100

Bank overdrafts are normally included as part of cash, rather than treated as financing items.

CHAPTER 6 **Tangible non-current assets**

Task 1

£	350,000

Cost of offices:

	£'000
Building	300
Legal fees	5
Alterations (£50 – £5)	45
	350

Task 2

Journal

Account name	Debit	Credit
	£	£
Freehold property: cost/valuation	100,000	
Freehold property: accumulated depreciation	31,250	
Revaluation reserve		131,250

Working

Accumulated depreciation at 31 December 20X5:

£250,000 × 5/40 =   £31,250

Task 3

£	4,000

Carrying amount at 1 January 20X3:

	£
Cost	20,000
Accumulated depreciation (£20,000 × 2/10)	(4,000)
	16,000

Depreciation charge for the year ended 31 December 20X3 is 25% × £16,000 = £4,000.

Task 4

£ | 3,200

Carrying amount at 1 January 20X3:

	£
Cost	20,000
Accumulated depreciation (£20,000 × 2/10):	(4,000)
	16,000

Depreciation charge for the year ended 31 December 20X3 is £16,000 ÷ 5 = £3,200.

Task 5

£ | 240,000

Gain on disposal:

	£'000	£'000
Sales proceeds		700
Less: carrying amount		
Valuation	500	
Accumulated depreciation (500 × 4/50):	(40)	
		(460)
		240

Task 6

True	✓
False	

IAS 23 states that borrowing costs can only be capitalised for the period during which construction was actually taking place, ie 1 April to 30 September, even though interest expense was incurred for the whole year. Therefore borrowing costs of £30,000 (750,000 × 8% × 6/12) are capitalised, while the remainder (750,000 × 8% – 30,000) must be recognised in profit or loss.

Task 7

Profit or loss	Other comprehensive income	
Expense of £10,000	Nil	
Net gain of £40,000	Nil	
Gain of £50,000	Nil	✓
Expense of £10,000	Gain of £60,000	

The company has adopted the fair value model, so:

- No depreciation is charged
- The gain on remeasurement is recognised in profit or loss

CHAPTER 7 **Intangible assets and inventories**

Task 1

True	
False	✓

Assets are rights or other access to future economic benefits controlled by an entity as a result of past transactions or events. Although the staff give the company access to future economic benefits (revenue from selling the products that they develop), the company almost certainly does not control these benefits. Employees are normally free to leave the company and work elsewhere.

Therefore neither the staff, nor their skills, can be recognised as assets in the company's statement of financial position and IAS 38 specifically states that a workforce cannot be treated as an intangible asset.

Task 2

Recognised as an intangible asset in the statement of financial position	
Recognised as an expense in profit or loss	✓

The expenditure does not meet the IAS 38 criteria for capitalisation, as the technical feasibility of the project and the entity's ability to use or sell it are uncertain. Therefore the expenditure must be recognised as an expense in profit or loss in the period in which it is incurred.

Task 3

True	✓
False	

IAS 38 prohibits the recognition of internally generated brands as assets.

Task 4

£Nil	✓
£10,000	
£40,000	
£60,000	

Recoverable amount is £110,000 (the higher of fair value less costs to sell and value in use).

Therefore the impairment loss is £40,000 (£150,000 – £110,000).

Because the property has been revalued, the loss is recognised in other comprehensive income. (Because recoverable amount is higher than depreciated historic cost; therefore none of the loss needs to be recognised in profit or loss.)

Task 5

£11,099	✓
£11,590	
£11,639	
£11,690	

Inventory valuation:

	Cost	NRV	Lower of cost and NRV
	£	£	£
A	2,880	3,420	2,880
B	5,500	5,034	5,034
C	3,310	3,185	3,185
Closing inventories are valued at			11,099

CHAPTER 8 **Liabilities**

Task 1

Journal

Account name	Debit	Credit
	£	£
Tax expense (profit or loss)	150,000	
Tax payable (statement of financial position)		150,000

Task 2

	True	False
The tax expense for the year ended 30 June 20X5 is £48,000	✓	
The tax liability at 30 June 20X5 is £48,000		✓

Corporation tax charge for the year ended 30 June 20X5:

	£
Tax expense based on profits for the year	50,000
Adjustment in respect of prior period (overprovision)	(2,000)
	48,000

The tax liability at 30 June 20X5 is £50,000.

Task 3

(a)

£ | 175,000

Working

	£'000
Tax expense based on profits for the year	150
Adjustment in respect of prior period	5
Deferred tax	20
	175

(b) **Statement of financial position as at 31 December 20X4 (extract)**

	£'000
Non-current liabilities:	
Deferred tax	130
Current liabilities:	
Tax payable	150

Task 4

True	
False	✓

This is a finance lease.

The following factors suggest that the risks and rewards of ownership have been transferred:

- The lease term is for the whole of the asset's useful life (five years)

- The present value of the minimum lease payments (£95,500) amounts to substantially all the fair value of the leased asset (£98,000)

Task 5

£	27,357

Interest is calculated as 10% × £34,870 **less** the first instalment of £10,000 payable **at the start of the year**.

Working

What happens over the whole term of the lease is shown below:

	Liability at 1 January £	Repayment 1 January £	Balance £	Interest at 10% £	Liability at 31 December £
20X1	34,870	(10,000)	24,870	2,487	27,357
20X2	27,357	(10,000)	17,357	1,735	19,092
20X3	19,092	(10,000)	9,092	908*	10,000
20X4	10,000	(10,000)	–	–	–

* There is a rounding difference of £1 and this has been deducted from the interest charge for 20X3.

Task 6

True	✓
False	

Is there a present obligation as the result of a past event? Yes. The company has a legal obligation under the guarantee.

Is the transfer of economic benefits in settlement probable? Yes. IAS 37 states that in this and similar situations, the individual obligations should be considered as a whole.

Can a reliable estimate be made of the amount of the obligation? Yes. The company should be able to use its past experience to predict the percentage of items that will need to be repaired or replaced.

Conclusion: recognise a provision for the best estimate of the costs of repairing or replacing items sold before the year-end under the guarantee.

Task 7

1 only	✓
2 only	
Neither 1 nor 2	
Both 1 and 2	

Sale of land and buildings: this is a non-adjusting event because it does not concern conditions that existed at the year-end.

Liquidation of a major customer: this is an adjusting event; it provides evidence of conditions that existed at the year-end (a trade receivable is worthless).

CHAPTER 9 **Further accounting standards**

Task 1

True	
False	✓

Revenue does **not** include items such as profits from the sale of the entity's own property, plant and equipment. This is because this kind of income does not arise from the company's ordinary activities.

Task 2

It should recognise a liability	✓
It should recognise revenue	

The advance payment is recognised as a liability, not as revenue. The goods have not yet been transferred to the buyer. Only when the goods are delivered should revenue be recognised.

Task 3

£Nil	
£6,250	
£15,000	✓
£25,000	

IAS 20 states that government grants should be recognised in profit or loss on a systematic basis over the periods in which the entity recognises the related costs for which the grants are intended to compensate.

The company will incur expenditure on training the new members of staff from 1 October 20X2 to 28 February 20X3. Therefore £15,000 (£25,000 × 3/5) should be recognised in profit or loss in the year ended 31 December 20X2, and the remaining £10,000 should be treated as deferred income.

Task 4

89.4 pence

$$\text{Earnings per share} = \frac{760,000}{850,000} = 89.4\text{p}$$

Weighted average number of ordinary shares

	£'000
1 July – 31 March (800,000 × 9/12)	600
1 April – 30 June (1,000,000 × 3/12)	250
	850

CHAPTER 10 Group accounts: the consolidated statement of financial position

Task 1

True	✓
False	

Although Moat Ltd only holds 20% of the total share capital, it holds 60% of the voting rights. Therefore it has the majority of the voting rights and Grange Ltd is a subsidiary according to the definition in IAS 27.

Task 2

£ | 1,226,000

Consolidated retained earnings:

	£'000
Church Ltd (1,080 + 96)	1,176
Steeple Ltd	50
	1,226

Task 3

£ | 400,000

Goodwill:

	£'000
Cost of investment (price paid)	4,000
Share capital attributable to Thatch Ltd (60% x 1,000)	(600)
Retained earnings attributable to Thatch Ltd (60% × 5,000)	(3,000)
	400

Task 4

£	1,444,000

Consolidated retained earnings:

	£'000
Valencia Ltd (1,250 + 110)	1,360
Vella Ltd (90% × 60) (20X6 only)	54
Add: gain on bargain purchase (W)	30
	1,444

Working: Gain on bargain purchase

	£'000	£'000
Price paid		600
Less: Fair value of net assets acquired:		
Share capital attributable to the parent (90% × 200)	180	
Retained earnings attributable to the parent (90% × 500)	450	
		(630)
		(30)

Task 5

£	33,500

Trade receivables:

	£
X Ltd	20,000
Y Ltd	15,000
Less: inter-company balance	(1,500)
	33,500

Task 6

£	144,000

Inventories:

	£
Kilvert Ltd	100,000
Woodford Ltd	50,000
Less: provision for unrealised profit (30,000 × 25/125)	(6,000)
	144,000

CHAPTER 11 **Group accounts: further aspects**

Task 1

Consolidated statement of comprehensive income for the year ended 30 June 20X9 (extract)

	£'000
Profit before tax	775
Tax	(180)
Profit for the year from continuing operations	595
Attributable to:	
Equity holders of the parent	580
Non-controlling interests (25% × 60)	15
	595

Task 2

Reduce by £25,000	
Reduce by £30,000	
Reduce by £35,000	✓
Reduce by £40,000	

To cancel the sale: reduce both revenue and cost of sales by £40,000.

To eliminate the unrealised profit: increase cost of sales by £5,000 (£10,000 ÷ 2)

Task 3

£	575,000

Investment in associate

	£'000
Cost of investment	500
Add: share of associate's profit since acquisition (30% × 250)	75
	575

Working
Alternative calculation (proof)

	£'000
Group share of net assets of associate (30% × 1,250)	375
Goodwill (W)	200
	575

Goodwill	
Cost of investment	500
Less: net assets acquired (30% × 1,000)	(300)
	200

CHAPTER 12 **Interpreting financial statements**

Task 1

True	
False	✓

The *Conceptual Framework* states that the objective of general purpose financial reporting is to provide financial information about the reporting entity that is useful to **existing and** potential investors, lenders and other creditors in making decisions about providing resources to the entity.

Task 2

(a) **ROCE**

20%

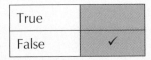

$$\frac{\text{Profit from operations}}{\text{Total equity + Non-current liabilities}} \quad \frac{300}{1,500} \times 100\% = 20\%$$

(b) **Operating profit percentage**

15%

$$\frac{\text{Profit from operations}}{\text{Revenue}} \quad \frac{300}{2,000} \times 100\% = 15\%$$

(c) **Asset turnover**

$$1.33 \text{ times}$$

$$\frac{\text{Revenue}}{\text{Total assets less Current liabilities}} \quad \frac{2,000}{1,500} = 1.33 \text{ times}$$

Task 3

Current ratio

$$2.0:1$$

Quick ratio

$$1.5:1$$

Current ratio $\quad \dfrac{\text{Current assets}}{\text{Current liabilities}} \quad \dfrac{4,750 + 11,350 + 2,900}{7,400 + 2,100} = 2$

Quick ratio $\quad \dfrac{\text{Current assets} - \text{Inventories}}{\text{Current liabilities}} \quad \dfrac{11,350 + 2,900}{7,400 + 2,100} = 1.5$

Task 4

$$3.5 \text{ times}$$

Inventory turnover $\quad \dfrac{\text{Cost of sales}}{\text{Inventories}} \quad \dfrac{4,200}{1,200} = 3.5$

Task 5

True	
False	✓

The irrecoverable debt is not the reason for the increase. In fact, a large debt write-off at the year-end would decrease trade receivables and, thereby, receivables days.

Possible reasons (only **one** was required):

- Some customers have been allowed extended credit terms (for example, because they are so significant that the business needs to maintain good relations with them).
- Sales were unusually high just before the year-end or were increasing throughout the year. If this were the case, receivables at the year-end would be high in relation to total sales for the year.
- Credit control procedures have not been applied during the last few months of the year.

Task 6

	True	False
Asset turnover is higher		✓
Gearing is higher		✓
Operating profit percentage is lower	✓	
Return on capital employed is lower	✓	

Revaluation of assets normally increases asset values. This means that the depreciation charge also increases. The revaluation surplus is taken to a revaluation reserve, which increases equity. There is no effect on sales.

As a result:

- Profit is reduced
- Capital employed is increased

This means that:

- Return on capital employed (ROCE) is lower
- Asset turnover is lower
- Operating profit percentage is lower

However, gearing is reduced, because assets and equity have increased and there is no effect on liabilities.

The company may appear to be less efficient and less profitable, but also less risky as an investment or as a loan creditor.

TEST YOUR LEARNING – ANSWERS

CHAPTER 1 Limited companies

Test 1

True	✓
False	

Limited liability means that the owners' liability is limited to the amount that they have paid for their shares.

Test 2

True	
False	✓

Shares are stated in the statement of financial position at their nominal value, not their market value.

Test 3

Accruals	
Drawings	
Loan stock	✓
Sales	

Test 4

The general reserve is non-distributable	
The retained earnings reserve is non-distributable	
The revaluation reserve is non-distributable	✓
The share premium account is distributable	

Although the directors may not intend to distribute the general reserve it is still legally distributable.

Test 5

£40,000	
£52,500	✓
£66,000	
£126,500	

Working

	£
Profit from operations	140,000
Loan stock interest (150,000 × 9%)	(13,500)
Profit before tax	126,500
Tax	(74,000)
Profit for the year	52,500

Dividends are not deducted as an expense from profit for the year.

Test 6

(a) **Hearts Ltd: Income statement for the year ended 31 December 20X2**

	£'000
Revenue	16,100
Cost of sales (4,515 + 10,493 – 5,292)	(9,716)
Gross profit	6,384
Operating expenses	(3,912)
Profit from operations	2,472
Finance cost	(105)
Profit before tax	2,367
Tax	(280)
Profit for the year	2,087

(b) **Hearts Ltd: Statement of financial position as at 31 December 20X2**

	£'000	£'000
Assets		
Non-current assets:		
Property, plant and equipment		5,852
Current assets:		
Inventories	5,292	
Receivables	3,578	
		8,870
Total assets		14,722
Equity and liabilities		
Equity:		
Share capital		840
Revaluation reserve		1,365
Retained earnings (3,955 + 2,087)		6,042
		8,247
Non-current liabilities:		
Bank loan		2,100
Current liabilities:		
Trade payables	3,675	
Tax payable	280	
Bank overdraft	420	
		4,375
Total liabilities		6,475
Total equity and liabilities		14,722

CHAPTER 2 **The frameworks**

Test 1

The four bodies that form part of the international standard-setting structure are:

- The International Accounting Standards Board (IASB)
- The International Financial Reporting Standards Foundation (IFRS Foundation)
- The IFRS Advisory Council
- The International Financial Reporting Standards Interpretations Committee (IFRS Interpretations Committee).

(The IASB is the body that actually develops and issues accounting standards.)

Test 2

True	
False	✓

Test 3

The objective of general purpose financial reporting is to provide financial information about the reporting entity that is useful to existing and potential investors, lenders and other creditors in making decisions about providing resources to the entity.

Test 4

A	Employees	
B	Government	
C	Investors	✓
D	Lenders	✓

Test 5

A	Accruals	
B	Consistency	
C	Going concern	✓
D	Reliability	

Test 6

A	Consistency	
B	Going concern	
C	Relevance	✓
D	Timeliness	

Test 7

Elements:

- Assets
- Liabilities
- Equity
- Income
- Expenses

Test 8

True	
False	✓

Although the contract looks like a liability it does not meet the definition in the *Conceptual Framework*. The business has an obligation to transfer economic benefit but only if the managing director actually does work for the business for the next five years. Therefore there is no *past* 'obligating event' that would result in a liability.

CHAPTER 3 **The statement of financial position**

Test 1

True	
False	✓

If the end of the reporting period (year-end) changes so that the financial statements are prepared for a different period, the entity should disclose: the reason for the change; and the fact that the comparative figures are not entirely comparable.

Test 2

Current assets:

Inventories

Trade and other receivables

Cash and cash equivalents

Test 3

Financial liabilities	
Investment properties	
Prepayments	✓
Trade and other payables	

Test 4

Statement of financial position as at...

	£'000
Assets	
Non-current assets:	
Property, plant and equipment (W1)	11,407
Current assets:	
Inventories	3,061
Trade and other receivables (W2)	4,217
	7,278
Total assets	18,685
Equity and liabilities	
Equity:	
Share capital	3,000
Share premium	1,950
Revaluation reserve	525
Retained earnings	4,503
Total equity	9,978
Non-current liabilities	
Bank loan	5,400
Current liabilities	
Trade and other payables (W3)	1,375
Tax payable	1,458
Bank overdraft	474
	3,307
Total liabilities	8,707
Total equity and liabilities	18,685

Workings

(1) Property, plant and equipment

	£'000
Land and buildings: Cost	7,724
Plant and machinery: Cost	6,961
Accumulated depreciation: Buildings	(468)
Accumulated depreciation: Plant and machinery	(2,810)
	11,407

(2) Trade and other receivables

	£'000
Trade receivables	4,294
Allowance for doubtful debts	(171)
Prepayments	94
	4,217

(3) Trade and other payables

	£'000
Trade payables	1,206
Accruals	169
	1,375

Test 5

Journal

Account name	Debit	Credit
	£	£
Bank	160,000	
Share capital		100,000
Share premium		60,000

CHAPTER 4 **The statements of financial performance**

Test 1

True	
False	✓

Test 2

£147,000	
£215,000	
£223,000	✓
£239,000	

Working

	£'000
General administrative expenses	155,000
Depreciation of office furniture	76,000
Prepayment (24,000 × 1/3)	(8,000)
	223,000

Test 3

Tarragona plc
Statement of comprehensive income for the year ended 30 September 20X3

	£'000
Continuing operations	
Revenue (33,202 – 748)	32,454
Cost of sales (W)	(17,377)
Gross profit	15,077
Distribution costs (6,165 – 165)	(6,000)
Administrative expenses (3,386 – 146)	(3,240)
Profit from operations	5,837
Finance costs	(279)
Profit before tax	5,558
Tax	(1,333)
Profit for the period from continuing operations	4,225
Discontinued operations	
Profit/(loss) for the period from discontinued operations (238 – 26)	(212)
Profit for the period	4,013
Other comprehensive income	
Gain on revaluation of land (5,800 – 4,800)	1,000
Total comprehensive income for the period	5,013

Working

Cost of sales	£'000
Opening inventories	8,570
Purchases	19,480
Discontinued operation	(411)
Closing inventories	(10,262)
	17,377

Test 4

> 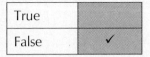 are the specific principles, bases, conventions,
> rules and practices applied by an entity in preparing and presenting
> financial statements.

Test 5

IAS 8 states that an entity should only change an accounting policy if the change:

- is required by a standard; or
- results in the financial statements providing reliable and more relevant information.

Test 6

True	
False	✓

If a change arises from a new standard, the transitional provisions may require prospective application (so that the effect of the change is dealt with in the current period).

Test 7

1 only	
2 only	✓
Both statements	
Neither statement	

Statement 1 is incorrect because only material prior period errors are corrected.

Test 8

Statement of changes in equity for the year ended 31 December 20X5:

	Share capital £'000	Share premium £'000	Revaluation reserve £'000	Retained earnings £'000	Total equity £'000
Balance at 1 January 20X5	1,000	300	0	700	2,000
Changes in equity for 20X5					
Total comprehensive income	0	0	150	300	450
Dividends	0	0	0	(50)	(50)
Issue of shares	100	20	–	–	120
Balance at 31 December 20X5	1,100	320	150	950	2,520

CHAPTER 5 **The statement of cash flows**

Test 1

True	✓
False	

Test 2

Bank current account in foreign currency	
Bank overdraft	
Petty cash float	
Short-term deposit	✓

Deposits must be repayable on demand to qualify as cash. A deposit is repayable on demand if it can be withdrawn without notice. A short term deposit normally has a fixed maturity date and cannot be withdrawn earlier without incurring a penalty. However, depending on the term of the deposit, it could be part of cash equivalents.

Test 3

Classification	Items
Operating activities	(d)
Investing activities	(c)
Financing activities	(b)
Increase/decrease in cash and cash equivalents	(a)

Test 4

(a)

The direct method	✓
The indirect method	

(b)

True	
False	✓

IAS 7 allows either method.

Test 5

(a)

Cash inflow of £5,600	
Cash outflow of £64,400	
Cash outflow of £94,400	✓
Cash outflow of £100,000	

Cash flows from investing activities:

	£
Payments to acquire property, plant and equipment (W)	100,000
Receipts from sale of property, plant and equipment	(5,600)
	94,400

Working

Property, plant and equipment: Cost	£
Opening balance	400,000
Disposals	(20,000)
Closing balance	(480,000)
Cash paid (balancing figure)	(100,000)

(b)

£6,000	
£18,000	
£26,000	
£30,000	✓

Working

Property, plant and equipment: Accumulated depreciation	£
Opening balance	68,000
Disposals (20,000 – 8,000)	(12,000)
Closing balance	(86,000)
Depreciation charge (balancing figure)	(30,000)

Test 6

(a) **Reconciliation of profit from operations to net cash from operating activities for the year ended 30 June 20X5**

	£'000
Profit from operations (270 + 62)	332
Depreciation	305
Increase in inventories (1,009 – 960)	(49)
Increase in receivables (826 – 668)	(158)
Increase in trade payables (641 – 563)	78
Cash generated from operations	508
Interest paid	(62)
Tax paid	(53)
Net cash from operating activities	393

(b) **Statement of cash flows for the year ended 30 June 20X5**

	£'000	£'000
Net cash from operating activities		393
Investing activities:		
Purchase of property, plant and equipment (W)	(559)	
Net cash used in investing activities		(559)
Financing activities:		
Increase in long-term loan (610 – 460)	150	
Dividends paid	(59)	
Net cash from financing activities		91
Net increase (decrease) in cash and cash equivalents for the year		(75)
Cash and cash equivalents at the beginning of the year		100
Cash and cash equivalents at the end of the year		25

Working

Property, plant and equipment	£'000
Property, plant and equipment at the beginning of the year	1,776
Depreciation	(305)
Property, plant and equipment at the end of the year	(2,030)
	(559)

Alternative working

Property, plant and equipment

	£'000		£'000
Balance b/f	1,776	Depreciation	305
Additions (bal fig)	559	Balance c/f	2,030
	2,335		2,335

Test 7

There has been a decrease in cash of £238,000 and this has reduced the company's cash balance from £240,000 to only £2,000.

However, there are many positive signs:

- Cash generated from operations is more than £5,000,000 (compared with profit from operations of £4,214,000). If the company can regularly generate this amount of cash, it should be able to avoid serious cash flow problems. There are no signs of problems in managing working capital; only receivables have increased in the period.

- The main reason for the net cash outflow is that there have been asset purchases of nearly £3,000,000. This means that the company should be able to continue to generate profits and cash inflows in future periods.

- Cash has also been used to repay some of the company's loan stock. Therefore cash outflows to pay interest will reduce in future periods.

- The company still has a positive cash balance; it has not overdrawn its bank account.

Conclusion: the company is probably managing its cash flow well and there appear to be no liquidity problems.

CHAPTER 6 Tangible non-current assets

Test 1

True	✓
False	

IAS 16 states that as well as its purchase price, the cost of an asset includes any further costs directly attributable to bringing the item to the location and condition necessary for it to be capable of operating in the manner intended by management.

Test 2

True	✓
False	

This is routine maintenance expenditure and must be recognised as an expense in profit or loss in the period in which it was incurred. It cannot be added to the cost of the building (IAS 16).

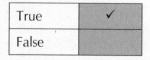

Test 3

(a)

True	
False	✓

IAS 16 states that where an item of property, plant and equipment is revalued, all assets of the same class should be revalued.

(b)

True	
False	✓

The company must keep the valuations up to date, but IAS 16 does not require annual revaluations. Revaluations should be carried out with sufficient regularity to ensure that the value at which an item is carried in the statement of financial position is not materially different from its actual fair value at the end of the reporting period.

(c)   Journal

Account name	Debit £	Credit £
Freehold property: Cost/valuation	70,000	
Freehold property: Accumulated depreciation	30,000	
Revaluation reserve		100,000

Test 4

True	
False	✓

IAS 16 does not prescribe a method of depreciation. Management should select a suitable method that reflects as fairly as possible the pattern in which the asset's economic benefits are consumed by the entity.

Test 5

£20,000	
£24,000	
£30,000	✓

Depreciation must be based on the revalued amount. Therefore the charge for the year ended 31 December 20X6 is £30,000 (600,000 ÷ 20).

Test 6

True	
False	✓

Only borrowing costs directly attributable to the acquisition, construction or production of a **qualifying asset** should be capitalised.

Test 7

(a) Investment property is property held to earn rentals or for capital appreciation or for both, rather than for:

- use in the production or supply of goods or services or for administrative purposes; or

- sale in the ordinary course of business.

(b) IAS 40 explains that owner-occupied property is not investment property.

Therefore the property that will be used as a hostel for employees would not be an investment property as this counts as being owner occupied.

The property that will be let out to other businesses would meet the definition of an investment property.

Test 8

(a) An entity should classify a non-current asset as **held for sale** if its carrying amount will be recovered principally through a sale transaction rather than through continuing use.

(b) An asset that is held for sale should be measured at the lower of its carrying amount and its fair value less costs to sell. It should not be depreciated.

An asset that is held for sale should be presented separately from other assets in the statement of financial position.

CHAPTER **7 Intangible assets and inventories**

Test 1

Recognise expenditure on both projects in profit or loss	
Recognise expenditure on Project X in profit or loss; Recognise expenditure on Project Y as an intangible asset	✓
Recognise expenditure on Project Y in profit or loss; Recognise expenditure on Project X as an intangible asset	
Recognise expenditure on both projects as an intangible asset	

IAS 38 states that an intangible asset arising from development should be recognised if an entity can demonstrate all of the following:

- the technical feasibility of completing the asset;
- its intention to complete the asset and its ability to use or sell it;
- how the asset will generate probable future economic benefits;
- the availability of adequate resources to complete the development;
- its ability to measure the expenditure reliably.

Both projects appear to meet some of the IAS 38 conditions.

There is a possibility that adequate resources will not be available to complete Project X as the company still has to obtain external funding. Therefore the expenditure must be recognised immediately in profit or loss.

Project Y is likely to be completed within the next few months and funding to complete the project appears to be available. On the basis of the information provided all the conditions appear to be met. Therefore the company should recognise the expenditure as an intangible asset.

Test 2

	True	False
An intangible asset may have an indefinite useful life	✓	
An intangible asset should always be amortised over its useful life		✓
Internally generated goodwill should never be recognised	✓	
No internally generated intangible asset may be recognised		✓

Intangible assets with an indefinite useful life are not amortised. Development expenditure should be recognised as an intangible asset if the project meets certain conditions.

Test 3

True	
False	✓

IAS 36 states that most assets should be reviewed for impairment only where there is some indication that impairment has occurred. However, two types of assets must be reviewed at least annually: intangible assets with an indefinite useful life; and goodwill acquired in a business combination.

Test 4

(a) An impairment loss is the amount by which the carrying amount of an asset exceeds its recoverable amount.

(b) The recoverable amount of an asset is the higher of its fair value less costs to sell and its value in use.

(c) An impairment loss should be recognised in other comprehensive income if the asset has previously been revalued upwards.

The loss is recognised in other comprehensive income (set against the revaluation reserve) until the carrying amount of the asset falls below depreciated historical cost; then the remainder of the loss is recognised in profit or loss.

Test 5

(a) Financial statements are prepared on an accruals basis. This means that the effects of transactions and other events are recognised when they occur and they are recorded in the accounting records and reported in the financial statements of the periods to which they relate. In addition, IAS 2 states that the carrying amount of inventories is recognised as an expense in the period in which the related revenue is recognised. Closing inventories are therefore recognised as an asset in the statement of financial position and carried forward to the next period, when they will be sold and the revenue will be recognised.

(b) The cost of inventories comprises all costs of **purchase**, costs of **conversion** and other costs incurred in bringing the inventories to their present **location** and **condition**.

(c) Closing inventories are valued at the lower of cost and net realisable value.

(d) Inventories are an asset because:

– they are the result of a past event (the purchase of goods); and

– the purchase of inventories gives rise to future economic benefits because it results in a future inflow of cash when the inventories are sold.

Test 6

£2,170	
£2,225	
£2,295	✓
£2,670	

Gross profit for April (FIFO):

	£
Sales	5,000
Cost of sales	(2,705)
	2,295

FIFO

Closing inventories are £625 (25 × £25).

Cost of sales is £2,705 (3,330 – 625).

CHAPTER 8 **Liabilities**

Test 1

£74,500	
£99,900	✓
£110,900	
£121,900	

Tax charge:

	£
Tax on profits for the year	85,500
Adjustments relating to previous years	(11,000)
Transfer to deferred taxation	25,400
	99,900

Test 2

(a) Deferred tax is not an actual tax. It can be thought of as a way of applying the accruals concept to accounting for corporation tax.

IAS 12 *Income taxes* defines deferred tax liabilities as the amounts of income taxes payable in future periods in respect of taxable temporary differences.

(b) IAS 12 defines taxable temporary differences as temporary differences that will result in additional taxable amounts in future periods when the carrying amount of the asset or liability is recovered or settled.

Another way of thinking of taxable temporary differences is that they are differences between taxable profit and reported profit which arise because some items are charged to tax or allowed for tax in a period that is different from the one in which they are recognised in the accounts.

Test 3

A finance lease	✓
An operating lease	

The note shows that leased assets have been capitalised (recognised as an asset).

Test 4

£ | 57,600

Working

	Liability at 1 January £	Interest £	Repayment £	Liability at 31 December £
20X1	76,000	1,600	(20,000)	57,600
20X2	57,600	1,200	(20,000)	38,800
20X3	38,800	800	(20,000)	19,600
20X4	19,600	400	(20,000)	–
		4,000		

Test 5

Legal proceedings:

Because the company will probably not be found liable, there is only a possible obligation to pay damages. Therefore the company should not recognise a provision.

However, there is a contingent liability, and information about the case should be disclosed unless the possibility that the company will have to pay damages is remote.

Staff retraining:

There does not appear to be any kind of obligation to carry out the retraining. The directors could still decide not to retrain the staff and to avoid the expense. Therefore no provision for training costs or loss of income should be made.

Because there is no obligation, there is no contingent liability.

Test 6

Damage to inventory as a result of a flood	
Discovery of a fraud committed by one of the accounts staff	✓
Issue of new share capital	
Sale of a freehold property	

CHAPTER 9 **Further accounting standards**

Test 1

(a) Revenue is the gross inflow of economic benefits during the period arising in the course of the ordinary activities of the entity.

(b) An entity should recognise revenue from the sale of goods when **all** the following conditions have been satisfied:

- The entity has transferred to the buyer the significant risks and rewards of ownership of the goods;

- The entity retains neither continuing managerial involvement to the degree usually associated with ownership nor effective control over the goods sold;

- The amount of revenue can be measured reliably;

- It is probable that the economic benefits associated with the transaction will flow to the entity; and

- The costs incurred or to be incurred in respect of the transaction can be measured reliably.

Test 2

True	
False	✓

IAS 20 allows two methods, either:

- Deduct the grant from the cost of the asset and depreciate the amount over the asset's useful life (so that the grant is recogni' profit or loss as a reduction in the depreciation expense); or

- Recognise the grant as deferred income (a liability) and reco' asset at its actual purchase price; then recognise the grant' profit or loss over the asset's useful life.

Test 3

	True	False
All companies must calculate and present earnings per share.		✓
Earnings per share is disclosed in the statement of comprehensive income.	✓	
The calculation is always based on profit after tax.		✓
The calculation is based on the number of shares in issue at the end of the year.		✓

IAS 33 only applies to companies that publicly trade their shares or have chosen to disclose earnings per share.

In practice the calculation **is** normally based on profit after tax, but earnings per share must be based on profit for the year attributable to equity (ie ordinary) shareholders. This may not be the same as profit after tax if there are preference shareholders, as preference shareholders are entitled to receive their dividends first.

Where ordinary shares have been issued during the year, the calculation is based on a weighted average.

Test 4

35.0 pence	
37.6 pence	
41.2 pence	✓
43.7 pence	

Net profit attributable to ordinary equity holders = £1,750,000

$$
\begin{aligned}
\text{Number of shares} &= 4{,}000{,}000 \times 9/12 + 5{,}000{,}000 \times 3/12 \\
&= 3{,}000{,}000 + 1{,}250{,}000 \\
&= 4{,}250{,}000 \\
\text{EPS} &= \frac{1{,}750{,}000}{4{,}250{,}000} \\
&= 41.2 \text{ pence}
\end{aligned}
$$

Test 5

True	
False	✓

Northern, Eastern and Southern are the only segments for which revenue exceeds 10% of total revenue. However, IFRS 8 also states that the total **external** revenue reported by operating segments must be at least 75% of the entity's total external revenue. The total revenue of these three segments is only £295,500 (145,000 + 42,500 + 108,000), which is 74% of the total. Additional operating segments must be identified as reportable until the 75% threshold is reached.

CHAPTER 10 Group accounts: the consolidated statement of financial position

Test 1

C Ltd only	
B Ltd and C Ltd	
C Ltd and D Ltd	✓
All four companies	

The following are subsidiaries of A plc:

- C Ltd (majority of equity shares)
- D Ltd (a member and can appoint a majority of the directors)

B Ltd and E Ltd are not subsidiaries because the investor does not have a majority of voting rights. (Neither preference shares nor loan stock carry voting rights.)

Test 2

(a) A subsidiary is an entity that is controlled by another entity.

(b) Control is presumed to exist where the parent owns more than half the voting power of an entity, unless it can be clearly demonstrated that such ownership does not constitute control.

Control also exists when the parent owns half or less of the voting power of an entity when there is:

- Power over more than half of the voting rights by virtue of an agreement with other investors;

- Power to govern the financial and operating policies of the entity under a statute or an agreement;

- Power to appoint or remove the majority of the members of the board of directors; or

- Power to cast the majority of votes at meetings of the board of directors.

Test 3

(a)   Goodwill

£1,000,000	
£1,400,000	
£2,000,000	
£2,350,000	✓

	£'000
Price paid	9,000
Less: fair value of net assets acquired	
Share capital attributable to Left plc (95% × 5,000)	(4,750)
Retained earnings attributable to Left plc (95% × 2,000)	(1,900)
	2,350

(b)   Consolidated retained earnings

£28,950,000	✓
£29,000,000	
£30,850,000	
£31,000,000	

	£'000
Left plc	28,000
Right Ltd attributable to Left plc	
(95% × (3,000 – 2,000))	950
	28,950

(c)   Non-controlling interest

£250,000	
£300,000	
£350,000	
£400,000	✓

	£'000
Share capital attributable to NCI (5% × 5,000)	250
Retained earnings attributable to NCI (5% × 3,000)	150
NCI share	400

Test 4

Why fair value adjustments should be made.

- The consolidated statement of financial position should reflect the assets and liabilities of the subsidiary at their cost to the group.

- If the subsidiary's assets and liabilities are not adjusted to fair value, goodwill will be over-stated.

Test 5

True	✓
False	

None of the goods remain in inventory at the year-end, so there is no unrealised profit.

Test 6

Consolidated statement of financial position as at 31 March 20X7

	£'000
Assets	
Non-current assets:	
Intangible assets: Goodwill (W2)	1,200
Property, plant and equipment (8,000 + 6,000)	14,000
	15,200
Current assets:	
Inventories (2,400 + 1,440)	3,840
Trade and other receivables (2,640 + 2,400 – 960)	4,080
Cash and cash equivalents (480 + 360)	840
	8,760
Total assets	23,960
Equity and liabilities	
Equity attributable to owners of the parent	
Share capital	5,000
Retained earnings (W3)	10,920
	15,920
Non-controlling interest (W4)	1,440
Total equity	17,360
Non-current liabilities (1,200 + 1,080)	2,280
Current liabilities:	
Trade payables (2,500 + 1,700 – 960)	3,240
Tax payable (860 + 220)	1,080
	4,320
Total liabilities	6,600
Total equity and liabilities	23,960

Workings

(1) Group structure

Salt plc owns 80% (800,000/1,000,000) of the equity share capital of Pepper Ltd.

(2)

Goodwill	£'000
Price paid	4,000
Share capital attributable to Salt plc (80% × 1,000)	(800)
Retained earnings attributable to Salt plc (80% × 2,500)	(2,000)
	1,200

(3)

Retained earnings	£'000
Salt plc	7,960
Pepper Ltd attributable to Salt plc (80% × 6,200 – 2,500)	2,960
	10,920

(4)

Non-controlling interest	£'000
Share capital attributable to NCI (20% × 1,000)	200
Retained earnings attributable to NCI (20% × 6,200)	1,240
	1,440

CHAPTER 11 **Group accounts: further aspects**

Test 1

The consolidated financial statements must reflect the operations of the group. If a company sells goods to another company in the same group, the group has not made a sale and no profit has been earned. Sales and profits should only be recognised when the goods are purchased by a customer external to the group.

Any purchases that are unsold at the year end will be included in inventories. The value of the inventory should be its cost to the group, not its cost to the individual group company that purchased it.

Test 2

True	✓
False	

The parent sold goods to the subsidiary and therefore non-controlling interests are not affected by the provision for unrealised profit on inventories.

Test 3

£1,250,000	
£1,340,000	
£1,450,000	✓
£1,540,000	

	£
Denston Ltd	950,000
Hawkedon Ltd	500,000
	1,450,000

Test 4

£1,250,000	
£1,275,000	
£1,300,000	✓
£1,400,000	

Working

	£	£
Aldeburgh plc		800,000
Southwold Ltd		600,000
Adjustment: intra-group sale	(125,000)	
Provision for unrealised profit	25,000	
		(100,000)
		1,300,000

Test 5

(a) An associate is an entity (other than a subsidiary) over which the investor has significant influence.

(b) Significant influence is the power to participate in the financial and operating policy decisions of the investee.

(c) An investor is presumed to have significant influence if it holds 20% or more of the voting power of the investee, unless it can be clearly demonstrated that this is not the case.

However, it is possible for an investor to exercise significant influence with a shareholding of less than 20%. IAS 28 *Investments in associates* explains that an investor usually has significant influence if:

- It is represented on the board of directors;

- It takes part in policy making processes, including decisions about dividends and other distributions;

- There are material transactions between the investor and the investee;

- There is interchange of management personnel;

- It provides essential technical information to the investee.

Test 6

Consolidated statement of comprehensive income for the year ended 31 December 20X3

	£000
Continuing operations	
Revenue (W)	2,880
Cost of sales (W)	(1,380)
Gross profit	1,500
Other income	0
Operating expenses (360 + 180)	(540)
Profit before tax	960
Tax (240 + 120)	(360)
Profit for the year	600
Attributable to:	
Equity holders of the parent	564
Non-controlling interest (240 × 15%)	36
	600

Workings

Group structure

Thames Ltd owns 85% of the equity share capital of Stour Ltd.

Workings

Revenue	£'000
Thames plc	2,280
Stour Ltd	1,200
Total intercompany adjustment	(600)
	2,880
Cost of sales	£'000
Thames plc	1,320
Stour Ltd	660
Total intercompany adjustment	(600)
	1,380

CHAPTER 12 Interpreting financial statements

Test 1

8%	
10%	✓
15%	
40%	

Operating profit percentage is $\dfrac{\text{Profit from operations}}{\text{Revenue}}$

Revenue is 80,000 (20,000 × 100/25)

Operating profit percentage is $\dfrac{20,000 - 12,000}{80,000} \times 100\% = 10\%$

Test 2

True	
False	✓

ROCE = Operating profit percentage × asset turnover

Therefore asset turnover $= \dfrac{\text{ROCE}}{\text{Operating profit percentage}} = \dfrac{20\%}{10\%} = 2$ times

Test 3

(a) Return on capital employed

$$\dfrac{\text{Profit from operations}}{\text{Total equity} + \text{non - current liabilities}} \times 100\%$$

(b) Acid test ratio

$$\dfrac{\text{Current assets} - \text{Inventories}}{\text{Current liabilities}}$$

(c) Inventory holding period

$$\dfrac{\text{Inventories}}{\text{Cost of sales}} \times 365 \text{ days}$$

(d) Interest cover

$$\frac{\text{Profit from operations}}{\text{Finance costs}}$$

Test 4

40%	
60%	✓
80%	
150%	

Gearing ratio:

$$\frac{\text{Non-current liabilities}}{\text{Total equity } + \text{ non-current liabilities}} = \frac{39,000}{26,000 + 39,000} \times 100\% = 60\%$$

Test 5

True	
False	✓

Test 6

	Formula	Calculation
Gross profit percentage	$\dfrac{\text{Gross profit}}{\text{Revenue}} \times 100\%$	$\dfrac{1,475}{4,100} \times 100\% = 36.0\%$
Inventory turnover	$\dfrac{\text{Cost of sales}}{\text{Inventories}}$	$\dfrac{2,625}{480} = 5.5 \text{ times}$
Trade receivables collection period	$\dfrac{\text{Trade receivables}}{\text{Revenue}} \times 365 \text{ days}$	$\dfrac{956}{4,100} \times 365 = 85 \text{ days}$
Trade payables payment period	$\dfrac{\text{Trade payables}}{\text{Cost of sales}} \times 365 \text{ days}$	$\dfrac{267}{2,625} \times 365 = 37 \text{ days}$

Test 7

True	✓
False	

Reducing administrative expenses will increase operating profit.

Test 8

REPORT

To: Michael Beacham

From: Accounting Technician

Subject: Interpretation of the ratios of Goodall Ltd

Date: October 20X3

As requested, I have analysed the financial performance and position of Goodall Ltd for 20X2 and 20X3. This analysis has been based on the ratios calculated by your financial adviser, which have been compared with industry averages.

Gearing ratio

This ratio is often used as a measure of the risk involved in investing in or lending to a business. The company's gearing has risen fairly sharply in 20X3 and is considerably higher than the industry average of 41%. Goodall Ltd has evidently taken out an additional long term loan during the year or increased an existing loan. The ratios show that the company is a much riskier investment than other businesses in its industry sector and that the position is deteriorating. It may be harder for the company to raise additional finance in the future, as potential lenders are normally reluctant to lend to a company that is already heavily in debt.

Interest cover

Interest cover has almost halved in the period, so that in 20X3 the company's profit from operations was only very slightly more than its interest payable. This is very low indeed compared with the industry average of 4.6.

This fall in interest cover has probably occurred partly because the company has increased its long term loans and will now be paying more interest as a result. However, the ratio has deteriorated so sharply (compared to the rise in the gearing ratio) that there must be additional factors at work. Interest rates may have risen (lenders may be demanding higher rates because the company is now very heavily indebted). Alternatively, it is possible that profit from operations has fallen. A combination of lower profits and higher interest costs would be extremely worrying.

Quick ratio/Acid test

This ratio has decreased in the two-year period and it is now much lower than the industry average of 1.1. At its last year-end the company's current liabilities were twice as great as its 'quick' current assets. The industry average shows that Goodall Ltd does not operate in an industry where a low quick ratio is the norm.

A possible reason for the fall is that there have been high cash outflows during the year, either changing a positive cash balance to a bank overdraft, or increasing an existing overdraft. This worsening of the quick ratio suggests that the additional long term loan has not been sufficient to meet the company's need for cash. Goodall Ltd does not have enough cash available to meet its current liabilities and it may have significant liquidity problems.

Return on equity

Return on equity has fallen sharply over the period, suggesting that there is less profit available for equity shareholders. This means that they are unlikely to receive much immediate return on their investment (in the form of dividends) and that there is little profit available for reinvestment in the company to generate better returns in future. The return on equity of Goodall Ltd is considerably lower than the industry average of 19%, which means that the company is much less likely to attract equity investors than other companies within the sector.

The increase in long-term loans will not have affected shareholders' equity. Therefore the lower return on equity has probably been caused by increased interest costs, possibly combined with lower profit from operations.

Conclusion

Goodall Ltd is already very highly geared, its interest cover is deteriorating and it appears to be suffering liquidity problems. All these things suggest that there would be considerable risk in lending money to this company, unless the loan is almost certain to generate increased profits in the short term. It is quite possible that the company will be unable to meet its interest payments in future as neither the profits nor the cash may be available. Return on equity is very low, which means that the company is unlikely to be able to raise additional finance from investors. On the basis of the limited information provided, it would not be advisable to make a loan to this company.

INDEX

REVIEW FORM

How have you used this Text?
(Tick one box only)

☐ Home study

☐ On a course_____

☐ Other _____

Why did you decide to purchase this Text?
(Tick one box only)

☐ Have used BPP Texts in the past

☐ Recommendation by friend/colleague

☐ Recommendation by a college lecturer

☐ Saw advertising

☐ Other _____

During the past six months do you recall seeing/receiving either of the following?
(Tick as many boxes as are relevant)

☐ Our advertisement in Accounting Technician

☐ Our Publishing Catalogue

Which (if any) aspects of our advertising do you think are useful?
(Tick as many boxes as are relevant)

☐ Prices and publication dates of new editions

☐ Information on Text content

☐ Details of our free online offering

☐ None of the above

Your ratings, comments and suggestions would be appreciated on the following areas of this Text.

	Very useful	Useful	Not useful
Introductory section	☐	☐	☐
Quality of explanations	☐	☐	☐
How it works	☐	☐	☐
Chapter tasks	☐	☐	☐
Chapter Overviews	☐	☐	☐
Test your learning	☐	☐	☐
Index	☐	☐	☐

	Excellent	Good	Adequate	Poor
Overall opinion of this Text	☐	☐	☐	☐

Do you intend to continue using BPP Products? ☐ Yes ☐ No

Please note any further comments and suggestions/errors on the reverse of this page or e-mail them to: paulsutcliffe@bpp.com

Please return to: Paul Sutcliffe, Senior Publishing Manager, BPP Learning Media Ltd, FREEPOST, London, W12 8BR.

REVIEW FORM (continued)

TELL US WHAT YOU THINK

Please note any further comments and suggestions/errors below.

Notes

Notes

Notes

Notes

Notes